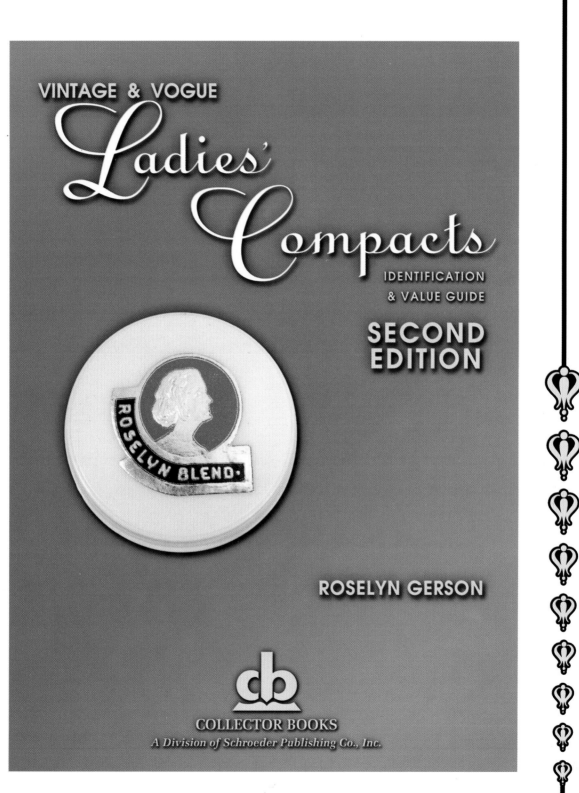

VINTAGE & VOGUE

Ladies' Compacts

IDENTIFICATION
& VALUE GUIDE

SECOND EDITION

ROSELYN GERSON

COLLECTOR BOOKS

A Division of Schroeder Publishing Co., Inc.

On Front Cover:
Lower left: Stunning unmarked hallmarked sterling compact, light blue enameled lid designed to resemble a butterfly, black accents, interior reveals mirror framed by decorative twisted wire, perforated metal revolving powder well, 2" dia., $650.00 – 750.00.
Center left: Volupté rare polished and brushed goldtone Golden Gesture hand-shaped compact, lid decorated with cards and card suits, interior reveals powder well, and puff, 4¾" x 2", NPA.
Upper left: Estee Lauder, 1999, round crystal encrusted goldtone Golden Millennium compact, lid enhanced with stylized hourglass filled with crystals and imprinted with the year 2000, round crystal Millennium charm decorates thumbpiece, 2¼" dia., $100.00 – 125.00.
Upper right: Square goldtone compact/bracelet, green enamel border on lid which is centered with an applied bow decorated with marquisettes, green composition strips on either side of the compact, interior reveals beveled mirror and sifter, compact 1¼" sq. with green strips, 2", $275.00 – 375.00.
Center: Black Bakelite vanity/folding fan combination, lid of vanity reveals mirror, powder well, puff, and lipstick, complete with silk tassel and carrying cord, vanity 3¼" x 1", ivory sticks 4". Shown with fan open. $700.00 – 900.00.
Lower right: Estee Lauder, 1996, small round goldtone compact, lid designed to resemble roulette wheel enhanced with red and black enamel, and crystals, and small pearl on lucky number seven, 2¼" dia., $125.00.

On Back Cover:
Lower left: Robert Original signed mini goldtone compact chair, coin decorates top lid, cabriole legs, interior reveals beveled mirror, puff, and sifter, 3½" h x 2½" w. Shown closed. $350.00 – 450.00.
Upper left: Estee Lauder, 1998, pave golden crystal Golden Pear compact, in the form of a pear enhanced with green pave crystal leaves, interior contains powder, puff, and mirror, 2½" x 2", $150.00 – 175.00.
Center: Volupté beautiful round brooch/pendant compact, lid decorated with applied blue enamel design enhanced with crystals, removable pin is decorated with an enlarged version of design on lid, compact 2¼", pin 1", length 3½", $175.00 – 225.00.
Upper right: Kigu highly engraved goldtone basket with swinging handle, white duck revealed under plastic domed lid, plastic interior, 2⅛" dia. x 1½" deep, England, $175.00 – 225.00.
Lower right: Estee Lauder, 1994, round goldtone Honeycomb compact, lid designed to resemble honeycomb with bumblebee on the honeycomb, bee decorated with crystals, 2¼" dia., $75.00 – 125.00.

PHOTOGRAPHY BY ALVIN GERSON
Cover design by Beth Summers
Book design by Joyce Cherry
Searching for a Publisher?

We are always looking for people knowledgeable within their fields. If you feel there is a real need for a book on your collectible subject and have a large comprehensive collection, contact Collector Books.

Collector Books
P. O. Box 3009
Paducah, KY 42002-3009

www.collectorbooks.com

Copyright © 2001 by Roselyn Gerson

Autographed copies may be ordered from:
Roselyn Gerson
P.O. Box 40
Lynbrook, NY 11563

Contents

Dedication

I dedicate this book to my husband, Alvin, without whose encouragement, support, understanding, great patience, enthusiasm, and sense of humor this book would still be a dream and not a reality; to our children, Robin and Denis, Roy, Ira and Gayle, for their patience and understanding, and to our grandchildren, Ilyse, Sarah, Shayna, Katerina, and Andrew and to the compact collectors.

In memory of our beloved firstborn grandchild
PAMELA BETH GERSON
1979 – 1981
Leukemia

About the Author
Roselyn Gerson

Roselyn Gerson, affectionately referred to as "The Compact Lady" by compact collectors and dealers, is the founder of the Compact Collectors Club and editor and publisher of the newsletter, *Powder Puff*. She is the author of the first book written on, and devoted solely to ladies' compacts, entitled *Ladies' Compacts of the Nineteenth and Twentieth Centuries*, 1989; *Vintage Vanity Bags & Purses*, 1994; *Vintage Ladies' Compacts*, 1996, and *Vintage and Contemporary Purse Accessories*, 1997. She has been an avid researcher and collector since 1976, and has completed the Appraisal Studies Certification course at New York University. She lectures widely and is a compact research consultant for Christie's Auction House, Estee Lauder Companies, Texas State Treasury, 20th Century Fox Films, Sotheby's, Christian Duncan, Inc., and Soller, Shayne & Horn, attorneys. She is on the Board of Advisors, Accessory Division, of the Museum of Vintage Fashion, CA. Gerson is a professional member of The National Writers' Club, and has written articles on compacts, solid perfumes, and, vanity bags/purses for *Collectrix Magazine*, *Antiques & Auction News*, *Vintage Fashions Magazine*, *Manhattan Antiques and Collectibles Directory*, *The California Purse Collector's Club*, *Lady's Gallery*, *American Country Collectibles*, *Head Hunters Newsletter*, *Mini-Scents*, *Collector Magazine*, and the *New England Antiques Journal*. She is also a member of the Society of Jewelry Historians, U.S.A. and the Long Island Professional Antiques Dealers Association. She is also the ladies' compact advisor for *Schroeder's Antique Price Guide* and their companion book, *Flea Market Trader*, *Antique Trader Antiques & Collectibles Price Guide*, and *Harry Rinker's Official Price Guide to Flea Market Treasures*. She is also on the board of advisors for both *Warman's Americana & Collectibles* and *Warman's Antiques and Their Prices*. Gerson is listed as compact expert in the CIC *Antiques & Collectibles Resource Directory*. She is an active fund-raiser for the Leukemia Research Foundation and is past president of the South Nassau (New York) Chapter of the Nassau Center for Emotionally Disturbed Children, Inc.

Acknowledgments

My sincere heartfelt thanks to the many wonderful compact collectors for their continued friendship, support, loyalty, encouragement, and enthusiasm My grateful appreciation to the collectors who shared their one-of-a-kind compacts to be photographed, and the collectors who shared their experiences, valued resources, research information, and vintage ads: Brenda Baceda, Laurel Bailey, Nathalie Bernhard, Marion Cohen, Nelda Davis, Ann Dowsett, Cynthia Fleck, Ellen Foster, Lenore Hiers, Brenda Lever, Joan Orlen, Barbara Schwerin, Ruth Wacker, and to Deborah Krulewitch, Sue Grundfest, Cheri Flannigan, Gayle Fox, Liz Lisotta, Lori Diamond, Geraldine Martin, Marion Jaye, and Susan Kretchner.

A very special thank you to my editor, Lisa Stroup, and the entire Collector Books staff for their continued encouragement, enthusiasm, and confidence in me.

To our dearest children, Robin and Denis, Roy, Ira and Gayle, and wonderful grandchildren, Ilyse, Sarah, Shayna, Katerina, and Andrew.

And most of all to my very best friend and photographer extraodinaire, Alvin.

Pricing Information

It is impossible to give absolute prices for articles as varied as compacts. Dealers' retail prices are determined by a number of factors:

Condition: Mint? Scratched, dented, cracked, or chipped? Mirror intact? Original puff, mirror, chain, and powder sifter? Original pouch and presentation box?

Production: Handmade? Mass produced? Hand painted? Commissioned? Personalized? Limited Edition?

Decoration: Precious metals, gold, silver? Silver plate, base metals? Precious stones — diamonds, rubies, emeralds, sapphires? Gemstones? Synthetic stones? Enameled? Man-made materials?

Maker or Manufacturer

Date of Manufacture

Place of Purchase: Demand and selection varies from one part of the country to another.

This is merely an "average price range" value guide and not a price list. Prices may be higher or lower than listed depending on the above conditions. Values given for items in mint condition, with original parts and presentation box.

NPA: No Price Available. Not enough examples of specific items evaluated to obtain fair median value. There may also be a large disparity of prices for identical items — prices for these items not yet stabilized.

Foreword
by Alvin Gerson

Antiquing — that's the one word that made me cringe. The weekend would begin with my wife's favorite request, "Let's go antiquing; it's fun." I always begged off saying that I had work that had to be ready for Monday.

I never found out what "fun" she had until the summer of 1976. It was the bicentennial year and, we went to a July 4th celebration in Sparrowbush, New York. There were antique vendors and flea market booths offering all kinds of "bargains." Now, don't get me wrong, I like a bargain as well as the next guy, but spending $25.00 for an old cake plate was not my idea of fun (or a bargain either, for that matter).

As I wandered from table to table watching the excitement on the face of my wife, I noticed a box with some small trinkets that were being sold as "collectibles." While my wife looked at the articles that were "bigger than a breadbox," I rummaged through the small items. That's when it happened! Here they were, the answer to my space problems (antiques take up a lot of room) and a way to save money.

"Look at these great collectibles," I shouted. She put down the item she was ready to purchase and came to see the "specials" I had discovered.

They were two ladies' compacts. One was black enamel, and the other was silver with a cloisonné center. The price was right, since the enamel was 50 cents and

the silver was 25 cents. Not only were these inexpensive, but how much room would a little compact need? I had to convince her to give up antiquing and take up collecting.

"Let me buy these for you as the start of your new collection and let's see if we can add to them at other markets," I pleaded. I was happy when she agreed. Look at how much money and room I saved just in that one trip alone. LITTLE DID I KNOW!

Here we are almost 20 years later, and we now have compacts displayed on walls, in cases, and in trays. So much for the room saving. I also defy anyone to find a silver or enamel compact for 50 cents today.

But I have to admit this small venture into the land of antiques and collectibles has changed our lives for the better. Now I look forward to spending my weekends with my lovely wife traveling from market to market in search of that one elusive different compact. In the past two decades we have traveled to many parts of the U.S. and enjoyed each other's company and mutual interests.

There are other benefits as well … I can honestly say that I am having "fun" and the work I saved for the weekend now gets done at the office.

Speaking of benefits, I have the sole distinction of being called "Mr. Compact Lady."

Onward
by Alvin Gerson

A funny thing happened on the way to the millennium. I guess it all began when I met Roselyn as we were both growing up in Brooklyn. She was 15 and I was 16, it was the beginning of a lifetime of sharing. I served in the Navy and Roselyn waited for me. (Did I tell you that she was the barracks pin-up girl when I was on Guam?) Soon after I was discharged, we were married. We raised three "exceptional" children (parents' pride allowed), and we were blessed with six "extraordinary" grandchildren. The years moved along sometimes slowly, most times too quickly.

Then came that fateful year, 1976. It was fateful because fate showed us the smile that is usually hidden by the mask of mystery. What a year! It was the United States Bicentennial, the year Roselyn started to collect compacts, and it was the year I built my first computer. Now you can see the directions we both were heading — Roselyn back into the past and me traveling into the future. Will our paths ever cross within these endeavors?

As the years passed, Roselyn started her newsletter, *Powder Puff,* and the Compact Collectors Club. I started a

computer user's group and a series of computer journals. I started to use the online services of CompuServe to obtain information for my journals. Roselyn started to use the computer to write her books. (She loves to cut and paste.) Through the years Roselyn was always there to help me with my work. She not only managed a club and her newsletter, she also raised three kids while her mother lived with us. Now that the kids are grown and sadly, her mother is gone, it was time for me to switch roles. Now that I'm retired, I'm her helper and number one "go-fer."

Meanwhile, back to the computer. Roselyn now uses the Internet for research for her collection, her books, and for *Powder Puff.* I still use the computer for graphic design and also the Internet to help research the past. So I guess our circle of life is represented by three Cs:

Children
Compacts
Computers.

Confessions of an Obsessive Compact Collector

Most compact collectors at one time or another have said to me, "Roz, you must have every compact that there is. (Not.) Is there a special compact that you are looking for that you don't have?" My usual answer to that is, I am looking for a a compact that doesn't look like a compact, one that sings or dances, plays music or twists and turns, a show stopper. So now I tell you, be careful what you wish for! Several months ago, Margaret Lipitch, a compact collector friend from England, sent me a picture of a unique compact that she had just bought. I wrote and told her that I would love to have one like it and if she did see another one to let me know. Well, she did, she found one for me. Another British collector, Suzanne Chestnut, was looking at it, and Margaret said to her, if you are not interested in it, Roz is. To make a long story short, it arrived in the mail. So by now you are probably saying to yourself, well, enough already, tell us about it! O.K. Picture this...a 14" x 3½" wide x 5¼" high mother-of-pearl pique tortoise shell revolving ballerina musical gondola/compact combination. The canopy on the gondola opens up to reveal a mirror and powder well, and the

"Spellbound – Paula Abdul" written in gold lettering on the top lid and a sticker that reads, "For Promotional Use

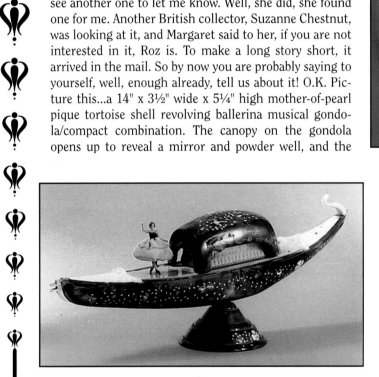

gondola has a dancing ballerina spinning around when the music box is turned on. It needs a table or shelf no less than 15" in diameter because the gondola spins completely around. So be forewarned, wishes can come true!

Recently my dear collector friend Debbie Matheney e-mailed me to let me know that there was a compact on eBay that she was sure I would be interested in. She had just won the bid on one just like it, and there was another one on then. I checked the item number and, of course, I bid on it. Much to my dismay another collector outbid me. But I did not despair because I kept checking and saw another one on the next day, and I won the bid. (I should also tell you that it was at ⅓ the price of the one that I was outbid on.) O.K., again so what is it? It is a Paula Abdul Compact Disc Compact!

It comes complete with black box with the title

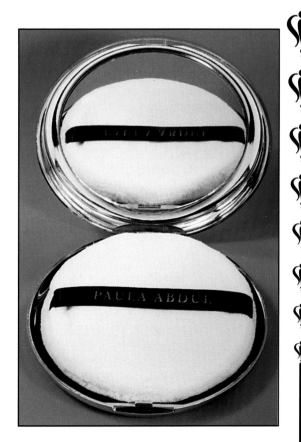

elry cuffs for cosmetic containers. Her jewelry line has cuff bracelets for compacts, rouge, and lipstick. The cuff slips around the outer rim of the compact and acts as a frame for the compacts. The lipstick tube needs two cuffs. The bracelets and lipstick tubes come in a variety of very beautiful colors and designs — circles, diamond shapes, solids, and stripes. I bought the Rossellini lipstick tube because I did not know if I had a lipstick tube that would fit the cuffs. Now of course begins the search through my compacts, powder, and rouge for the right sizes to fit these bracelets. Oh yes, I was told by the salesperson that the larger cuff could be worn as a bracelet, the smaller cuff could be used as napkin holder, and the lipstick cuffs could be put on a string and worn as a necklace. So there you have it, Compact Jewelry!

Alvin and I were at a very large antique show and spent 4 or 5 hours walking up and down the aisles, looking for that "special" compact. We found none. But while I was walking around I did see something that did catch my eye (aha!). It was a marbleized,

Only." Inside the box there is a black velvet pouch for the large beautiful 5½" diameter silvertone compact. The interior of the compact reveals a mirror and puff with "Paula Abdul" written in gold on a black ribbon across the top of the puff. Lift off the puff and you find a circular Paula Abdul advertising fold-up booklet. Finally under all of that is the "Spellbound" CD by Paula Abdul 1991, Virgin Records. So here is the compact/compact that plays music! This time Alvin said, "This is a compact?"

When I made the next purchase, Alvin did not say a word — he was in shock. I read in one of the 18 or 20 magazines that I receive that Isabella Rossellini had just come out with a new line of cosmetics and jewelry for cosmetic containers. Isabella is an avid collector of Bakelite jewelry, especially bracelets, and because of her love for Bakelite jewelry, she created Bakelite jew-

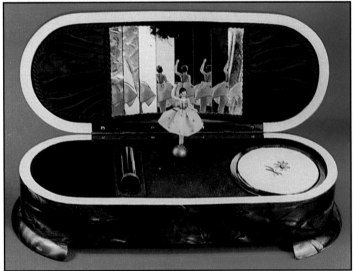

tortoise colored celluloid jewelry box, 4½" x 3"h x 13½". I know that by now you are probably thinking, a celluloid jewelry box? Yes, a celluloid musical jewelry box that when opened reveals a twirling dancing ballerina. Yes, again the dancing ballerina! The back of the open jewelry box is mirrored and reflects the ballerina twisting and turning to the music, the interior also reveals a white enamel compact and lipstick well with a lipstick tube, and an additional opening for personal necessities. When Alvin met up with me after I had purchased the box, he asked me what kind of compact I bought that needed such a large box? I told him it was a surprise and that I would show it to him when we got home. Surprise was an understatement, when I showed the jewelry box to Alvin he rolled his eyes and said, "Oh noooo."

Several months ago one of our new members, Noelle Soren, sent me a letter with photocopies of some of her compacts. She described them and mentioned that one of the compacts, a very pretty plastic blue compact designed to resemble the sun, was purchased in Italy and that these types of compacts were all the rage there. I mentioned to her that if she went back to Italy and saw another one to please buy one for me and I would gladly reimburse her. Sure enough, several months later I received a package from her with a short note. The note read, "I don't know

if you remember, but you asked me to pick up a sun compact for you when I visited Italy again. Well, I could not get the sun for you but got the Devil instead! Hope you like it." Like it, I love it! It is an adorable 6" h x 3½" diameter. red plastic cosmetic box shaped like the Devil, complete with cape, white horns, and pitch-fork! When opened, a mirror is revealed on one side, and the other side reveals three sliding cosmetic compartments in addition to an eyebrow pencil and blush applicator. So please, do be careful what you wish — you may wish for the sun and get the Devil instead.

I really do love all of them, but Alvin did ask me please not to make wishes like that again. Read on and see whether I did or not!

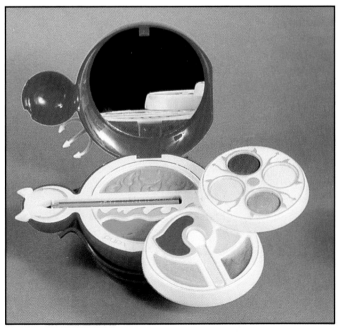

Preface

The first book, *Ladies' Compacts of the Nineteenth and Twentieth Centuries,* was published in 1989, and my second book, *Vintage Ladies' Compacts,* was published in 1996. These books devoted solely to compacts were received enthusiastically and warmly by compact collectors, dealers, costumers, historians, fashion designers, museums, and costume jewelry collectors. Since then, I have received countless letters, e-mails, and telephone calls from both collectors and dealers, strongly encouraging me to do a book with a value guide update with additional color pictures of compacts. Hence this book, *Vintage & Vogue Ladies' Compacts.* Since writing my first two books, I have acquired or have access to many more beautiful and unusual compacts, so naturally I was thrilled to do a third book. However, I could not write a completely new book because there is very little additional historical information available about compacts. Most of the manufacturers of ladies' vintage compacts are no longer in existence. Unfortunately, there were few records kept by these manufacturers. Many of these firms moved, changed hands or were absorbed by other companies and if there were any records, they were lost in the shuffle. Information relating to compacts was compiled from catalogs, magazines, advertisements, antique trade papers, antique books, the dictionary, encyclopedias, patents, and trademarks sources. Also researched were museums, libraries, auction houses, and antique shows. There are many compacts that have no identifying marks such as patent numbers, manufacturer's name or place of origin on them. In order to determine the dates of these compacts, their designs, mirrors, backs, clasps, powder sifters, puffs, composition, and motifs were examined and compared with similar examples of compacts whose dates were known. Many compact manufacturers spanned two or three decades and rather than speculate on the exact manufacture date of a specific compact, only the name of the manufacturer, if known, was listed. Therefore, I felt it was necessary to retain the pertinent compact information that appeared in the first book. However, throughout this book, I have added information and over 300 compacts in full color, many of which have never appeared in print.

Compact collecting has become overwhelmingly popular in the last few years and many compact articles have appeared in magazines, trade papers, and newspapers in both the United States and Europe. There are also several other books on compacts that have been published since my first book.

In recent years, compact collecting has become recognized as a separate collectible area. Price guides now have a compact category listing; in fact, in 1994, for the first time the Texas State Fair had a separate category for compacts in its Antique Round-Up. Because the interest in compact collecting was so intense, in 1987, *Powder Puff,* the Compact Collectors Chronicle, was created! This quarterly newsletter for compact enthusiasts has an international readership and also sponsors an annual Compact Collectors Convention and auction; proceeds from the auction go to the Pamela Beth Gerson Chapter for Leukemia Research.

Vintage compacts are now being featured in prestigious auction houses and the first museum compact exhibit. "Compacts of Character" featuring compacts manufactured by Stratton, Kigu, and U.S. manufacturers, was held July 1 through July 31, 1994, at The Manor House Museum, Suffolk, England.

Compacts have also been recognized by other authorities in popular trends. Enesco and Hallmark, manufacturers of collectible Christmas ornaments, limited editions of adorable compact Christmas ornaments.

Vintage and vogue compacts and vanity cases are one of the most sought after new collectibles today by both men and women. Men who collect ladies' compacts are usually interested in their intricate mechanisms or the secondary accessories that the compact might be combined with, i.e., watches, music boxes, compasses, etc. Motif of the compact might align with their primary collection, such as Empire State Building, World's Fair, ships, etc. Combination compacts are also eagerly sought by the secondary accessory enthusiasts.

Vintage compacts are especially desirable since the workmanship, design, technique, and materials used in the execution of these compacts would be very expensive and virtually impossible to duplicate today. Vintage compacts are reminders of another era, they have a history, uniqueness, and patina. They are a nostalgic romantic link in miniature with the past. They were made in a myriad of shapes, styles, materials, and motifs, made of precious metals, base metals, fabrics, plastics, and almost every conceivable natural or man made medium. Commemorative, premium, patriotic, figural, combination, Art Deco, and enamel compacts are examples of the most desirable collectible vintage compacts. Collectible also are compacts whose lids are decorated with hand-painted reproductions of priceless paintings by famous artists. Some of the subjects of the Louvre compact series are Romeo and Juliet, Wood by the Winds, A Gallant Gentleman, April Showers, etc. A hand-painted reproduction of the French artist Hardouin Coussin's rendition of Napoleon Bonaparte's sister, Marie Pauling, also graced many lids of the popular Mondaine compacts.

History once again repeats itself, the "old" compacts

are the "new" collectibles. Vintage compacts are becoming more and more precious and are rapidly appreciating in value and desirability. Yet, we cannot ignore the fabulous figural compacts that are being produced today in limited editions; they are tomorrow's contemporary collectible compacts. Many of the giants of the beauty industry presently feature unique, delightful, figural collectible compacts. Each year Estee Lauder, currently the most prolific manufacturer of beautiful and affordable compacts, creates limited editions of fabulous figural compacts. Yves St. Laurent's heart-shaped compacts with matching lipsticks feature a different colored center stone each year. Debbie Palmer introduces several lovely compacts each year, and Katherine Baumann creates stunning colored crystal compacts. Many firms commission artists to create compacts for them. Sculptor Robert Lee Morris created a compact and matching lipstick for Elizabeth Arden. In fact, would you believe, Tweety Bird and Sylvester compacts made exclusively for Warner Bros. stores, and Minnie and Mickey Mouse compacts made exclusively for Disney stores are very coveted and collectible. Many of these contemporary compacts will be the collectibles of the future, especially the ones made in limited editions. Whether you decide to include these limited edition contemporary compacts in your collection or purchase them for investment purposes is strictly a matter of personal choice. Because there is a resurgence in the manufacture of figural compacts today, these unusual, figural contemporary compacts will likely be the coveted compact collectible of tomorrow.

I hope that you will enjoy this book as much as I enjoyed collecting, researching, and writing on one of my favorite subjects, vintage and vogue compacts.

The Hagn Merchandiser, Chicago

COMPACTS AND CIGARETTE CASES

EVERY NUMBER IS AN OUTSTANDING VALUE

No. 723J89—"Marie Antoinette" Compact. Genuine tapestry covered top in an attractive floral pattern with black enamel border. Full size non-glare magnifying mirror on back. Yellow embossed edge. Contains full size regular mirror, powder container and large puff. Diameter, 3 9/16 ins.

Each .... **75c** | Price, per dozen **$8.40**

No. 723J155—Lightweight Double Compact. The catalin border comes in assorted colors—red, green, crystal and shell—and shapes, and is a very effective contrast to the genuine tapestry covered top. Has a large size non-glare magnifying mirror on back. Contains cake rouge, powder sifter, 2 puffs and double unbreakable mirror. Diameter, 3 ins. Try an assortment today. Each.. **60c**

No. 723J154—Velvet Topped Compact. Assorted beautiful colored scenes done in a special Viennese process which cannot rub off. To appreciate the beauty and coloring of these compacts, they must be seen. Full size non-glare magnifying mirror on back, yellow embossed edge. Contains full size regular mirror, powder sifter and large puff. Diameter, 3 9/16 ins. Each **$1.00**

No. 723J153—Always Popular, Double Pouch Powder Compact. Yellow lightweight armour mesh combined with genuine tapestry top makes it one of our most outstanding numbers. The effect is both beautiful and rich. Contains cake rouge, 2 puffs, double unbreakable mirror and loose powder sifter.

Each .... **85c** | Price, per dozen **$9.00**

No. 727J35—Extremely Smart Ladies' Cigarette Case. Your choice of either crystal or shell, cross bar deep cut pattern. The polished yellow band, hinges and lock make a very effective contrast. Holds 10 cigarettes. **$1.00** Size, 3¾x3 ins. Each................

No. 723J156—Stylish Loose Powder Compact with Genuine Tapestry covered top in a beautiful floral pattern. The yellow polished sides and shell back give it the appearance of a much higher priced piece of merchandise. Contains full size mirror, powder container and large puff. Size, 2⅞x2⅜x½ ins. Each............ **85c**
No. 823J157—As above, with simulated cloisonne top in assorted colors. Each.............. **85c**

1938 Hagn Merchandiser Catalog.

A Brief History of Compacts

Dating back to the ancient civilizations of the world, the use of cosmetics and cosmetic containers was commonplace in all climes and sections of the globe. The word "cosmetics" is derived from the Greek word *kosmein,* meaning to decorate or adorn. Cosmetics were used as an artificial means to enhance and embellish the natural beauty of both men and women. The oldest known surviving cosmetic is powder which was originally made by pulverizing flowers and fragrant leaves.

The predecessors of the present day powder compact were the Oriental ointment container, the Egyptian kohl-pot (Figure 1), the Etruscan cosmetic jar, the French unguent jar, and the English sweet coffer. Although cosmetics originated in the Orient, the Egyptian tombs yielded the first evidence of the use of cosmetics. In the days of antiquity it was customary for kings and queens to be buried with their personal artifacts and most valued possessions. When Egyptian tombs were excavated, archaeologists discovered cosmetic containers known as kohl-pots and applicators known as cosmetic spoons. Kohl-pots or containers were found in various sizes and were made of onyx, glass, ivory, bone, alabaster, steatite, and wood. Kohl was a black mineral substance used to embellish the

Figure 1 — Egyptian kohl-pots, obsidian with gold mountings, Twelfth Dynasty. Courtesy of Metropolitan Museum of Art, Purchase, Rogers Fund, and Henry Walters Gift, 1916 (16.33–35).

lashes and lids of the eyes. The kohl was applied with an elaborately carved ivory or wood cosmetic spoon (Figure 2) or kohl-stick. In addition to being used as a cosmetic, kohl protected the eyes from insects which caused eye diseases and shielded the eyes from the desert's glaring sun.

In ancient Greece, Rome, and China, carbonate of lead was used to whiten the face, and alkanet was used for rouge. Queen Jezabel is believed to have introduced cosmetics to the Hebrews. In India, both men and women used cosmetics after the bath.

Cosmetics were used throughout the Middle Ages.

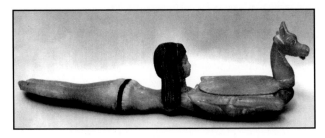

Figure 2 — Egyptian covered cosmetic spoon, alabaster and slate, c. Eighteenth Dynasty. Courtesy of the Metropolitan Museum of Art, Rogers Fund, 1926 (26.2.47).

The Crusaders returning to Britain brought back cosmetics from the harems in the East. Cosmetics were used extensively by men and women alike in Renaissance Italy and France. In Britain during Queen Elizabeth's reign, cosmetics were in fashion and were kept in sweet coffers that were restricted to the boudoir.

In the late eighteenth century the use of cosmetics in England was so widespread, Parliament passed a law that made the use of cosmetics and other seductive ploys akin to witchcraft:

"That all women of whatever age, rank, profession, or degree, whether virgins, maids, or widows, that shall, from and after such Act, impose upon, seduce, and betray into matrimony, any of His Majesty's subjects, by the scents, paints, cosmetic washes, artificial teeth, false hair, Spanish wool, iron stays, hoops, high heeled shoes, bolstered hips, shall incur the penalty of the law in force against witchcraft and like misdemeanors, and that the marriage, upon conviction, shall stand null and void."

Women who used cosmetics were suspected of being "ladies of the night" and it was suggested in "Eve's Glossary" by the Marquise de Fontenoy in 1897 that women, instead of using harmful artificial and poisonous substances, use only natural substances.

In the late nineteenth century, the use of cosmetics in Europe, particularly in France, Italy, and Austria experienced a revival. The most precious, stunning, and exquisitely executed compacts were made in Europe at the turn of the century. Italy produced sterling silver compacts with a robust gilt overlay and colorful painted enamel scenes on the lids (Figure 3), and also produced engraved sterling silver compacts resembling hand mirrors with a lipstick concealed in the handle. French compacts or vanity cases were finished in a matte gilt and encrusted with gems or stones set in prongs, with either a wrist chain or finger ring chain attached (Figure 4). Austrian compacts were elaborately made enamels with a finger ring, chain, or lipstick attached.

During the Victorian era the use of artificial beauty

Figure 5 — Elizabeth Arden "The Ardena Patter." An instrument for applying stimulation to facial muscles, in original patter box, 1920s.

Figure 3 — Antiqued sterling silver enameled lipstick case; painted scene on lid lifts to reveal mirror, Italy. Antiqued sterling silver enameled compact with painted scene on lid and gilded interior, Italy.

Figure 4 — Matte goldtone-finish vanity case with enameled lid encrusted with pronged blue and pink cabochon stones; carrying chain and tassel, goldtone interior, and compartment for powder, lipstick, and eye makeup, France, turn of the century.

aids was frowned upon in polite society, a conservative attitude that was also adopted in America. Before World War I the use of make-up was considered immoral. Instead, proper diet, fresh air, and exercise were recommended as the only way to improve on

nature. In the early twentieth century women were advised to pinch their cheeks to obtain a natural, rosy glow. In the 1900s both the Dorothy Gray and Elizabeth Arden cosmetic firms introduced the "face patter" to stimulate circulation and thereby make the cheeks naturally pink (Figure 5).

Attitudes regarding cosmetics changed drastically in the first quarter of the twentieth century. The use of make-up during the day became accepted and was no longer looked upon with disdain. The practice had finally achieved an element of respectability and acceptability. The trend-setting silver screen stars played an important part in the acceptance of make-up. The word "make-up" was in fact coined by Max Factor, beauty consultant to the stars. Women began to recognize the importance of personal beauty and opted to adopt a "modern" image aided by the use of cosmetics. As women became liberated and more women entered the business world, the use of cosmetics became a routine and necessary part of a woman's grooming. Subsequently, compacts, portable containers for cosmetics, became a necessity. Because of this, the basic compact, an easy-to-carry container for cosmetics complete with mirror and cosmetic applicator or puff, emerged.

Before World War I, women smoking in public were universally frowned upon. In fact, an Italian composer, Ermanno Wolf-Ferrari, wrote an opera in 1909 called "Il Segreto di Susanna" (The Secret of Susanna). Susanna's secret was not that she was unfaithful to her husband, but rather that she smoked cigarettes without her husband's knowledge. After the war when it became acceptable and fashionable for women to smoke and wear make-up publicly, accessories that accommodated both makeup and cigarettes emerged. Ronson, Elgin American, Evans, Volupté, Richard Hudnut, and others made these compact/cigarette cases in a variety of combinations, designs, and materials. These cases not only conserved space in a purse but also allowed a woman to light a cigarette and at the same time have access to her compact.

The umbrella term "compact" is generally used to designate a

Figure 6 — Elgin American square brushed goldtone Aquarius Zodiac compact, 2¼" x 2¾". c. 1949.

Figure 8 — Sterling silver hallmarked octagonal mesh vanity bag with goldtone interior and finger ring chain.

Figure 7 — Royal blue Bakelite vanity case decorated with red dots and raised Egyptian figure on front and back lids. Silk carrying cord and tassel. Interior reveals powder, rouge, and lipstick compartments, mirror, and shirred pocket for bills.

Bakelite vanity bag shown open.

portable cosmetic container. The nomenclature soon broadened for the various styles of cosmetic containers:

COMPACT: A small portable make-up box (Figure 6) containing a mirror, puff, and powder with either screw-top, slip-cover, or piano-hinge lid.

VANITY CASE: A powder compact (Figure 7) that also contains rouge and/or lipstick.

VANITY BAG: A dainty evening bag (Figure 8), usually made of mesh, incorporating a compact as an integral part of the bag.

VANITY CLUTCH: A small clutch bag with specific compartments for compact, lipstick, and rouge. These cases can be removed and replaced.

VANITY PURSE: A leather, fabric, metal, or beaded purse that contains a vanity case as an integral part of the purse.

VANITY RETICULE: A bag with designated compartments for compact, lipstick, and rouge cases, which can be removed and replaced.

VANITY BOX: A fitted traveling cosmetic case.

VANITY POCHETTE: A drawstring powder pouch with a mirror located on the outside base.

VANITY POUCH: A compact with shallow powder pouch.

MINAUDIÈRE: A rigid metal box-shaped evening bag made of precious metals, some set with precious stones or gemstones, with compartments for powder, lipstick, rouge, mirror, coin holder, comb, cigarettes, and small watch or any combination of the above.

NECESSAIRE: A smaller version of the minaudiere, cylindrical in shape, made in precious metals, base metals, or synthetic materials.

CARRYALL: A mass-produced, inexpensive version of the minaudiere.

PLI: A make-up tube containing powder at one end and a push puff at the other end.

POWDERETTE: A pencil-shaped powder container that releases powder when the tip is pressed, sometimes contains lipstick at other end.

PUFF KASE: A tubular powder container with sliding removable puff.

TANGO CHAIN: Lipstick or rouge container attached to a compact or vanity case by a short chain.

FLAP JACK: Slim, flat, round compact resembling a "flapjack" pancake.

Portable containers for cosmetics enjoyed immense popularity and became an indispensable fashion accessory. Fashion setters dictated that a woman have a different compact or vanity case for each outfit in her wardrobe. The Elgin American Co. promoted a popular boxed set of three different compacts, one for daytime, playtime, and nighttime (Figure 9).

Compacts were made to suit every taste and to fit every price range. The price of compacts varied depending on the manufacturer and the materials used. The prestigious jewelry houses such as Cartier, Hermes, Boucheron, Tiffany, Van Cleef & Arpels, Aspreys, Maubousson, Chaumet, Faberge, Black, Starr, and Frost were often commissioned to manufacture exquisite compacts in precious metals, many encrusted with precious gems. Some of these compacts were so elegantly made that they were considered a form of jewelry or dress accessory as well as a portable container for cosmetics.

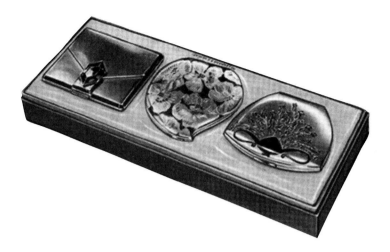

Figure 9 — Triple Compact Ensembles,
Elgin American Catalog, 1949.

Cosmetic houses such as Coty, Evening in Paris, Tre-Jur, Charles of the Ritz, Colleen Moore, Dorothy Gray, Helena Rubinstein, Jonteel, Lady Esther, Richard Hudnut, Princess Pat, Ritz, Tangee, Woodbury, Yardley, and Elizabeth Arden jumped on the bandwagon and mass produced affordable compacts in many different styles. Even though these compacts were made of less expensive materials, they could equal the beauty of the most expensive compacts. In fact Van Cleef & Arpels, the famous jewelry house, designed affordable compacts for Revlon. These compacts came complete with powder, either pressed or loose, which could be refilled when necessary.

The costume jewelry houses and fashion designers such as Trifari, Eisenberg Original, Coro, Robert, Ciner, Hobé, Hattie Carnegie, Schiaparelli, Monet, Lilly Dache, and Gloria Vanderbilt, to mention just a few, also featured a selection of beautiful, affordable compacts. These compacts are now eagerly sought after by both compact and costume jewelry collectors.

Many cosmetic houses contracted metal and paper firms to manufacture empty compact cases to be filled with their own cosmetics. The most popular compact manufacturers in the twentieth century were Elgin American, Volupté, Evans, Whiting & Davis Co., and Stratton of London, Inc. The Elgin National Watch Co., Wadsworth Watch Case Co., and the Illinois Watch Co. were all subsidiaries of Elgin American in Elgin, Illinois. Elgin American manufactured compacts, compact/watches, and compact/music boxes, and was the forerunner in the manufacture of the affordable "carryall."

The Volupté Co. in Elizabeth, New Jersey, was one of the most prolific manufacturers of ladies' compacts during the late thirties and forties. Volupté manufactured compacts in every conceivable style, design, and shape.

The Evans Co. in North Attleboro, Massachusetts, manufactured cigarette cases, compacts, vanity pouches, mesh vanity bags, and vanity purses. They were reputed to be the largest manufacturer of vanity accessories.

The Whiting and Davis Co. in Plainville, Massachusetts, has been the leader in the manufacture of mesh bags and vanity bags since the latter part of the nineteenth century. The company's exquisite mesh evening bags and compacts are still being manu-

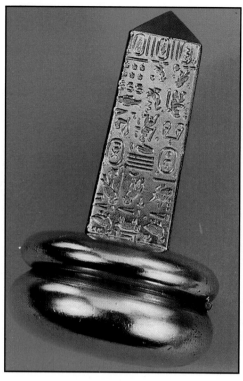

Figure 10 — Silver metal compact with Cleopatra's needle motif; hieroglyphics inscribed on obelisk.

Figure 11 — Volupté Gone With the Wind square silvertone compact; black enamel lids; interior mirror and powder well, 2⅞" square; front lid decorated with the name "Scarlett O'Hara" hand painted enamel Southern scene.

factured today.

It is unusual that an article that was essentially utilitarian be produced in such a diversity of materials, styles, shapes, decoration, motif, and combinations, with such painstaking detail. Cosmetic containers were executed in almost every natural and man-made material, from precious metals and gems to paper, damascene, enamel, gemstones, plastics, pewter, fabrics, lacquer, wood, mother-of-pearl, petit point, leather, butterfly wings, and papier-maché.

The kaleidoscope of shapes and motifs used in the manufacture of compacts reflected the mood and spirit of the times. Compacts came in a variety of shapes: square, rectangular, round, triangular, oblong, oval, crescent-shaped, fan-shaped, and hexagonal. Some were shaped as hand mirrors with a lipstick or perfume vial concealed in the handle, round balls, bells (to be used as holiday tree ornaments), hearts, walnuts or acorns, baskets, animals, and birds.

Tutankhamen's tomb, unearthed in 1922, set off an Egyptian revival, with the emergence of many souvenirs. One of them was a Cleopatra's needle compact with hieroglyphics inscribed on the obelisk (Figure 10).

During World Wars I and II, compacts displayed patriotic motifs. Compacts made in the shape of the Army, Navy, and Marine hats were popular. The flag, inscribed messages from loved ones, and emblems of the armed forces were also part of the design on the patriotic compacts. The compact was one of the most popular gifts a serviceman could give to his loved ones waiting at home. President Jimmy Carter as an ensign at the Naval Academy in Annapolis gave Rosalynn Smith, his future wife, a beautiful compact for the holidays. The compact was engraved "ILYTG," a Carter family endearment which stands for

"I love you the goodest."

Famous fictional and cartoon characters also appeared on the lids of the compacts. Charlie McCarthy, Mickey and Minnie Mouse, Alice in Wonderland, Popeye, and Little Orphan Annie were just a few. One of Candice Bergen's mementos of her ventriloquist father's most famous dummy is a Charlie McCarthy compact! The original movie press book for the epic film "Gone With the Wind" made in 1940, advertised Volupté's "Scarlett O'Hara compact – $2.00 at all department, novelty, etc. stores (Figure 11). Three styles — Southern scenes — inspired by the picture."

There are ingenious three-inch Teddy Bear and Monkey compacts manufactured by Schuco in the 1920s that contain a lipstick tube which is revealed when the head is removed. Their centers open to reveal a powder compartment, puff, and mirror.

In 1940 Volupté manufactured several versions of the hand-shaped compact that were adorned with a black or white lace glove, red manicured nails, a faux engagement ring, a rhinestone tennis bracelet, an unadorned goldtone hand, and various combinations of these versions. In the 1940s Volupté also made several types of "Lucky Purses." Henriette, Kigu, and K & K made several basket-shaped and ball-shaped compacts, some of them are an eight-ball, a ball with a pair of dice on the lid, a roulette ball, and floral baskets with handles. Marhill, one of the leading manufacturers of mother-of-pearl compacts, made mother-of-pearl compacts in a checkerboard design (Figure 12).

Mondaine made beautifully tooled leather compacts that resembled miniature books. Exquisite handmade petit point compacts with labels attached to the inner mirror indicating the exact number of stitches per inch were made in Austria by Schildkraut in a variety of shapes and sizes. Although the floral

Figure 14 — Volupté silvertone "Petite Boudoir" compact, designed to resemble vanity table with collapsible cabriole legs, shown open, with original presentation box.

Figure 12 — Marhill compact and matching pill box; lids decorated with mother-of-pearl enhanced with goldtone bands and raised painted flowers set with sparkle; 2¾" x 2½", pill box 1¼" square.

petit point compacts are lovely, the scenic petit point compacts are less plentiful and are considered more desirable.

The designs and decorations of compacts became more and more ingenious. Some were shaped as musical instruments — drums, guitars, pianos — or as miniature suitcases and cameras, such as the Kamra-Pak. Padlock-shaped ones opened when the hasp was pressed (Figure 13). A silver triple-tiered compact was manufactured in the 1920s that swivels open to reveal multiple make-up compartments. Some compacts in the 1930s had an interior windshield wiper to clean the mirror. There were telephone dials made with a goldtone cartouche on the lid that could be personalized with your name or telephone number. And there were miniature vanity tables and a grand piano with collapsible legs that fold flat on the underside of the compact (Figure 14).

Also in demand were souvenir compacts of the states and

Figure 13 — Zell goldtone compact designed to resemble padlock; picture locket under flower decorated lid; 2½" dia.

foreign countries, scenic spots, historical areas, and commemorative events. College and fraternal organization emblems also appeared on the lids of compacts. Political compacts had candidates' names, Wilkie, Stevenson, Eisenhower, or Roosevelt, imprinted on the compacts in color combinations of red, white, and blue. The political compact is another "crossover collectible" — for the compact collector and political memorabilia enthusiasts. Premium compacts were popular during the commercial age and manufacturers had their slogans, logos, or names imprinted on compacts. These premium compacts kept the manufacturer's product in the public eye.

Some of the most stylized, colorful, and desirable compacts were made during the heydays of Art Nouveau and Art Deco. The Art Nouveau style was free flowing with the emphasis on curved lines, natural motifs, and female faces. The Art Deco style was angular with the emphasis on geometric patterns and abstract designs.

These affordable compacts could be purchased over the counter at any novelty, five and dime, drug store, or department store. Women who did not live in an urban area could buy compacts through the mail-order catalogs of Sears Roebuck, Montgomery Ward, Baird-North, Pohlson, and the Boston Shepard Stores.

Many vintage compacts were multipurpose and were combined with other accessories. The combination and gadgetry compacts that include watches, music boxes, barometers, cigarette cases, lighters, canes, hatpins, cameras, mesh bags, and bracelets cross over into other fields of collecting and are very desirable and eagerly sought after by both the compact collector and the secondary accessory collector. Some compacts concealed manicure sets, sewing kits, ivory slates and slim pencils for jotting down notes, dance programs, combs, coin holders for "mad money," compartments for calling cards and pills. The Segal Key Company made a compact with a concealed blank key that slides

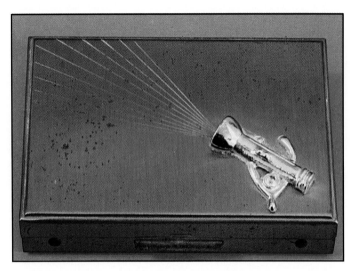

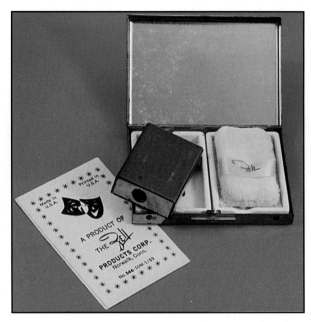

Figures 15 & 16 — Zell "First Nighter" goldtone compact/flashlight combination; brushed goldtone lid decorated with applied wishbone and flashlight; interior reveals mirror, powder compartment with puff, and removable flashlight; insert reads "Easily removed for regular flashlight use to illuminate locks, keyholes, programs, nameplates, maps, etc."; 3¼" x 2¼". Shown closed on left, open on right.

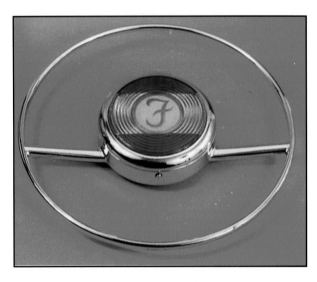

Figure 17 — Automobile steering-wheel compact; compact designed as the horn; silvered metal red and white letter F on compartment lid; interior has mirror and lights, 1920s.

out by pressing a button. Ladies' fans had a hidden compact on the base so that make-up could be applied discreetly. There were also compacts that came complete with a flashlight (Figure 15, 16), one version lit up the interior of the compact, another version had an exterior flashlight to help you find your way in a darkened theater. Compacts made for automobiles were incorporated in the visor, steering wheel, and on the gear-shift handle for easy access and an impromptu and hasty touch-up (Figure 17).

The vanity hatpin was popular in 1910 and was considered a dangerous and lethal weapon because of its long steel shank. The ladies' compact cane was popular in France and was sold by prestigious jewelry houses such as Hermes, Paris, in the early 1900s.

During Prohibition, many necessaires concealed whiskey flasks and some compacts could even be attached to a woman's garter underneath her dress. There was even a water-proof compact bracelet that could be worn on the beach and into the water.

There were several versions of a ladies' "pistol" compact, and there were compacts manufactured by Dunhill and by Evans that resemble cigarette lighters.

Today, the pendulum is swinging back to the time when ladies' compacts were all the rage. Present day compact manufacturers are producing lovely affordable compacts, some in limited editions; these compacts should also be seriously considered by compact collectors.

Vintage compacts whose intricate and exacting workmanship, design, and technique made them works of art in themselves, some even worthy of museum display, are still the most desirable, with contemporary compacts running a close second. For the collectors, compacts, whether they be vintage or contemporary, are miniature treasures, small jewels of the past, present, and future.

A Guide for the Collector

Three Little Words

Three terms you should be familiar with when discussing antiques or collectibles are nomenclature, provenance, and attribution.

NOMENCLATURE is the defining word for an article within a category. For example, in the over-all category of jewelry, the nomenclature for a specific item of jewelry would be ring, bracelet, brooch, pendant, etc.

PROVENANCE is the history or background of an article. Authenticated proof of the manufacturer, country of origin, date of manufacture, and a receipt showing date and place of purchase would be evidence of provenance. Having the original presentation box or pouch enhances the provenance. Knowing the provenance of an article allows you to command a greater price.

ATTRIBUTION denotes the previous owner of an item, either a family, museum, gallery, or corporation. An item has greater value if a famous — or infamous — person previously owned the object. Items belonging to Andy Warhol and the Duchess of Windsor were recently sold at auctions far above the actual value of the items simply because of their attribution. The attribution of an article is usually included in its provenance.

The Famous Coty Powder Puff

The Coty trademark No. 158,435 was registered in France on September 15, 1914, by Francois Joseph de Spoturno Coty. This trademark is for the Airspun Face Powder and Compact container that is covered with white and gold powder puffs on an orange background. Rene Lalique, the famous French glassmaker, and Leon Bakst, the renowned designer of stage settings and costumes for the Ballet Russe, collaborated on this creation. The powder puff trademark has been used since 1914 on Coty's cosmetic products.

Figure 18 — Coty powder and powder-compact advertisement from a 1926 issue of Theatre Magazine.

Whiting & Davis Company Mesh Bags

The Whiting & Davis Co. originally known as Wade Davis, was founded in 1876 in Plainville, Massachusetts, and is the oldest ongoing handbag manufacturer in North America. The vanity bags created by Whiting & Davis between 1896 – 1935 have become sought after collectors' items because of their intricate craftsmanship, beautiful colors, and delicate patterns.

The mesh bags were handcrafted from 1892 to 1912 when the first automatic mesh machine was made. Two popular types of mesh ring designs that Whiting & Davis manufactured were the star-shaped mesh (1900 – 1915) and the tiny mesh (1910 – 1925) (Figure 19). Metal tags with the familiar Whiting & Davis Co. trademark were attached to the mesh bags from 1908 until 1925. After 1926 the Whiting & Davis trademark was imprinted on the frame of the mesh bag.

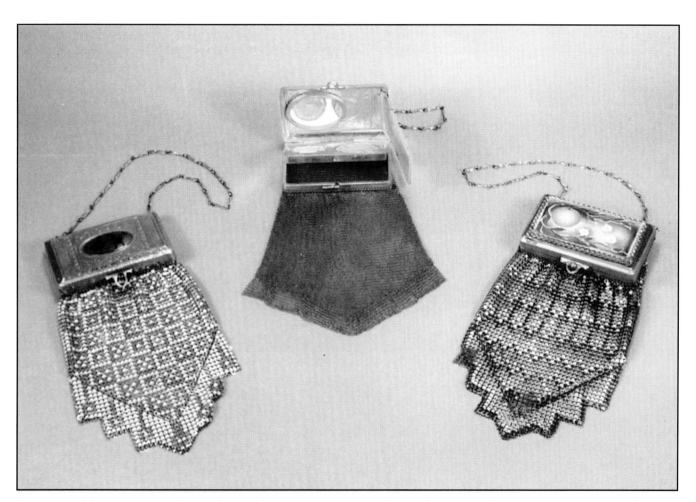

Figure 19 — Whiting & Davis "Elsa" mesh vanity bags with compartments for powder, rouge, and comb. Left, copper disc on silvertone lid decorated with black silhouette of man and woman; center, shown open, soldered baby mesh; right, multicolor mesh, lid decorated with painted fruit.

A Vanity Bracelet Compact

On November 23, l926, Elijah L. Johnson was granted a patent for a wrist cosmetic holder #1,607,985 (Figure 20). His justification for the need of such a product is as follows:

"Modern usage of cosmetics by the feminine sex demands that certain necessary cosmetics be carried on the person so that they may be conveniently and promptly applied whenever the situation demands it. Cosmetics are usually kept in a vanity case, but places are often frequented by the feminine sex where cases cannot be conveniently carried. One example of this is in a ballroom where a vanity case would be very much in the way. Another example of its utilities is automobile driving where a lady driver's attention is detracted from her driving while searching for cosmetics in a vanity case. With my invention the cosmetics are handy and may be readily applied with little distraction and little danger of accidents which might occur from inattention to driving. It is the object of this invention to provide a cosmetic holder which is adapted to be secured to the wrist. The cosmetic holder of my invention is in the form of a bracelet which will be very convenient for use and will in no manner interfere with a person's activity. It is quite essential to a lady's appearance and particularly to her self-satisfaction that she be able to inspect her countenance at various intervals. A lady, however, is often constrained from such an inspection, since considerable attention might be attracted by opening a vanity case and she might suffer considerable embarrassment. It is another object of my invention to provide a cosmetic holder which is adapted to be secured to the wrist and which has a mirror, by means of which a person's appearance may be very readily inspected without attracting attention."

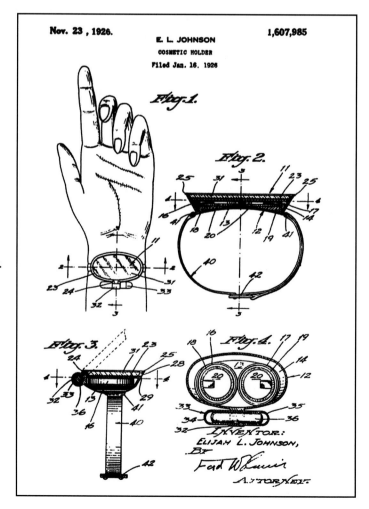

Figure 20 — Wrist Cosmetic Holder Patent.

Chatelaines, Chatelettes, and Coach Chatelaines

In medieval times when the Crusaders were away fighting the wars, they entrusted the keys to the many rooms in their castle to their ladies. The ladies carried the keys on chains attached to their belts and were called chatelaines. Eventually the name "chatelaine" became associated with an article of jewelry rather than a person.

Chatelaines were popular during the Victorian era as a decorative, utilitarian piece of jewelry. They were made in a variety of shapes, materials, and sizes and consisted of several chains suspended from a hook or clasp that was attached to the belt (Figure 21c). The vanity chatelaine usually had a powder compact, lipstick holder, writing slate, slim pencil, coin holder, vinaigrette, or perfume container suspended from these chains.

Chatelettes are chatelaines with shorter and fewer chains (Figure 21a & b).

Coach chatelaines were made with hooks that could be hung inside a coach so the ladies could avail themselves of this portable vanity while they were traveling.

a.

b.

c.

Figure 21 — (a) Antique silver filigree coach-chatelette with compact, perfume bottle, and swivel mirror suspended from chain with filigree hook.
(b) Antique silver filigree engraved belt chatelette with matching writing slate, perfume or smelling salts holder, pencil, and round compact suspended on filigree chain from belt hook.
(c) German silver fluted chatelaine, oval locket/pin container, oblong stamp holder, round compact, oval coin holder, and oblong memo pad, all suspended from ring.

Salvador Dali's "Bird-In Hand" Compact

Salvador Dali, the Spanish surrealist painter, sculptor, and illustrator (May 11, 1904 – January 23, 1989), was born in Figueras, Catalonia, Spain, and studied in Barcelona and Madrid. He became known as the "enfant terrible" of surrealism, as well as its best-known exponent. Since 1932 Dali's works have been shown throughout Europe, the United States, and the Orient.

In the 1940s and 1950s, Dali designed many commercial

There has always been a great demand for the works of Salvador Dali. The Dali "Bird-In-Hand" compact is very desirable because of its beauty, rarity, and uniqueness. It is sought after by compact collectors, collectors of Dali's works, objects d'art, and figural items.

A "Bird-in-Hand" compact is on display in the Salvador Dali Museum, 1000 3rd Avenue South, St. Petersburg, FL 33701.

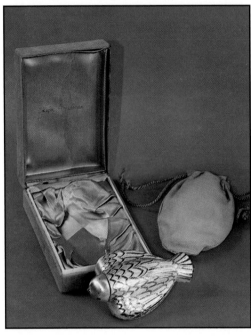

Figure 22 — Elgin American Dali "Bird-in-Hand" compact with turquoise drawstring carrying case and turquoise suede fitted presentation box.

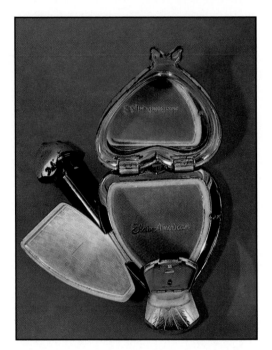

Figure 23 — Elgin American Dali "Bird-in-Hand" compact opened to reveal lipstick holder, powder, and pillbox compartments.

works of art. In 1950 he was commissioned to design a compact for Elgin American, which became known as the "Bird-in-Hand" compact.

The "Bird-In-Hand" compact is 4½" x 2½" with ruby red eyes and was manufactured in three different finishes — satin bronze, silver, and sterling silver — with a 14k gold overlay effect on the wings. The compact contains a powder compartment, a pillbox, and a lipstick. The bird's head holds the slide-out lipstick and the body contains the powder box, which is revealed when the wings are spread apart (Figure 23). The tailpiece conceals the pillbox. Dali's signature appears on the underside of the bird's head (Figure 24). The compact comes with a turquoise drawstring carrying case and a suede turquoise Elgin American fitted hinged presentation box (Figure 22).

The minimum prices for the "Bird-in-Hand" compact were listed in Elgin American's 1952 – 1953 catalog:

Satin bronze finish . . . . .Dealer $7.50 . . .Retail $15.00
Silver finish . . . . .Dealer $12.50 . .Retail $25.00
Sterling silver . . . . .Dealer $50.00 .Retail $100.00

Figure 24 — Elgin American Dali "Bird-in-Hand" compact; silver finish on left, satin bronze finish (goldtone) on right.

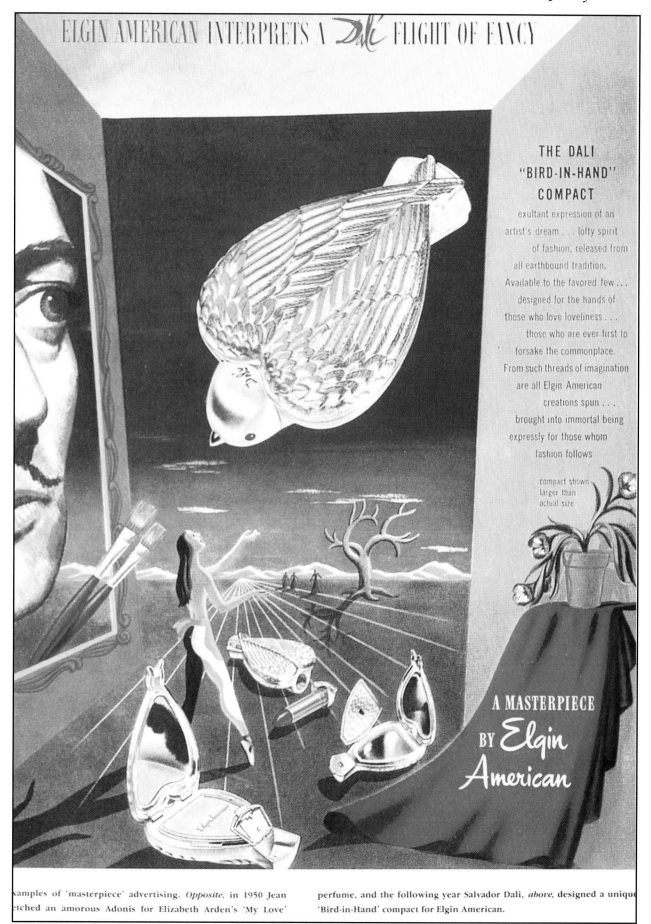

ELGIN AMERICAN INTERPRETS A *Dali* FLIGHT OF FANCY

THE DALI "BIRD-IN-HAND" COMPACT

exultant expression of an
artist's dream . . . lofty spirit
of fashion, released from
all earthbound tradition.
Available to the favored few . . .
designed for the hands of
those who love loveliness . . .
those who are ever first to
forsake the commonplace.
From such threads of imagination
are all Elgin American
creations spun . . .
brought into immortal being
expressly for those whom
fashion follows

compact shown
larger than
actual size

A MASTERPIECE
BY *Elgin American*

Examples of 'masterpiece' advertising. *Opposite*, in 1950 Jean
etched an amorous Adonis for Elizabeth Arden's 'My Love'
perfume, and the following year Salvador Dali, *above*, designed a unique
'Bird-in-Hand' compact for Elgin American.

Vogue *ad for "Bird-In-Hand" compact, 1951.*

25

Minaudières, Carryalls, and Necessaires

In the 1930s women customarily wore evening gowns to dinner parties and the theater. Since women often traveled in the same social circles, the well-dressed woman needed several different gowns with matching bags to wear to these functions. To resolve the problem of changing evening bags to match each costume, Van Cleef & Arpels invented the minaudière (Figure 25b), the one evening bag that could harmonize and complement each dress. The minaudiére is a rigid metal box-shaped evening bag, really a super compact with specific compartments for cosmetic and personal necessities — powder, lipstick, coins, a watch, cigarettes, and comb. It was Estelle Arpels, co-founder with her husband Alfred Cleef of Van Cleef & Arpels, who inspired the name for the firm's jeweled evening bags. Her brothers, Julien, Charles, and Louis, who were also partners, used to say that no one could minauder, or charm, in society as their sister Estelle. Thus, the name minaudière. The original minaudières were sold at fashionable, expensive jewelry houses. They were usually made of gold or silver and sometimes encrusted with precious gems.

The carryall (Figures 25a), an affordable mass-produced version of the minaudière, was manufactured in a variety of beautiful and inexpensive finishes by many popular compact manufacturers.

The necessaire (Figures 25c) is cylindrical or bolster-shaped, a smaller version of the minaudière with fewer compartments, made in either precious metals or inexpensive finishes.

a.

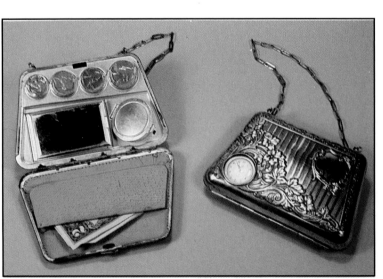

b.

c.

Figure 25 (a) — Evans carryall with dual openings, white enamel lids decorated with red and clear rhinestones, interiors reveal cigarette holder, cigarette compartment, coin holder, lipstick holder, compact, and comb. Rigid braided goldtone handle.
(b) Engraved and engine-turned decorated silvertone minaudière with watch incorporated in lid with carrying chain. Interior reveals coin holder, mirrored cigarette compartment, powder well, and leather pocket for incidentals.
(c) Webster Company sterling silver necessaire with lipstick suspended from bottom. Gilded interior; mirror separates powder and rouge compartments, second opening reveals cigarette compartment. Black wrist carrying cord.

Tips From a Compact Collector

Compacts are found in many different places. Flea markets, and tag and garage sales usually have the best prices but may be time consuming. The best source is still either an antique shop or antique show if you are looking for a specific collectible. The antique dealers have already scouted the garage sales and flea markets and will therefore save you time. Compacts may also be found in thrift stores, vintage clothing stores, and consignment shops. Quality vintage compacts may now be found at many auction houses as well, and many antique papers advertise compacts for sale.

Presently auctions on computers are also a very popular source for compacts. In addition to finding compacts from the comfort of your own home, the auction prices usually indicate current values for your collectibles. Collectors now make printouts of current completed auctions of compacts that they own that may be used for insurance purposes.

When purchasing a compact by mail, always inquire as to the compact's condition and age, and request a complete description including price. Find out whether you may return the compact if you are not satisfied.

Always request a receipt when making a purchase. The receipt should describe the compact in as much detail as possible. The price, condition, composition, and name and address or phone number of the vendor should also be included.

When traveling to different parts of the country, "let your fingers do the walking." Check the Antique section in the Yellow Pages of the local telephone directory for antique shops and the local paper's daily-event section for flea markets, tag sales, and street fairs.

Another source is *Powder Puff*, the International Compact Collectors Chronicle, P.O. Box 40, Lynbrook, NY 11563. The newsletter features a Seekers, Sellers, and Swappers column which is offered free to members.

If a compact comes in the original box or pouch, do not destroy or discard it. The value of the compact is increased if it has its original presentation box.

Original parts of a collectible should always be left intact. Missing, broken, or torn parts such as colored stones, tassels, mirrors, or carrying cords may be replaced with parts that will adhere to and not alter the style or original design. Check to see whether there has been a "marriage" between two compacts — one part of a compact attached or inserted in a compact of like design. Lipsticks are sometimes removed from an inexpensive compact and inserted in a more expensive compact. A reputable dealer will tell you if this has been done.

Enameled compacts purchased for investment purposes should be in mint condition. Minor flaws in a compact purchased for your collection and not for resale may be repaired. Repairing chipped or scratched enamels may be costly and decrease the value of the compact.

Only mirrors that are broken should be removed and replaced in a vintage compact. I prefer not to replace a mirror that is discolored, flawed, or in need of resilvering. The original mirror always enhances the value of the compact.

It is advisable to remove loose powder from your compact before adding it to your collection. Loose powder will inadvertently spill when the compact is opened. Solid powder, rouge, and lipstick should never be used but may be left in the compact.

Never apply a sticker directly to the surface of a compact. The acids from the glue may discolor or irreparably damage the finish, especially an enamel finish. Apply a price or identification sticker to the metal or mirror inside the compact or on a string-tag attached to the compact.

Parts of a vintage compact may sometimes be very fragile and should be handled as little as possible. The best way to display, share, and enjoy your collection is in a glass-enclosed cabinet or case. Compacts may be displayed in a revolving lighted curio cabinet or in a showcase such as those used to display watches. Another way to display compacts is in a viewing table that can also serve as a coffee or cocktail table, or in a 3" to 5" deep shadow box. The compacts can be suspended from hooks or placed on shelves inside the framed box. Several shadow boxes mounted on the wall produce an interesting and unusual wall arrangement.

Keep a running inventory of your collection. List the items on index cards and keep them in a file box. Note the date, price, and place of purchase and the name of the seller. Also include any information on the history, previous owner, or background that you can obtain from the seller. Include a full description including size, finish, and condition, and a photograph of the compact.

Photograph or videotape your collection so that you will have a complete and accurate record of your collection for insurance purposes. Don't forget to keep adding pictures as your collection grows. Keep the photos in a safe place in your home and a duplicate set in a friend's home or in a safety deposit box.

Always use a certified appraiser when you have your collection appraised. Your local Society of Appraiser Referral Services will supply you with information about an appraisal specialist in your area. An appraisal should be typewritten, dated, and signed and contain a complete and accurate description of the collection (not a "laundry list" type that uses description such as "round," "small," "red," "compact," etc.). It is very important that your appraisal be current. If you should sustain a loss, your insurance company will pay only the latest amount listed by the appraiser.

Vanity Reflections

Inflated Flatos

Paul Flato's compacts made in the 1940s and 1950s are pretty, whimsical, and eagerly sought after by compact collectors. Flato's compacts, either goldtone or silvertone, are decorated with an applied whimsical object usually set with beautiful colored stones. The majority of Flato's compacts also come with a matching lipstick. The matching lipstick has a miniature replica of the theme that decorates the front lid applied to the end of the tube. The set comes complete with a fitted case that holds the compact and lipstick. The cases come in a variety of colors and materials — satin, moire, grosgrain, leather. Flato patented many of his compact designs and also had a patent for the fitted slip case, "Compact and Lipstick Receptacle" Des. 154,670, filed on Feb. 28, 1948 (Figure 32). These vintage compacts were affordable and could be found priced from $40.00 to $140.00 depending on whether they had original box, puff, lipstick, and case. Now they are going for $300.00 and $400.00 (complete). One of the reasons could possibly be that there have been several articles on jewelry that mention Paul Flato prominently. On October 21, 1991, Christie's American Jewelry Auction catalog had bibliographies on the foremost American jewelers, and Flato was one of the jewelers included. Perhaps this write-up, in addition to several other articles on Flato, has made the public again aware of this designer.

Below, reprinted with permission, from Christie's American Jewelry, October 21, 1992, auction catalog is Paul Flato's biography, written by Janet Zapatta.

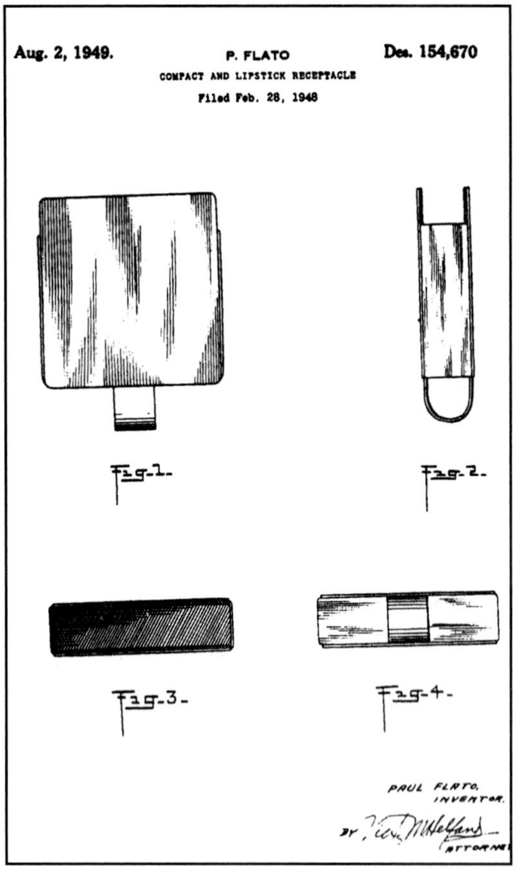

PAUL FLATO

Paul Flato was born in 1900 in Flatonia, Texas, amid the expectation of a new century, and, in three decades, would become one of the foremost American jewelry designers. Flato's introduction into the jewelry field started in the role of salesman for Edmond E. Frisch. In the late 1920s, he opened his own shop at 1 East Fifty-Seventy Street in New York City, several years before Tiffany & Co. relocated to their current address just across the street. His design-oriented style, often bordering on the humorous, reached its peak in the 1930s when all the fashionable people of New York gathered at his salon. Adolph Kleaty, George Headley, and Fulco di Verdura were among his designers. Two prominent clients, Mrs. James V. Forrestal and Millicent Rogers Balcom, were responsible for his whimsical creations such as the "wiggly clips" and the "puffy heart" series.

In 1937, Flato opened a branch in Beverly Hills, at 8657 Sunset Boulevard, with Fulco di Verdura in charge. He is credited with designing the jewelry Katherine Hepburn wore in "The Philadelphia Story." This branch remained open for only two years, frequented by such luminaries as Greta Garbo, Joan Crawford, Merle Oberon, and Marlene Dietrich. Later in life, Flato left this country, establishing a shop in Mexico City in the fashionable Zona Rosa district.

On Tuesday, December 6, 1994, Christie's, New York, had another important jewels auction. Approximately 2,000 original full-color drawings by Paul Flato, one of America's great jewelers, were offered (Figures 28, 29, 30). The artwork was in an attic for almost three decades and was sold in group lots. Flato covered every aspect of jewelry design, puffy hearts, animals, telephones, and body parts. In the early 1940s Flato closed his business. In Christie's December 6, 1994, auction, in addition to the drawings, one actual piece of Flato jewelry — a gold telephone dial compact — was offered (Figure 27).

Figure 26 — Paul Flato's Compact and Lipstick Receptacle Patent.

Amusing Retro Gold
Telephone Dial Compact

Of circular outline in 14K gold, the lid designed as a rotary dial, the finger holes engraved and enameled with the letters "I LOVE YOU" opening to reveal a mirror, in a suede slipcase, circa 1940. Signed by Flato. Estimated auction price $1,500.00 – $2,000.00 — actual price realized was $4,830.00 plus tax.

Figure 27 — Paul Flato's 14K gold telephone dial compact. Photograph reproduced with permission from Christie's, NY.

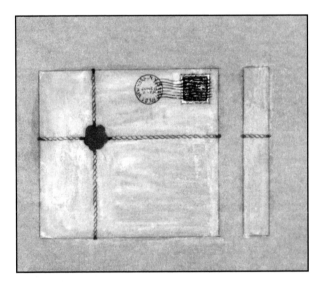

Figures 28, 29 & 30 — Paul Flato's original drawings of ladies' vanities. Photographs reproduced with permission from Christie's, N.Y.

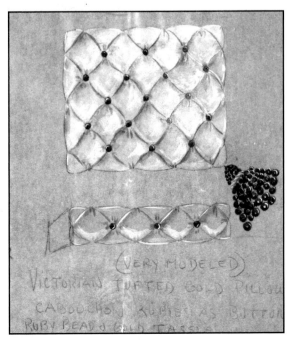

THE PICCADILLY VANITY BAG

The Piccadilly vanity bag, popular in the 1920s, incorporates a compact on the center of the outside frame. Opening the Piccadilly compact can sometimes be very tricky. Immediately underneath the compact there should be an engraved tab. To open the compact, gently pull down on the tab. If the compact resists or the tab is fragile, insert your fingernail between the compact and tab and press down on the tab (should be the same effect as pulling the tab). The compact should then pop open. Remember never use force to open any compact.

KIGU

The Kigu compact was crafted by Gustav Kiashek who was one of the first craftsmen ever to make a powder compact. He was a second generation master silver and goldsmith from Hungary. By the early twenties, he had set up a factory in Budapest to produce small quantities of these beautifully decorated compacts, establishing the firm's trade name KI-GU which is derived from KI-ashek and GU-stav. Gustav's son George came to England in 1939 and at the end of the war began to produce the compacts and cigarette cases that made the name of Kigu, as it became known, celebrated worldwide. While he was a goldsmith, George foresaw that powder compacts would become a necessity for every woman. He combined the craftsmanship of the artist with the skill of the engineer to produce compacts of character, and as his slogan put it, at a price which everyone could afford. Many patents, registered designs, and trademarks made Kigu features exclusive. Among these are the patented inner lid catch which makes for easy operation, the built-in mirror frame which guards the glass, and the spill-proof inner lid which prevents powder from escaping. The finish of the compacts is jewel-like and is protected by an invisible coating. Kigu compact shapes and motifs took on a new dimension. Some of these were the "Musical Flying Saucer," "Tennis Ball," "Flower Basket," and assorted "Suitcases." A costume jewelry factory was also acquired which produced decorative adornments for the compacts as well as for other fashion accessories. Kigu stopped making compacts and manufactured costume jewelry instead in the latter part of the 1950s and the early part of the 1960s when the au natural look took over, and compressed powder in disposable plastic compacts replaced the metal case. The beautifully crafted and figural vintage Kigu compacts are now much coveted collector items.

THE MAGIC MONOGRAM DIAL

The Zell monogram dial compact was one of their most popular designs. Since it could be personalized, it was a perfect gift. These compacts have two open panels on their lids and can be personalized by adjusting the moveable dials located on the rim of the compact. Compacts that are engraved "Happy Birthday" or "Congratulations" have two panels, one for the month and the other for the date. The style that comes with letters is designed for monogramming the compact (Figure 31).

VANITY KODAK ENSEMBLE

The October 1928 issue of the *Eastman Kodak Trade Circular* introduced the Vanity Kodak Ensemble (Figure 32). In addition to the Kodak camera, the ensemble contained a large mirror, change pocket, a Richard Hudnut combination powder and rouge compact, and lipstick tube. The grained leather strap-style carrying case came in three colors, gray, beige, and green. Production of this vanity ensemble continued through 1929 (for one year only) and the camera to 1933. This ensemble is very rare and is sought after by both vintage camera collectors and compact collectors (Figures 33, 34).

Prior to seeing this ad, I wasn't aware that a combination such as this one existed. One day when Alvin and I were out antiquing, Alvin spotted the case with the Kodak camera, minus the compact combination, in one of the showcases. He called me over and I remembered that I had the exact Richard Hudnut vanity and lipstick tube at home that would complete the ensemble. Because it was late in the day and the camera case was not complete, the price of the case with the camera was very affordable. I was thrilled when I came home and found the compact that completed the set. Exactly like the ad! If I had not seen the ad, I would have missed out on this great find. This is one of the reasons that vintage ads are very important; they help determine the date and manufacturer of unmarked compacts. They also illustrate what the original tassel or carrying chain looks like for replacement purposes.

CONVERTIBLE RING VANITIES

In the 1925 *Woman's World* magazine, an ad appeared offering Gift No. 559, a "Convertible Ring Vanity," sent prepaid, for a 2-year subscription — 50 cents for each year — total $1.00. "Useful, Beautiful and Brand New! By far the most convenient and most artistic innovation in the line of vanities which has yet been devised for milady's service and adornment. It was the sensation in the smart Parisian salons this season. These Convertible Vanities Are the Smart Thing Now — Three Combinations in One — Sautoir, Bracelet or Ring with Mirror, Compact and Puff. It may be worn on the finger as a handsome dinner ring, on a silk ribbon as a modish bracelet, or on a sautoir as an ornate and artistic appendage. But wherever it is worn, it is always ready for instant use as a vanity. Open the lid with its beautiful stone setting and, lo! there is revealed a diminutive mirror, a compact, and a powder puff large enough to render the full service that is expected of it. The rings are exquisitely etched, filled white gold, mounted with your choice of the following synthetic stones — jade, turquoise, emerald, ruby and onyx (Figure 35). The top of the ring measures one inch long by half inch wide. A handsome piece of workmanship throughout." (A smaller version comes with mirror and filled with lip rouge.)

Figure 31 — Zell "Initially Yours" dial-a-monogram round goldtone compact with complimentary goldtone powder spoon gift; two dials on exterior rim set first and last initials in panels on lid of compact; rhinestones frame panels; lid decorated with incised swirls; interior mirror, puff, and powder well; 3¼" dia.

Figure 33 — Kodak Vanity Ensemble; tan leather case contains Kodak camera and a Richard Hudnut Du Barry tango chain goldtone vanity; vanity contains mirror, rouge, and powder compartments; lipstick attached to vanity by link chain; case contains mirror and small shirred pocket; exterior carrying handle; compact 1⅜" x 3¼", case 3¾" x 7". Shown open.

Figure 32 — Eastman Kodak Company Trade Circular, October 1928.

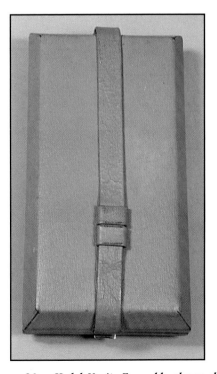

Figure 34 — Kodak Vanity Ensemble, shown closed.

Figure 35 — Two oval convertible compact/ring combinations; smaller ring is a rouge pot, interior contains rouge and mirror; stone centered on lid of smaller ring; larger ring interior has powder compartment, mirror, and puff; both can be converted to bracelets or worn on a chain as a neck pendant; larger one shown as bracelet with grosgrain wrist band; smaller one shown as ring; larger one $\frac{5}{8}$" x 1"; smaller one $\frac{15}{16}$" x $\frac{7}{8}$".

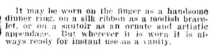

Woman's World magazine, 1925.

Gallery of Vintage Compacts

Rare, unusual museum quality verdigris metal compact designed to resemble a miniature dresser, top lifts up to reveal mirror, powder well and puff, drawer pulls out and framed hand painted picture of a period woman pops up. Reverse side shows fly in a spider web, 1¾" x 1¾" x ¾" deep. NPA.

Dresser compact with drawer partially open.

Dresser compact with drawer completely open.

Reverse side of dresser compact.

Extremely rare museum quality brushed goldtone scepter vanity case combination, c. 1935, sold exclusively at Bergdorf Goodman; sphere-shaped top opens to reveal metal mirror separating mini coin purse from rouge and powder wells; rhinestone decorated baton unscrews twice revealing cavities for personal necessities; lipstick tube pulls out from tip of scepter; complete with brown silk carrying cord, 10½" x 2½" dia. NPA.

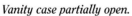

Vanity case partially open.

Vanity case completely open.

Prinzess goldtone compact designed to resemble purse; over-all engraved design; push-back handle reveals powder compartment; lid centered with colored stones and raised enamel flowers; Czechoslovakia; 3½" x 3". $150.00 – 200.00.

Goldtone Trinity Platé two sided vanity; lids and rim decorated with filigree overlay enhanced with cabochon and faceted blue and green colored stones; one side opens to reveal mirror and powder well; other side reveals pocket with pull-string powder puff; black tassel and carrying cord; 2½" dia. x 1¼". $325.00 – 500.00.

Antique goldtone filigree vanity case with multicolored stones on lid; opens on either side; two sliding lipsticks at sides; one side opens for powder compartment, other side for rouge; screw perfume knob at top conceals metal perfume wand; black tassel and carrying cord; 2" x 1¼". $350.00 – 450.00.

Small round goldtone vanity; applied raised star design enhanced with blue stones decorates top lid; goldtone filigree and blue stones encircle second lid opening; top opens to reveal lip rouge; second opening reveals mirror separating powder and rouge compartment; 2" dia. x 1¼". $250.00 – 350.00.

Left – Gilded-metal embossed vanity case; multicolored intaglio decorated lid; cameo disc centered on lid; metal tassel; carrying chain; velvet interior with compartment for powder, rouge, and lipstick tube; deeply beveled mirror framed with metal scallop; France; 3" x 2½". $300.00 – 400.00.

Top – Oblong gilded-metal embossed compact; multicolored intaglio decorated lid; prong set with red stones and painted cloisonne inserts; carrying chain; deeply beveled mirror framed with metal scallop; France; 1½" x 2½". $150.00 – 200.00.

Right – Gilded-metal embossed vanity case; multicolored intaglio decorated lid; prong set with pale pink stones; turquoise stones surround painted cloisonne centered disc; velvet interior with compartment for powder and lipstick tube; deeply beveled mirror framed with metal scallop; tassel; carrying chain; France; 2¾" x 2¾". $300.00 – 400.00.

Bottom – Gilded-metal embossed vanity case; multicolored intaglio decorated lid; prong set with blue stones; velvet interior with compartments for powder and two lipstick tubes; deeply beveled mirror framed with metal scallop; tassel; carrying chain; France; 2" x 2¾". $250.00 – 300.00.

Left – Brushed goldtone purse-motif vanity case; lid decorated with colored stones set on filigree plaque; interior reveals powder sifter, rouge compartment, and mirror; carrying chain; 3" x 2". $100.00 – 175.00.

Top – Antique goldtone vanity; lid set with colored stones; interior reveals compartments for powder, rouge, and lipstick tube; mesh carrying chain; 2¼" x 2½". $100.00 – 175.00.

Right – Purse-motif dark grained goldtone compact; interior reveals powder compartment, mirror, and coin and bill holders; blue stone centered on lid; carrying chain; 2¾" x 1¾". $75.00 – 100.00.

Bottom – Morss oblong brass compact; deeply engraved lid centered with pavé set rhinestones and green colored stones; 2⅞" x 2⅛". $100.00 – 125.00.

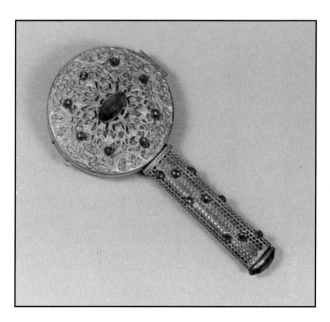

Goldtone vanity shaped as hand mirror; filigree lid and lipstick tube enhanced with red stones; interior opens to reveal mirror and powder and rouge compartments; lipstick slides out of handle; large faceted marquis red stone centered on lid and end of lipstick tube; 2" dia. x 4". $200.00 – 250.00.

Top – Gilded-metal compact; filigree lid decorated with prong set red and green cabochon stones and prong set pearls; dome-shaped painted enamel disc centered on lid; interior reveals mirror and powder compartment; France; 2¼" x 2¼". $175.00 – 225.00.

Top center – Horseshoe-shaped gilded-metal embossed compact; lid decorated with prong set red and green cabochon stones; blue disc with fleur-de-lis centered on lid; interior reveals beveled mirror and powder well; France; 1⅜" x 1⅜". $125.00 – 150.00.

Bottom center – Round embossed gilded-metal compact; lid set with dome-shaped painted enamel disc; interior contains mirror and powder well; France; 1½" dia. $40.00 – 60.00.

Bottom – Gilded-metal engraved comb case with comb; case decorated with enamel flower and bezel set colored stones; 4" x 1". $35.00 – 50.00.

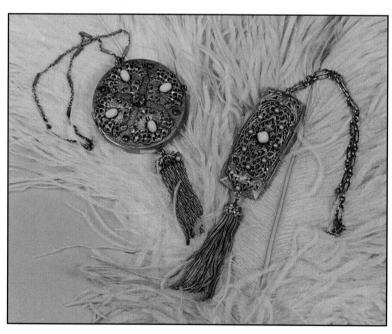

Left – Round antique goldtone compact; filigree lid set with pearls and yellow stones; interior reveals mirror and powder well; metal tassel and carrying chain; 2½" dia. $200.00 – 250.00.

Right – Oblong antique goldtone coin holder; filigree lid set with pearls; metal tassel and carrying chain; 1½" x 3¾". $175.00 – 225.00.

Left – Antique goldtone oblong filigree vanity; filigree lids set with pearls and yellow stones; interior reveals powder and rouge compartments and mirror; metal tassel and carrying chain; 1½" x 3". $350.00 – 400.00.

Right – Round antique goldtone filigree compact; filigree lids set with pearls; interior reveals mirror and powder compartment; metal tassel and carrying chain; 2" dia. $275.00 – 325.00.

Square mini goldtone compact, lid decorated with colorful crystal flowers and bees, push-down thumbpiece, interior powder well and mirror, 2" sq. $75.00 – 85.00.

Unmarked round goldtone compact, lid decorated with beautiful prong set multi-shaped colored stones, 3¼" dia. $75.00 – 125.00.

Germaine Monteil round, brushed goldtone Jeweled Lipstick and Jeweled Powder compacts, lids set with round mobe pearl framed by pronged, faceted turquoise stones, twist closures. Left, powder compact, 1¾" dia., $45.00 – 55.00; right, lipstick compact, 1" dia. $35.00 – 45.00.

Two 2" square compacts. Top, petit point lid framed with clear rhinestones; bottom, black enamel lid framed with clear rhinestones. $25.00 – 35.00 each.

Square goldtone compact lid decorated with black and clear crystal flowers, framed mirror and powder well, 2" sq. $35.00 – 45.00.

Volupté square goldtone compact, lid centered with crystals in the shape of a diamond, interior reveals powder compartment and mirror, 2½" x 2½". $45.00 – 55.00.

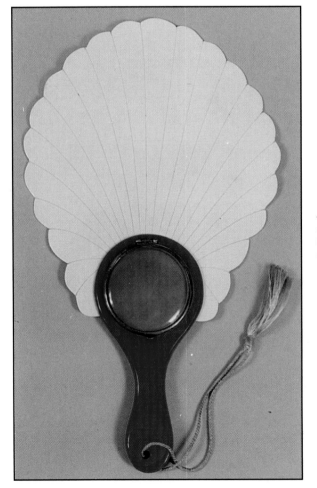

Ivorene and maroon plastic fan/compact combination; incised sunburst design on fan; maroon handle incorporates compact; interior reveals mirror and puff; exterior mirror on reverse side of compact; tassel; 7" x 11½", compact 2⅛", $375.00 – 475.00.

Square goldtone Ciner compact and lipstick, lid of compact centered with a beautiful enamel and colored crystal coat-of-arms, top of lipstick decorated with a crown set with clear crystals, complete with faille carrying case, interior of compact reveals signed puff mirror and powder well, 2¾" sq. $175.00 – 225.00.

Square polished goldtone Wadsworth compact, elaborately framed round mirror centered on top lid, 3" sq. $45.00 – 55.00.

Round goldtone Max Factor compact, lid decorated with dimensional fishes and centered with a cabochon green stone, 2" dia. $55.00 – 75.00.

Triangular-shaped brass compact, lid decorated with filigree design centered with green cameo, powder well, mirror, and puff, 1¾" x 1¾", $75.00 – 85.00.

Antique goldtone filigree vanity case; outer rims set with pearls and blue stones; openings on either side; one side powder compartment and mirror; other side rouge compartment and mirror; metal tassel and carrying chain; 2¾" dia. $300.00 – 400.00.

Antique goldtone vanity bag; filigree goldtone lid decorated with blue stones; moonstone centered on front lid of vanity; front lid opens to reveal framed mirror and compartments for rouge and powder; interior of bag silk lined with pockets on either side; silk back; jeweled carrying chain and tassel; Trinity Plate 2" x 3½" x 1". $450.00 – 550.00.

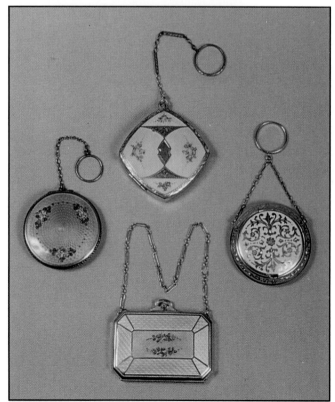

Left – Hallmarked sterling round compact; lavender cloisonné lid decorated with flowers; finger ring chain; 2" dia. $225.00 – 275.00.

Top – Silvertone and yellow enamel vanity; enamel lid decorated with flowers; interior reveals mirror and compartments for rouge and powder; finger ring chain; 2" x 2". $125.00 – 150.00.

Right – Green, off-white, and silvertone champlevé vanity; interior reveals mirror and compartments for rouge and powder; finger ring chain; 2¼" dia. $100.00 – 125.00.

Bottom – E.A.M. blue cloisonné enamel vanity; lid decorated with flowers; interior reveals metal mirror, powder, and rouge compartments; wrist chain; 2½" x 1½". $125.00 – 150.00.

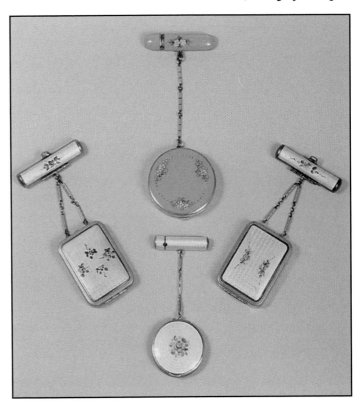

Left – Green enamel tango chain vanity; lid of vanity and lipstick holder decorated with flowers; lipstick holder suspended by two chains; interior of vanity reveals metal mirror separating powder and rouge compartments; lipstick holder opens up to accept slim lipstick tube; 1½" x 2" x 4½". $125.00 – 150.00.

Top – Hallmarked sterling green enamel tango chain vanity; enamel lid and lipstick holder decorated with flowers; lipstick suspended by green enamel link chain; interior of vanity reveals mirror and compartments for powder and rouge; engraved next to hallmark is date 3–4–15; 2" dia. x 5½". $350.00 – 450.00.

Right – Blue, same as compact on left.

Bottom – Round yellow enamel mini-tango chain vanity; enamel lid and lipstick decorated with flowers; lipstick suspended by link chain; interior of vanity reveals metal mirror separating powder and rouge compartments, $100.00 – 125.00.

Left – D.F.B. Co. blue enamel vanity case with painted windmill scene; wrist carrying chain with key; powder sifter and rouge compartment; "Pat'd Feb. 9, 1926"; 3" x 2". $150.00 – 250.00.

Right – Same as left compact except for unusual feature of finger carrying ring on underside of compact.

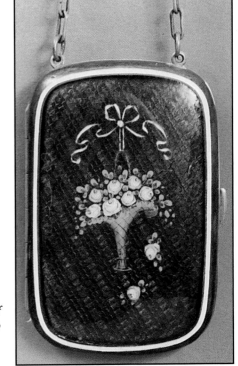

Stunning green enameled vanity, lid decorated with enameled basket of flowers, interior reveals beveled mirror, powder compartment, and two coin holders, complete with carrying chain, 3½" x 2¼". $225.00 – 275.00.

Round, peach enameled finger ring compact, lid decorated with Elk emblem, reverse side reads, "Carnival Ball, New Orleans, 30, March 2nd, 1916," interior mirror, puff, and powder well, 1½" dia. $85.00 – 100.00.

Pinaud cream-colored enamel compact/key-chain combination compact, bone-colored enamel lid with goldtone stripes, interior reveals mirror and puff, 1½" sq. $35.00 – 45.00.

Round silvertone finger ring compact, yellow enamel lid centered with pink enamel rose, interior reveals mirror and perforated powder well with rotating lid, 1⅞" dia. $85.00 – 100.00.

Silvertone octagon Art Deco yellow and black enameled compact and tango chain, matching lipstick connected from finger ring by yellow enameled chain; compact 2⅛", lipstick 2⅛". $225.00 – 275.00.

Desirable, unique green enameled octagon-shaped tandem powder compact and rouge compact, matching lipstick attached by two goldtone chains, enameled lid decorated with pink roses, 1¾" h x 3". $450.00 – 600.00.

Oval green and blue Art Deco enameled vanity and tango chain, matching lipstick, interior reveals beveled mirror, powder and rouge compartments with puffs; compact 2¾" x 1½", lipstick 2¼". $225.00 – 275.00.

Lower left – Lavender enamel vanity; enamel lid decorated with flowers; interior reveals metal mirror separating powder and rouge compartments; 2" x 1½". $80.00 – 100.00.

Top left – RAC octagon-shaped green enamel tango chain compact; center of lid decorated with transfer decal of man and woman; lipstick tube decorated with flowers; 2" x 2" x 5". $175.00 – 200.00.

Top center – Blue enamel octagon-shaped vanity; enamel lid decorated with flowers; finger chain; interior reveals powder well, metal mirror, and rouge compartment; 1¾" x 1¾". $80.00 – 100.00.

Top right – White enamel octagon-shaped tango chain vanity; enamel lid decorated with flowers; lipstick tube suspended by two chains; interior reveals metal mirror, powder, and rouge compartments; 2" x 2" x 5". $175.00 – 200.00.

Lower right – Blue, same as lower left compact.

Bottom center – Yellow enamel vanity; enamel lid decorated with flowers; interior reveals metal mirror separating rouge and powder compartments; 1¾" x 2¼". $80.00 – 100.00.

Center – Round green enamel mini compact; enamel lid decorated with goldtone star design; 1½" dia. $75.00 – 100.00.

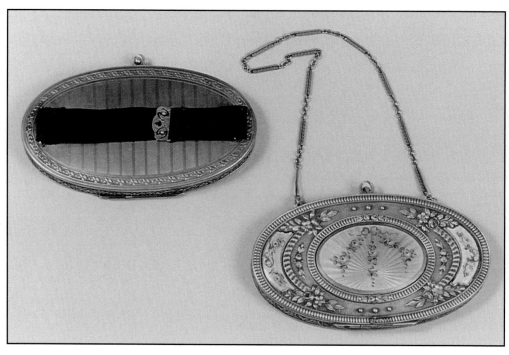

Left – Antiqued goldtone oval embossed vanity case; cloisonné lid decorated with flowers; compartments for powder sifter, rouge, lipstick, and coins; unusual grosgrain carrying handle on back lid; 4¾" x 2½". $350.00 – 500.00.

Right – Same as compact on the left except comes with carrying chain.

Foster & Bailey sterling silver green cloisonné vanity case suspended from enameled perfume container; powder and rouge compartments; lipstick attched at base; tassel and black enameled finger ring chain; 2" dia. x 8". $2,500.00 – 3,000.00.

Gilded turquoise enamel compact; turquoise lid decorated with a gold foliate overlay design; centered on lid is a hand-painted portrait on enamel; interior reveals beveled mirror; 2¾" x 2¼". $250.00 – 300.00.

Top – Semi-scalloped blue enamel and gilded compact; hand-painted pastoral scene centered on lid; engraved back lid; interior reveals deeply beveled mirror and powder well; 2¾" x 2¾". $250.00 – 300.00.

Bottom – Gilded oblong blue enamel compact; enamel lid framed by deeply etched design; engraved back lid; interior reveals deeply beveled mirror and powder well; 2" x 3⅛". $150.00 – 175.00.

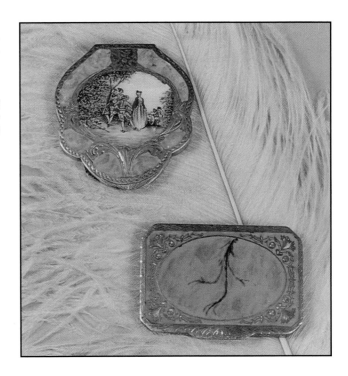

Gilded silver blue enamel compact; front lid decorated with exquisite hand-painted scene; back lid engraved; interior reveals deeply beveled mirror and powder well; carrying pouch reads "David Webb, Inc. New York"; 4" x 3". $450.00 – 550.00.

Left – Round gilt and enamel neck pendant compact with chain; colorful enameled lid decorated with Egyptian motif; interior reveals wire framed mirror, powder puff, and powder compartment; 1⅜" dia. $100.00 – 150.00.

Right – Round gilt and enamel neck pendant compact with chain; blue enameled lid decorated with green leaves; interior reveals wire framed mirror, powder puff, and powder compartment; 1⅜" dia. $100.00 – 150.00.

Sterling and enamel round minaudière; lid centered with stunning hand-painted pastoral scene; blue enamel dots encircle painting; interior reveals deeply beveled mirror; comb holder and comb swing down from mirror frame; lower center part for small necessities; flanked on either side by powder well and removeable lipstick tube and holder; interior lids, exterior back lid, and outer rim heavily engraved; decorative metal link chain; ornate clasp designed as bow; 3½" x 1". $650.00 – 850.00.

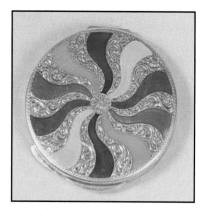

Round sterling compact; lid decorated with red, yellow, green, and blue enamel swirls; interior reveals beveled mirror and powder well; 2¾". $250.00 – 350.00.

Cobalt blue enamel coppertone compact designed to resemble an acorn; interior reveals mirror and powder well; matching enamel lipstick case concealed in tassel; carrying cord; Austria; 1½" x 2¾". $550.00 – 650.00.

Robert Original compact chair open.

Robert Original signed mini goldtone compact chair, coin decorates top lid, cabriole legs, interior reveals beveled mirror, puff, and sifter, 3½" h x 2½" w., $350.00 – 450.00.

Mini three-leg Duncan Phyfe style goldtone compact table, elaborately decorated with clear rhinestones and pearls, mirror replaced, very possibly a Robert Original, 3½" h x 2¾" dia. Shown closed. $300.00 – 375.00.

Compact table at left open.

Robert dresser vanity set; polished armchair-shaped compact; legs, arms, and back heavily engraved; filigree on back and skirt of chair elaborately decorated with pink flowers, rhinestones, and pink stones; lid of chair opens to reveal mirror, puff, and powder compartment; matching clock, perfume bottles, double-sided hand mirror, mirrored tray, and picture frame; label affixed to compact mirror reads "Original by Robert;" compact 2½" dia. x 5", clock 4½" x 3", perfume bottle holder 3" x 2½" x 2¾", hand mirror 4" dia. x 9", tray 6" dia. x 1½", frame 2¾" x 3½". NPA.

Left – Pygmalion goldtone compact designed to resemble grand piano; interior puff reads "Sonata;" cartouche on embossed lid; collapsible legs; 2¼" x 2¾" x 1½". $350.00 – 450.00.

Center – Pygmalion goldtone compact designed to resemble grand piano; interior puff reads "Sonata;" mother-of-pearl lid; sticker on interior mirror reads "Marhill Genuine Mother-of-Pearl;" collapsible legs; 2¼" x 2¾" x 1½". $450.00 – 550.00.

Right – Pygmalion goldtone compact/music box combination designed to resemble grand piano; interior puff reads "Sonata;" starburst design on lid; music box wind-up key located underneath compact; collapsible legs; 2¼" x 2¾" x 1½". $450.00 – 550.00.

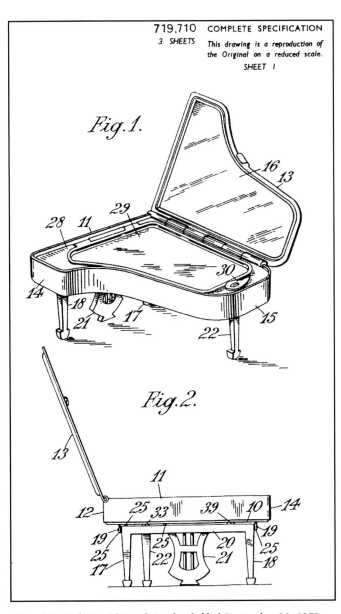

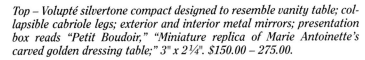

Patent By Salo David Rand, England, filed September 30, 1952.

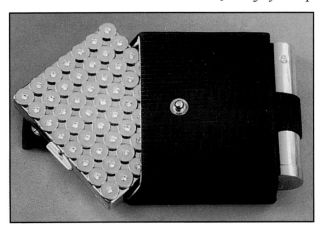

Paul Flato polished goldtone compact with matching lipstick, lid of compact decorated with raised round circles centered with clear rhinestones, lipstick decorated with matching rhinestones, complete with black faille case, 2" x 2½". $95.00 – 100.00.

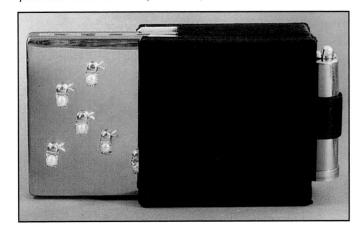

Flato square goldtone compact in slip case with matching lipstick, lid of compact and top of lipstick decorated with little birds and pearls, 2¾" sq. $95.00 – 110.00.

Top – Volupté silvertone compact designed to resemble vanity table; collapsible cabriole legs; exterior and interior metal mirrors; presentation box reads "Petit Boudoir," "Miniature replica of Marie Antoinette's carved golden dressing table;" 3" x 2¼". $150.00 – 275.00.

Bottom – Wadsworth goldtone compact designed to resemble vanity table; collapsible cabriole legs; interior and exterior mirrors; 3" x 2". $150.00 – 275.00.

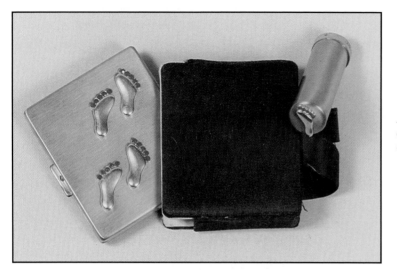

Flato goldtone compact, two sets of feet enhanced with red stones applied to lid; lipstick top has foot and red stones; complete with black satin case, 2½" x 2". $225.00 – 275.00.

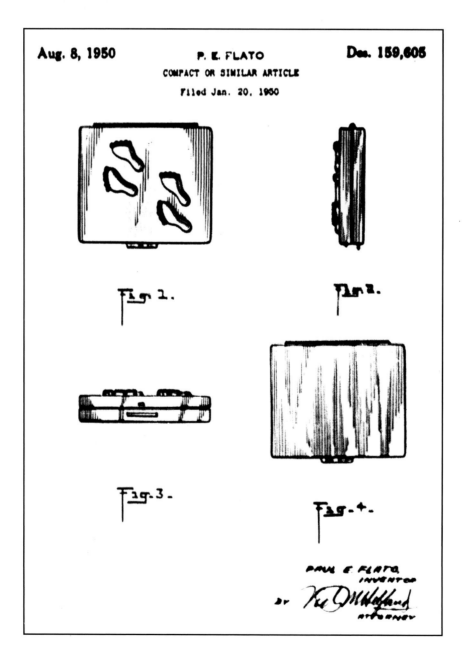

Round brushed goldtone Atomette compact, lid decorated with a beautiful crystal poodle, 2¾" dia. $90.00 – 120.00.

Ciner square brushed goldtone compact with matching lipstick, lid decorated with rhinestone poodle, matching rhinestone poodle head decorates lipstick, complete with black silk fitted carrying case, 2½" x 2½", $125.00 – 175.00.

Tokalon "Petalia" powder box; lid decorated with picture of Pierrot, collar design decorates sides of box; 2¼" dia. $150.00 – 200.00.

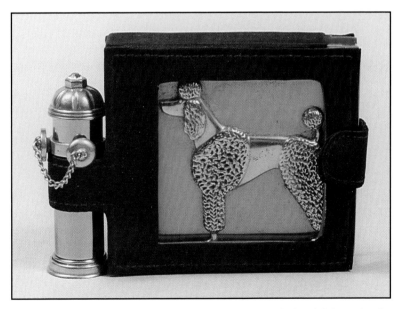

Robert square goldtone compact with large poodle applied to lid; lipstick takes the form of a fire hydrant; top of hydrant decorated with clear rhinestone; complete with black moire carrying case; Original by Robert logo imprinted on red carrying case lining and puff, 2¾" x 2¾". $350.00 – 400.00.

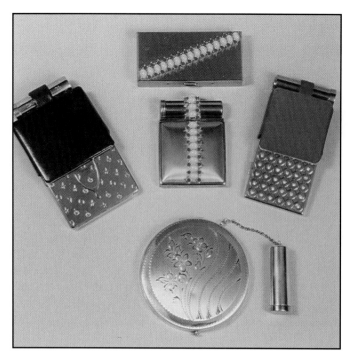

Left – Flato goldtone compact with blue leather case; lid of compact and lipstick tube engraved with good luck symbols; goldtone horseshoe affixed to lid; attached sleeve for lipstick; 2½" x 3 ". $175.00 – 250.00.

Top center – K & K brushed goldtone cigarette case; lid enhanced with band of turquoise and red stones; 3½" x 1½". $60.00 – 80.00.

Center – K & K brushed goldtone compact; compact opens when attached lipstick is pressed back; lid enhanced with band of turquoise and red stones; beveled mirror; Patent #1802795; 2½" x 3". $100.00 – 150.00.

Right – Flato goldtone compact; lid enhanced with raised circles centered with rhinestones; pink silk case with sleeve for lipstick; 2" x 2¾". $100.00 – 125.00.

Bottom center – Rex round brushed silver tango chain compact; lid decorated with polished goldtone flowers; lipstick attached by chain; 3½" dia. x 8". $125.00 – 200.00.

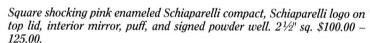

Square shocking pink enameled Schiaparelli compact, Schiaparelli logo on top lid, interior mirror, puff, and signed powder well. 2½" sq. $100.00 – 125.00.

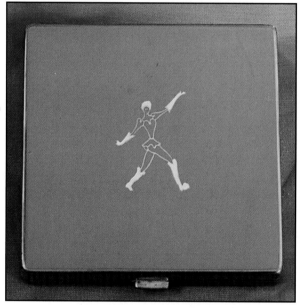

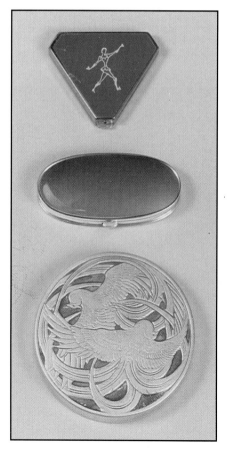

Top – Schiaparelli triangular goldtone rouge compact; dark pink lid decorated with goldtone feminine figure; interior reveals mirror, heart-shaped puff and rouge compartment; case signed; 2" x ⅜". $60.00 – 100.00.

Center – Tiffany & Co. sterling oval compact; interior mirror and powder well; case signed; 2¾" x 1¼". $100.00 – 125.00.

Bottom – Roger & Gallet "Lalique" designed round aluminum compact; lid decorated with embossed cut-out birds on a light orange background; interior mirror, powder compartment, sifter, and "Roger & Gallet" powder puff; inner rim signed; France; 3" dia. x ½". $200.00 – 250.00.

Yardley square silvertone Triple Compact, complete with two lipsticks, one for daytime and one for the evening, either one can be snapped tandem to the compact, lid of compact is centered with family picture. Interior metal mirror separates rouge from powder compartment, compact 1 ⅞" sq. with tandem lipstick 2 ¼". Shown closed in presentation box. $125.00 – 150.00.

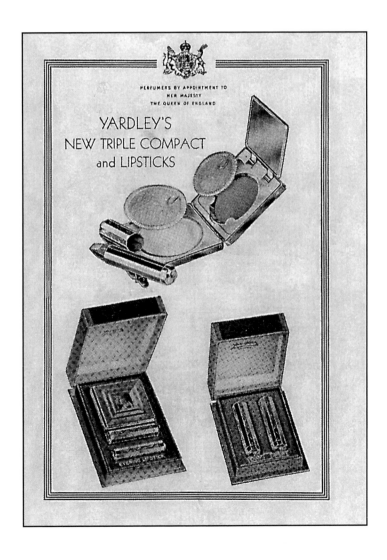

Left – Ciner square goldtone compact with matching lipstick; compact lid and lipstick top decorated with faux pearls; interior mirror and powder well; gold threads decorate black fitted case; powder lid signed; 2¾" square. $175.00 – 200.00.

Center – Ciner square goldtone mini compact with matching lipstick; compact lid and lipstick tube covered in brown alligator leather; interior mirror and powder well; goldtone alligator applied to the top of lipstick tube and centered on compact lid; brown corduroy fitted case; powder lid signed; 2" x 2". $175.00 – 200.00.

Right – Ciner square goldtone compact with matching lipstick; compact lid and lipstick top decorated with pale orange cabochon stones; interior mirror and powder well; gold threads decorated black fitted case; powder lid signed; 2¾" square. $150.00 – 175.00.

Left – Estee Lauder 1969 round silvertone Art Deco compact; lid decorated with light blue, gray, and white Art Deco design; interior reveals mirror and powder well; signed interior rim, beautiful blue suede fitted presentation box with tassel, 4" dia. $175.00 – 225.00.

Right – Estee Lauder 1969 round polished silvertone Heirloom compact; lid decorated with repoussé leaf and ball design; interior reveals mirror and powder well, signed interior rim; beautiful blue suede fitted presentation box with tassel, 4" dia. $175.00 – 225.00.

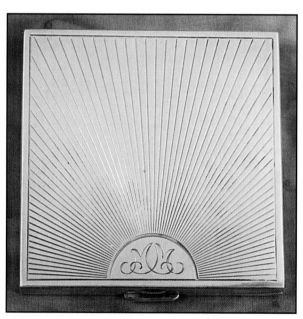

Square sterling silver Tiffany "window wiper" compact, lid decorated with inscribed sunburst pattern, monogram on lower lid, interior reveals beveled mirror, powder well, puff and "window wiper", 2¾" sq. $150.00 – 200.00.

Square silvertone compact/perfume combination, lids back and front decorated with beautiful design in high relief, perfume at top of compact, front opening compact, interior reveals powder well, puff, and mirror framed with rope design, 2" x 2". $175.00 – 200.00.

Compact at left shown open.

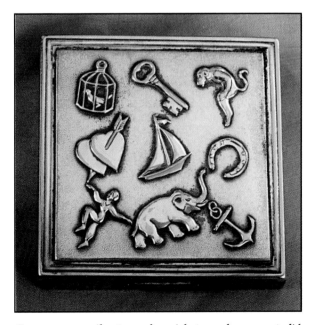

Square Volupté sterling silver compact, lid decorated with raised swirls and centered with a vase with flowers, interior contains mirror, puff, and powder well, 2½" sq. $100.00 – 125.00.

Evans square silvertone charm/photograph compact, lid decorated with nine charms in high relief, interior reveals metal mirror that swings open for photograph, powder well, puff, and sifter, 2½" sq. $75.00 – 95.00.

Left – Eisenberg Original brushed goldtone square compact; large emerald-colored stoned applied to outer lid; interior mirror and powder well; powder lid signed; 3" x 3". $125.00 – 200.00.

Right – Eisenberg Original brushed goldtone square compact; lid set with multicolored marquis and round faceted stones; interior mirror and powder well; powder lid signed; 3" x 3". $125.00 – 200.00.

Gloria Vanderbilt square goldtone compact; lid decorated with painted raindrops, umbrellas, and figures holding umbrellas; "Apres la pluie, le beau temps" painted on front lid; interior mirror and powder well; case signed; 3¾" x 3¾". $150.00 – 225.00.

Enameled light blue square Zell compact, lid decorated with goldtone vintage automobiles, interior mirror, puff, and powder well, 2¾" sq. $35.00 – 45.00.

Schildkraut hand engraved Kyoto Original mother-of-pearl inlay compact, lid decorated with Asian scene, beveled interior mirror, puff, and powder well, 2⅜" x 2¾", $55.00 – 65.00.

Volupté square brushed goldtone compact, lid decorated with engraved polished goldtone frame on artist's easel, enameled ice wagon centered in frame, 3" sq. $75.00 – 100.00.

Round, rare cork compact, goldtone metal lid decorated with a blue and orange abstract enamel design, 3" dia. $55.00 – 65.00.

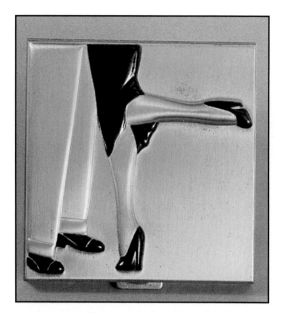

Volupté desirable square brushed goldtone compact, dancing legs in high relief, further enhanced with black enamel legs and skirt, 3" sq. $400.00 – 500.00.

Pilcher polished round goldtone compact, lid decorated with hands in high relief playing piano, 3" dia. $450.00 – 500.00.

Wadsworth goldtone vanity case designed to resemble large matchbook, complete with black striker and two applied matches with red tips, interior reveals beveled mirror, compartment for lipstick, powder well, and an added compartment, perhaps for eye make-up, "Ruth from Vic" engraved on front lid, 2½" x 3¾", $375.00 – 425.00.

White-enameled compact, lid decorated with colorful enameled musicians, 3" sq. $45.00 – 65.00.

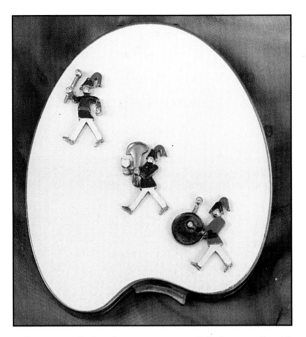

White-enameled Volupté compact, lid decorated with enamel Drum Major and two Marching Band musicians, 3¼" x 3". $85.00 – 95.00.

Heart-shaped goldtone compact, lid decorated with colorful enamel, "I Love You" in several languages, mirror, and powder well, 2½" x 2¾". $45.00 – 55.00.

Two wooden-lidded compacts, decorated with painted Asian scenes accented with gold sparkles, interior reveals mirror, powder well, and sifter, 2⅜" x 2¾". $25.00 – 30.00 each.

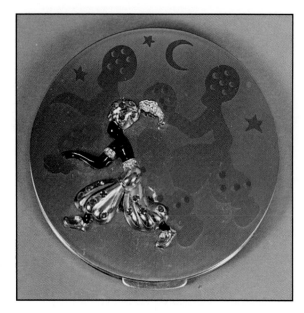

Round polished goldtone Columbia Fifth Avenue compact, lid decorated with a blackamoor elaborately decorated with rhinestones and blue crystals, background shows polished goldtone shadows of the blackamoor decorated with red enamel circles, 4" dia. $125.00 – 175.00.

Two oval-shaped enameled mini compacts, interiors reveal powder wells, sifters, and puffs. Upper left, white enamel compact lid decorated with young girl, dress enhanced with sparkles; right, black enamel compact lid decorated with young girl with umbrella and two red mushrooms, decorated with sparkles, 2¼" x 1½". $35.00 – 45.00 each.

Left – Hattie Carnegie round goldtone compact with matching lipstick; outer rim of compact and lipstick tube set with green pronged faceted stones; interior reveals mirror and powder well; compact lid and inner lipstick tube signed; 2" dia. $150.00 – 180.00.

Right – Hattie Carnegie goldtone compact with matching lipstick; polished strip with small applied goldtone knots set with colored stones decorate deeply incised compact lid; interior mirror and powder well; powder lid and lipstick tube signed; 3¾" x 2¼". $175.00 – 225.00.

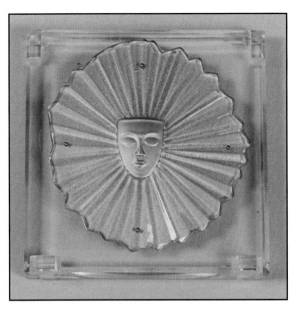

Roger & Gallet Lucite compact; sunburst medallion molded and painted separately; hand-applied to lid; two hinged closures on either side of front lid; interior reveals mirror and powder compartment; 4" x 4". $125.00 – 225.00.

Roger & Gallet round black plastic compact, lid centered with an applied goldtone sunburst medallion, 3" dia. $45.00 – 65.00.

Estee Lauder 1967 light blue and cobalt blue enamel goldtone "Boutique" compact, lid centered with turquoise cabochon stone, 1½" dia. $25.00 – 35.00.

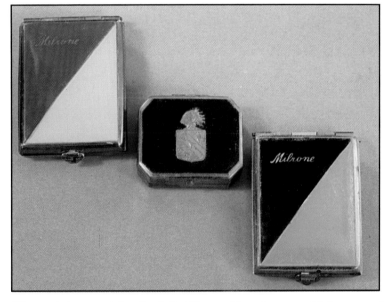

Three mini compacts/vanity. Left, Milrone oblong brown and beige enamel vanity, interior reveals metal mirror that separates powder/puff from rouge/puff section, 1½" x 1¼". $45.00 – 55.00. Center, black enamel oblong with cut corners compact, lid centered with goldtone crest, interior reveals framed mirror and powder well, ⅞" x 1¼". $20.00 – 30.00. Right, Milrone oblong black and orange compact, interior reveals mirror, powder well, and puff, 1½" x 1¼". $35.00 – 45.00.

Bourjois Evening in Paris square silvertone vanity/compact, enameled cobalt blue lid decorated with silvertone celestial moon and star, metal mirror separates powder compartment from rouge and lipstick compartments, 2¼" sq. $35.00 – 45.00.

Top – Trifari "lip-lock" brushed goldtone compact; lid decorated with applied framed disc of colored stones; pull-out lipstick opens compact; interior reveals signed powder well and mirror; 3¼" x 2¼" x 1". $175.00 – 200.00.

Bottom – Trifari square brushed goldtone compact; center of lid decorated with applied colored stones; interior reveals signed powder well and mirror; 3" x 3". $100.00 – 150.00.

Scalloped half-moon-shaped goldtone compact with two hand-stitched puppies on lid; scalloped interior mirror; reverse side engraved with wedding date of Tzeepa and Lenny 5/7/51 3¾" x 2" x ½". $125.00 – 175.00.

Round goldtone compact; plastic textured dog with moveable head applied to pearlized plastic lid; head moves right and left; Great Britain; 3" dia. $80.00 – 150.00.

Lilly Daché "Loving Touch" ivorene matching compact, lipstick, and rouge case; carved figures on a swing and foliage decorate round plastic compact lid, goldtone lipstick tube, and rouge case; compact interior reveals mirror and powder compartment; initials L.D. imprinted on compact and rouge lid; compact comes in hat box presentation box; compact 2¾" dia., rouge 4½" x 2½" x ⅞". $250.00 – 300.00 set.

Lower left – Round pink-enameled silvertone compact; three enameled dogs applied to center of lid; finger ring; 2⅛". $50.00 – 70.00.

Upper left – Coppertone compact with black enamel cat decorated with blue stars on lid; 2¾" x 2⅜". $40.00 – 60.00.

Top center – Square chrome vanity with cut corners; lid decorated with a three-dimensional blue elephant balancing on blue faceted ball; interior contains powder and rouge compartments; 2½" x 2½". $60.00 – 100.00.

Upper right – Shields, Inc. square compact; light yellow enameled lid decorated with brown wash tub and two three-dimensional dogs; 2½" x 2½". $100.00 – 125.00.

Lower right – Round coppertone compact with embossed black enamel cat centered on lid; finger ring chain; 1½" dia. x ½". $75.00 – 125.00.

Bottom center – Astor-Pak round plastic compact; silvertone Scottie dog centered on top of ivorene lid; bottom lid black; 3½" dia. $100.00 – 125.00.

Center – Round white enamel compact with mesh bottom; black poodle with raised fur centered on lid; 2½" dia. $60.00 – 80.00.

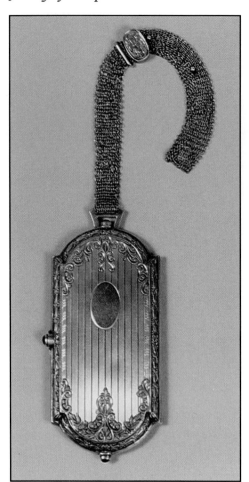

Tiffany & Co. sterling vanity case; exterior of case beautifully embossed; cartouche centered on both lids; interior reveals framed mirror, covered powder and rouge compartments; sapphire thumb-pieces; wide mesh adjustable wrist carrying chain; 1¾" x 3¾". $450.00 – 650.00.

Tiffany vanity case open.

Round dark green marbleized Bakelite compact; lid decorated with pink carved Bakelite roses and painted green leaves; interior reveals beveled mirror and powder compartment; plastic link carrying chain with finger ring; 2½" dia. $125.00 – 200.00.

Red and Black enamel goldtone vanity, interior reveals two mirrors, one on the powder compartment side and one on the rouge side, lipstick centered between mirrors, reverse side of each mirror reveals openings for photos, complete with carrying cord and tassel, 2½" x 2". Shown closed at left, open below. $200.00 – 250.00.

Orange Bakelite round compact, interior reveals mirror and powder well; carrying cord; concealed in orange silk side tassels, two silvertone metal lipstick tubes, and one goldtone metal tube containing perfume bottle concealed in center tassel, 2" dia. $650.00 – 750.00.

Navy blue Bakelite round compact, interior reveals mirror and powder well: carrying cord, concealed in faded blue tassels, two lipsticks tubes marked Novita, and one Bakelite tube containing perfume bottle concealed in center tassel, 2" dia. $650.00 – 750.00.

Black Bakelite museum quality vanity designed to resemble miniature dagger, brown leather sheath enhanced with antique embossed goldtone tip and collar, Bakelite vanity top unscrews to reveal mirror, powder well, and puff, second and third compartments unscrew to reveal cavity for personal necessities and curved comb, complete with brown tassel carrying cord, 7½" x 1½" x 1¼" dia. Shown closed. $1,400.00 – 1,700.00.

Black Bakelite vanity open.

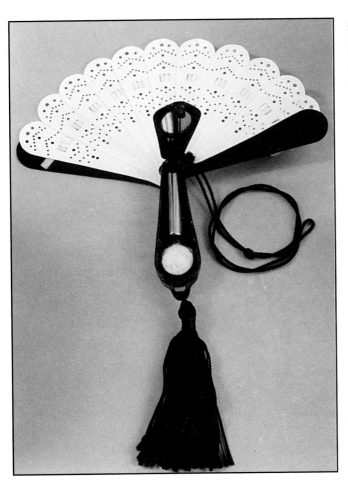

Black Bakelite vanity/folding fan combination, lid of vanity enhanced with rhinestones, pierced ivory sticks, black Bakelite guards, interior of vanity reveals mirror, powder well, puff, and lipstick, complete with silk tassel and carrying cord, vanity 3¼" x 1", ivory sticks 4". Shown with fan opened. $700.00 – 900.00.

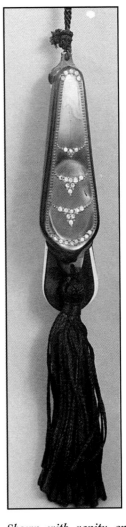

Shown with vanity and fan closed.

Round brushed goldtone compact, lid decorated with polished goldtone stars, black silk carrying wrist cuff, reverse side of cuff has snap-shut mini pocket for money, complete with black tassel, interior reveals mirror and powder well, 4" dia. $150.00 – 200.00.

Oval coral Bakelite vanity; lid decorated with painted flowers set with clear and blue rhinestones; interior reveals mirror and compartments for powder and rouge; carrying cord; tassel conceals lipstick tube; 2" x 3⅓". $225.00 – 300.00.

Round brown Bakelite compact; lids decorated with carved flowers; front lid further decorated with rhinestones; interior reveals mirror and powder compartment; carrying cord and tassel; 2" dia. $125.00 – 200.00.

Round yellow Bakelite compact; lid decorated with pink flowers; Bakelite tube (lipstick or perfume) concealed in tassel; carrying cord; interior reveals mirror and powder well; 1¾" dia., tube 2½". $150.00 – 190.00.

Chatain round red Bakelite vanity; lids decorated with carved goldtone highlights; interior reveals mirror, compartment for powder, and two Tokalon lipsticks, carrying cord and two tassels (replaced); Paris; 3¾" x 4". $250.00 – 350.00.

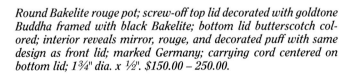

Round Bakelite rouge pot; screw-off top lid decorated with goldtone Buddha framed with black Bakelite; bottom lid butterscotch colored; interior reveals mirror, rouge, and decorated puff with same design as front lid; marked Germany; carrying cord centered on bottom lid; 1¾" dia. x ½". $150.00 – 250.00.

Left – Octagonal celluloid green marbleized compact; black compact lid decorated with rhinestones; interior reveals mirror and powder well; tassel; unusually long carrying cord; 2¼" x 2¼". $175.00 – 225.00.

Right – Black Bakelite compact; white engraved flowers on lid highlighted with colored stones; interior reveals mirror and powder compartment; tassel; unusually long carrying cord; 2¼" x 2¼". $125.00 – 175.00.

Left – Octagonal celluloid compact; sides ivorene colored; lids decorated with multicolored sparkle; interior reveals mirror and powder compartment; carrying chain and tassel; 2½" x 2½". $150.00 – 200.00.

Right – Oblong coral colored Bakelite compact; sides ivorene; front lid decorated with black enamel designs and red colored stones; interior contains mirror and powder compartment; carrying cord and tassel; 2" x 2½" x ¾". $175.00 – 225.00.

Brown plastic composition compact; lids decorated with embossed textured flying cranes; interior reveals mirror and powder well; carrying cord; tassel (replaced); 3" x 4". $275.00 – 375.00.

Black and ivorene Bakelite necessaire; front lid decorated with rhinestones; front opening reveals mirror and compartments for rouge and powder; back opening reveals fabric pocket for change, keys, etc.; carrying cord and tassel; 1¾" dia. x 4". $350.00 – 450.00.

Black triangle-shaped Bakelite vanity; lid decorated with painted silver leaves enhanced with rhinestones; interior reveals powder well and lipstick compartment; ivorene rim; carrying cord and tassel; $175.00 – 225.00.

Tan plastic vanity case; lid decorated with maroon flowers; interior reveals mirror, powder and rouge compartments, two lipsticks, noir and vif, and pocket for puff; carrying cord and two tassels (replaced); 3¾" x 5". $350.00 – 450.00.

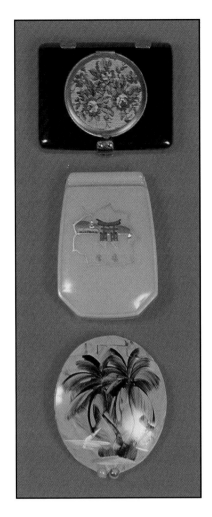

Top – Black Bakelite and tapestry vanity/cigarette case combination; black cigarette case lid incorporates tapestry-covered round vanity; interior of vanity reveals powder well, metal mirror, and rouge compartment in lid; Patent #2055389; vanity case, 2¼" dia.; cigarette case, 3¾" x 3". $150.00 – 175.00.

Center – Light green celluloid vanity case; lid decorated with hand-painted Asian scene; interior reveals compartments with removeable covered lip and cheek rouge containers, mirror, and powder compartment; 2¾" x 4". $125.00 – 175.00.

Bottom – Yellow marbleized oval-shaped plastic souvenir compact; Miami, Fla. and painted palm trees decorate lid; interior contains mirror and powder well; 3" x 3½". $40.00 – 80.00.

Green marbleized Bakelite stylized acorn-shaped compact; interior reveals mirror and large powder cavity; front decorated with silver etched designs enhanced with green colored stones; carrying cord; tassel (replaced); 2" dia. x 4½". $250.00 – 350.00.

Black oblong Bakelite vanity; exterior beautifully decorated with clear and green colored rhinestones; interior reveals mirror, covered removeable powder and rouge containers, and lipstick compartment; carrying cord; tassel (replaced); 2¼" x 4". $350.00 – 475.00.

Beautiful ivory, coral, and green colored plastic compact; lid decorated with a Bohidsattva in a lotus blossom; interior reveals mirror and powder well; carrying cord and tassel; 2½" x 3¾". $300.00 – 400.00.

Bone-colored octagon plastic compact; textured front lid decorated with carved red flowers and green leaves; green marbleized back lid; compact centered on front lid, interior reveals mirror and powder well; plastic carrying chain; tassel (replaced); 3" x 3¾". $250.00 – 350.00.

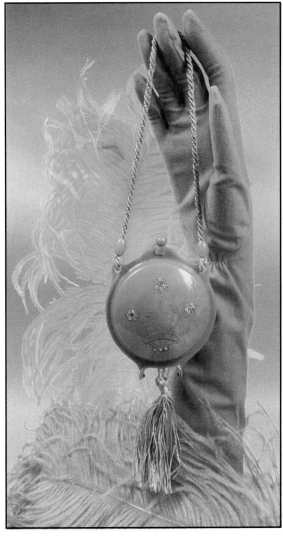

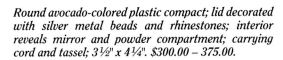

Round avocado-colored plastic compact; lid decorated with silver metal beads and rhinestones; interior reveals mirror and powder compartment; carrying cord and tassel; 3½" x 4¼". $300.00 – 375.00.

Bone-colored plastic compact; detailed figures of male and female carved on front lid; interior of compact reveals mirror and powder well; fancy braided carrying cord; two lipsticks and one perfume bottle concealed in tassels; glass perfume bottle decorated with blue enamel stripes, perfume label reads "Rose-Calderara-Bankmann-Vienne"; 2" dia. $700.00 – 900.00.

Black Bakelite compact; front lid decorated with rhinestones; interior of compact reveals mirror and powder well; carrying cord; two lipsticks marked Paris, and one Bakelite tube containing perfume bottle concealed in fancy tassels; 2" dia. $700.00 – 900.00.

Exquisite brown plastic vanity; exterior decorated with hand carved designs; top opening unscrews and reveals cheek rouge; second opening reveals mirror and powder well; third opening reveals cavity for change, keys, etc; lipstick tube concealed in silk embroidered tassel; rope carrying cord; 2¼" x 5". $900.00 – 1,200.00.

Black oblong Bakelite vanity and combination; front lid decorated with beautiful engraved silver roses enhanced with rhinestones; side closure rhinestone filigree clasp; removeable wrist watch; watch face shows through front lid; interior reveals mirror, powder compartment, two lipstick compartments, and watch compartment; Bakelite tube with perfume bottle concealed in silk tassel; fancy braided carrying cord; 2½" x 4". $650.00 – 750.00.

Black Bakelite vanity open.

Black Bakelite vanity closed.

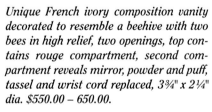

Unique French ivory composition vanity decorated to resemble a beehive with two bees in high relief, two openings, top contains rouge compartment, second compartment reveals mirror, powder and puff, tassel and wrist cord replaced, 3¾" x 2¼" dia. $550.00 – 650.00.

Beehive vanity open.

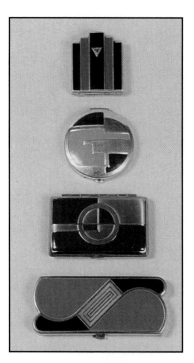

Left – Black shield-shaped Bakelite compact; lid enhanced with silver and gold metal beading and rhinestones; interior reveals beveled mirror, powder well, and second compartment; carrying cord and tassel (replaced); 3¼" x 5¼". $350.00 – 500.00.

Right – Green and black shield-shaped Bakelite compact; front and back lids green; lid decorated with metal beading and rhinestones; interior reveals beveled mirror, powder well, and second compartment; carrying cord and tassel (replaced); 3¼" x 5¼". $350.00 – 500.00.

Top – Fillkwik Co. Art Deco silvertone step pyramid-shaped black and red striped vanity; interior reveals metal mirror which separates powder and rouge compartments; small triangular fraternal emblem applied to lid; 1½" x 1¾". $75.00 – 100.00.

Top center – Round silvertone compact; orange, black, and silver Art Deco design on lid; 2" dia. $50.00 – 75.00.

Bottom center – Goldtone oblong vanity; lid decorated with blue and goldtone Art Deco design; interior reveals mirror and side-by-side rouge and powder compartments; 2¾" x 1½". $75.00 – 100.00.

Bottom – Zanadu goldtone vanity; beautiful orange, black, and goldtone Art Deco/Art Moderne design on lid; interior reveals mirror, powder and rouge compartments, and separate lipstick compartment with mini goldtone lipstick tube; 3½" x 1½". $100.00 – 125.00.

Karess round compact; goldtone top lid decorated with profile of woman, a rose, and a star on a dark blue and black background framed with goldtone bars; silvertone bottom lid; 1¾" dia. $80.00 – 150.00.

Octagon-shaped pewter tone compact, lid centered with octagon-shaped silvertone disc decorated with an enamel flower, latch closing, interior reveals mirror and perforated powder well that swivels to release powder, 2". $25.00 – 35.00.

Antonin of France round black celluloid compact lid decorated with a beautiful Art Deco woman's face looking into a hand mirror, hand engraved and hand painted, 3" dia. $150.00 – 200.00.

Silvertone octagon powder grinder "Flapper" compact; lid beautifully decorated with dancing couple and saxophone player and drummer in black and silvertone; U.S. Patent #1674525; 2" x 2". $150.00 – 200.00.

Antonin of France round black celluloid compact lid decorated with a beautiful Art Deco woman's face, hand engraved and hand painted, 3" dia. $150.00 – 200.00.

Round compact designed to resemble picture hat; lid covered with fabric resembling beads; lid further enhanced with colorful beads and mother-of-pearl petals; trimmed in pink velvet; reverse side black silk; 3" dia. $200.00 – 300.00.

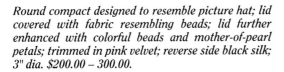

Miniature compact formed in the style of World War I helmet; strap on front of olive green helmet; Cherbourg written on side; bottom opens to reveal interior mirror; 1¾" x 2¼". $250.00 – 300.00.

Miref goldtone compact designed to resemble five-star general's cap; visor decorated with five green stones centered on five engraved stars; interior beveled mirror; France; 2 " dia. x 2¾". $250.00 – 350.00.

Polished goldtone jockey cap; black visor decorated with red plastic bow; interior mirror and puff; 2" dia. x ¾". $350.00 – 450.00.

Dorothy Gray round silvertone compact fashioned as picture hat; raised dome centered on lid; decorated with bow and flowers; 3⅞" dia. $125.00 – 175.00.

Top left – Round goldtone compass/compact combination; working compass on lid protected by beveled glass dome; glass bottom lid; interior reveals deeply beveled mirror and powder compartment; 2¾" dia. $150.00 – 200.00.

Top right – Agme "dial-a-scene" gold and silvertone compact; silvertone lid framed by goldtone border; centered on lid are two openings which reveal scenes of Paris; moveable dials on either side; Switzerland; 2" x 3¼". $125.00 – 175.00.

Center left – Elgin American brushed goldtone compact; thermometer centered on lid; incised polished goldtone figures of women playing tennis, golf, ice skating, and horseback riding decorate the four corners of lid; 2¾" x 2¾". $120.00 – 150.00.

Center right – Hingeco Vanities, Inc. "sardine can" compact; white enameled lid decorated with colorful scenes of Paris, London, New York, Swiss Alps, and Morocco; key on bottom of lid pulls out and turns to open compact; 2½" x 3". $150.00 – 200.00.

Bottom – Le Rage goldtone "dial-a-date" compact lid decorated with colorful activities; two moveable dials, one to indicate activity and the second one to indicate time; England; 4" dia. $250.00 – 300.00.

Left – Goldtone "dial-a-date" compact with appointment reminders printed on lid protected by clear plastic; two moveable dials, one to set time, one to indicate appointment destination; beveled mirror, France, 2½" x 3". $150.00 – 175.00.

Right – Schildkraut goldtone "dial-a-date" compact with two moveable clock hands centered on round raised dome which indicates different activities and times, 3" x 2½". $150.00 – 175.00.

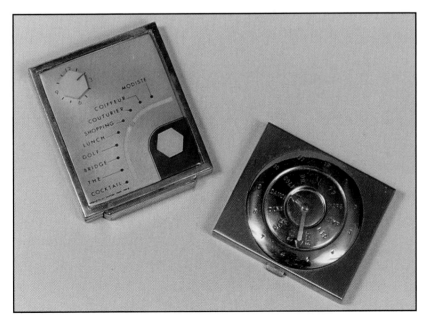

Lower left – Volupté brushed goldtone compact; lid decorated with red, white, and blue enamel stripes and red, white, and blue stones; 3" x 3". $60.00 – 80.00.

Top left – Plastic U.S. Navy hat compact; blue and black; lid decorated with goldtone navy insignia; 3" x 1¼". $75.00 – 90.00.

Top center – Photo cigarette and compact combination; light blue enameled lid with American flag and "God Bless America" and "Liberty" in goldtone; hinged mirror separates powder and cigarette compartments; photo slides into back of mirror; 2¾" x 2½" x ¾". $125.00 – 150.00.

Top right – Sterling U.S. Army hat compact; lid decorated with embossed insignia; interior lid of hat acts as mirror; 3" dia. x 1¼". $125.00 – 175.00.

Lower right – Elgin American goldtone compact; lid decorated with red, white, and blue enamel stripes; 2¾" x 2¾". $50.00 – 70.00.

Bottom center – White enameled vanity; U.S. Marine insignia centered on lid; interior reveals metal mirror which separates powder and rouge compartments; 2¼" x 2¼". $40.00 – 60.00.

Center – Volupté round white enameled compact; lid decorated with a red anchor and a blue rope; 2½" dia. $50.00 – 70.00.

Beautiful engine-turned goldtone Stratton Initial compact, rare to be complete with original goldtone key needed to set initials, interior reveals framed mirror, powder well, and puff, 2¾" x 3¼", England. $125.00 – 150.00.

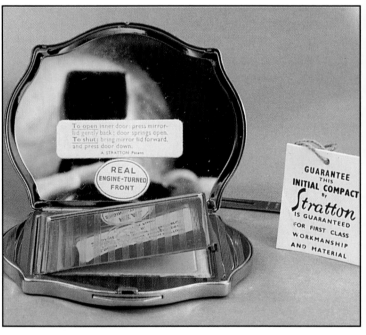

Stratton compact at left, open. Printed directions for opening powder well read, "To open: inner door, press mirror lid gently back; door springs open. To shut: bring mirror lid forward, and press door down."

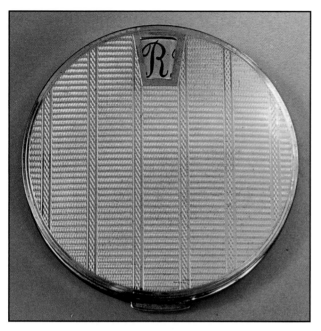

Stratton round engine-turned goldtone Initial compact, lid has dial that sets one letter, interior contains framed mirror, puff, and powder well, 3" dia., England. $75.00 – 125.00.

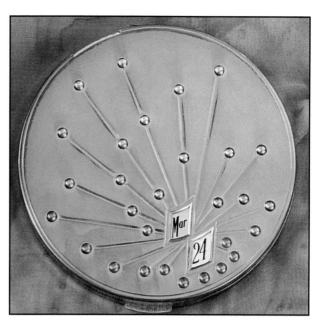

Zell Dial a Date round polished goldtone compact, lid decorated with decorative sunburst and raised tiny balls, lid has dials that set the month and day, interior contains framed mirror, puff, and powder well, 3¼" dia. $75.00 – 125.00.

Round brushed silvertone compact; lid decorated with applied goldtone sailor and heart inscribed with the word "Taken;" matching silvertone sailor pin; pin was a gift from Alvin to me when he was in the U.S. Navy in 1945. Set $150.00 – 200.00.

Evans square goldtone compact, lid decorated with a red, white, and blue enamel Union Jack flag, applied goldtone emblem, Dieu et Mon Droit centered on lid, 2½" sq. $75.00 – 125.00.

Henriette white enameled compact and matching cigarette case; matching pin by Accesscraft; lids decorated with goldtone lion centered on blue, white, and red ribbon; label affixed to compact mirror reads "Sole Authentic Case for Benefit of British War Relief Society and Bundles For Britain;" reverse side of pin reads "Official BWRS and BB;" compact 3" x 3", cigarette case 5¼" x 3". $175.00 – 225.00.

Volupté round goldtone compact, lid decorated with enameled red, white, and blue stars and stripes, centered with ROOSEVELT in blue enamel, 3" dia. $175.00 – 225.00.

Henriette square goldtone compact, red, white, and blue enamel lid decorated with a service emblem, souvenir from Camp Croft, 3" x 3", $35.00 – 45.00.

Silver compact designed to resemble drum; applied drumsticks on top lid; snares applied on bottom lid; tension wires encircle rims of drum; interior reveals metal mirror and powder well; 1½" dia. x 1". $275.00 – 325.00.

Polished silvertone officer's cap souvenir compact, interior reveals mirror, powder well, and puff, 1950s, 2½" dia. Front shown. $250.00 – 300.00.

Reverse of souvenir compact at left which reads "Strathaird," Souvenir, 1950, with repoussé map of Australia.

Black plastic compact designed to resemble guitar; plastic strings; interior reveals mirror, powder compartment, puff, and sifter; 2" x 5½". $175.00 – 225.00.

Lower left – Atomette goldtone suitcase compact; tan leather covers both front and back lids; metal handle, 3" x 2½" x ¾". $80.00 – $120.00.

Upper left – Marbleized tortoise-colored suitcase compact with goldtone hardware, 3" x 2½" x ½". $150.00 – 175.00.

Top center – Mini black enameled suitcase vanity with goldtone hardware; decorated with gold travel stickers; interior has metal mirror separating rouge and powder compartments, 2" x 2". $80.00 – 120.00.

Upper right – Kigu Compact of Character goldtone suitcase compact with lipstick encased in lid cover; marcasite horse and carriage decorate lid; interior mirror sticker reads, "The inner lid opens automatically if outer lid is eased back fully; to close, return outer lid to vertical position and then press down inner lid," 3" x 2½" x ½". $175.00 – 225.00.

Lower right – Goldtone suitcase compact decorated with B.O.A.C. travel stickers; push-back ridged handle, 3" x 2½" x ½". $160.00 – 180.00.

Center – Brown leather suitcase compact decorated with colorful travel stickers, double leather handles, 2¾" x 2½" x¾". $150.00 – 175.00.

Lower left – Blue enameled suitcase compact with goldtone snap opening, 3" x 2¼" x ¾". $80.00 – 120.00.

Upper left – Kigu goldtone suitcase compact; incised goldtone hardware; cartouche centered on lid; "Bon Voyage" and Kigu logo inscribed on inner powder lid; push-back handle; 3¼" x 2¼" x ½". $150.00 – 175.00.

Top center – Wadsworth two-sided tan leather mini hatbox vanity; polished goldtone lids on either side; powder/mirror compartment one side, rouge/locket compartment other side; leather finger carrying handle, 1½" dia. x 1". $50.00 – 75.00.

Upper right – Red marbleized suitcase vanity; goldtone hardware; colorful sticker scenes of New York applied to both lids; interior reveals powder and rouge compartments; patent #1883793 U.S.A.; 3" x 2½". $125.00 – 150.00.

Lower right – Brushed goldtone suitcase compact with blue and red straps and corners, U.S.A.; 3" x 2¼". $150.00 – 175.00.

Bottom center – Hingeco Vanities Inc. black enameled suitcase vanity; goldtone hardware; interior reveals compartment for rouge, powder, and beveled mirror; 2¾" x 1¾". $175.00 – 225.00.

Center – Zell round maroon hatbox compact; goldtone hardware; anchor and U.S.N. emblem centered on lid; 3" dia. $150.00 – 175.00.

Bottom – Green leather photo compact popular during the war years; beveled mirror; open slot on lid to insert picture; picture protected by clear plastic; goldtone frame around picture; 1940s; 3" x 3". $80.00 – 120.00.

Center – Round goldtone photo vanity; interior reveals powder well, mirror, and rouge compartment; interior compartment can be removed to insert photo which is protected by clear plastic; 1920s; 2" dia. x ½". $75.00 – 100.00.

Top – Red leather photo compact popular during the war years; beveled mirror; open slot on lid to insert picture; picture protected by clear plastic; goldtone frame around picture; 1940; 3" x 3". $80.00 – 120.00.

Left – Abarbanel Original Lucite photo compact; interior mirror slides out to permit insertion of picture; 3¾" x 3¾". $80.00 – 120.00.

Top – Lucite photo compact; picture placed behind removeable mirror; 3¼" x 3¼". $60.00 – 90.00.

Right – Ziegfeld Creation Lucite photo compact with scalloped edges; photo slides into slot behind interior mirror; 1940s; 4" x 4". $80.00 – 120.00.

Lower left – Elgin American round goldtone compact; lid decorated with a multicolored enamel Eastern Star emblem; 3". $40.00 – 60.00.

Center left – Parisian Nov. Co.; round promotional compact for Marksons Furniture; colored birthstones printed around outer lid; Pat. 11-2-15, 6-26-17; 2¼" dia. $80.00 – 100.00.

Upper left – Parisian Nov. Co.; round promotional compact for Christo Cola; green background; Pat. 11-2-15, 6-26-17; 2¼" dia. $80.00 – 100.00.

Top center – Brushed goldtone oblong compact; three transfers of cigarette packages on lid; 2⅜" x 3¼". $100.00 – 125.00.

Upper right – Cruver Manufacturing Co. round souvenir compact with picture of "House In Which Jenny Wade Was Shot," Gettysburg, PA; 2¼" x ¼". $80.00 – 100.00.

Center right – Parisian Nov. Co. round promotional compact for The Golden Pumpkin; Pat. 11-2-15, 6-26-17; 2¼" dia. $80.00 – 100.00.

Lower right – Stratton round blue enameled compact; multicolored enameled Eastern Star decorates lid; England; 2¾" dia. $60.00 – 80.00.

Center – Vashe round silvertone vanity green enameled promotional vanity for Howard's; lid decorated with palm trees; interior has powder and rouge compartments; puff reads "Dine and Dance;" 2¾" dia. $80.00 – 100.00.

Evans square goldtone compact, striated lid decorated with red, gold, and blue mini Pepsi-Cola cap, 2½" sq., $75.00 – 95.00.

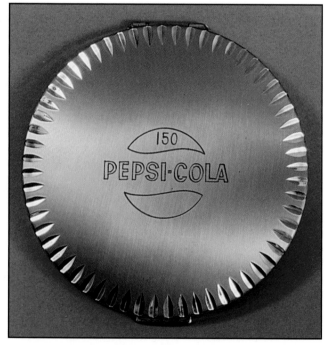

Stratton round brushed goldtone compact, PEPSI-COLA engraved on lid, upper rim of compact decorated with polished goldtone design, 3¼" dia., Patent #764125, England. $75.00 – 95.00.

Lower left – Ritz goldtone souvenir compact of Hawaii; brushed goldtone lid decorated with polished goldtone map of the Hawaiian Islands; side clip for lipstick tube; 3½" x 2½". $60.00 – 100.00.

Top left – Stratton souvenir compact from England; Queen Elizabeth and Prince Philip pictured on lid under clear plastic protector; England; 3" dia. $150.00 – 175.00.

Upper right – Volupté goldtone souvenir compact of Brooklyn; silvertone compact lid decorated with polished goldtone famous Brooklyn sites; 3" x 3". $80.00 – 125.00.

Lower right – Gwenda silvertone souvenir compact of Scotland; plaid lid decorated with stitched heather; back lid black enamel, matching plaid powder puff; England; 3" dia. $125.00 – 150.00.

Center – Black enameled souvenir compact of Paris; front lid decorated with goldtone Paris sites; France; 3½" x 2¾". $125.00 – 175.00.

Left – Round silvertone souvenir compact of Disneyland; polished goldtone Disneyland scene centered on brushed silvertone lid; 3½" dia. $60.00 – 100.00.

Top – Chrome octagonal-shaped souvenir of Canada; lid decorated with colorful flags; 2½" x 2½". $80.00 – 120.00.

Right – Rosenfeld blue round leather souvenir compact of Israel; zipper closure; gold-colored disc with dancing man and woman centered on lid; 3" dia. $60.00 – 100.00.

Bottom – Heart-shaped silvertone souvenir compact of Washington, D.C.; polished goldtone D.C. attractions on lid; 2¾" x 3". $40.00 – 60.00.

Center – Round green enameled souvenir compact with goldtone "U.S. Zone Germany" map and Army insignia on lid; polished goldtone scalloped edges frame lid; reverse side goldtone; 4" dia. $250.00 – 300.00.

Square polished goldtone Volupté souvenir compact of San Francisco, lid decorated with engraved points of interest, 3" sq. $35.00 – 55.00.

Square goldtone souvenir of Hollywood compact, lid decorated with points of interest, mirror, and powder well, 3" sq. $35.00 – 55.00.

Pilcher round goldtone Texas souvenir compact, front lid shows map of Texas and adjacent territories, United States & Mexico, reverse side shows a humorous Texas Conversion Table, interior reveals framed mirror, sifter, and puff, 3¾" dia. $175.00 – 225.00.

Reverse side of Texas souvenir compact.

Round blue cobalt enamel Stratton Canadian souvenir compact, lid decorated with colorful maple leaf, interior reveals framed mirror, puff, powder well, and sifter, 2¾" dia. $75.00 – 125.00.

Very rare Kigu round brushed goldtone royal commemorative compact with picture of Prince Charles and Princess Diana on the lid, "H.R.M. The Prince Charles – Lady Diana Spencer, 1981" printed around edge of picture, 3" dia. NPA.

Unmarked, much coveted round goldtone compact with picture of The Beatles on the lid, 2⅞" dia. $375.00 – 475.00.

Square goldtone souvenir compact from the New Rosslyn Hotels, Los Angeles, CA, plastic lid decorated with photo of hotels, interior contains powder well, puff, and mirror, 2½" sq. $35.00 – 45.00.

Round ball-shaped pink suede compact with goldtone trim around decorative closure; three bands of Austrian crystals encircle suede ball; pink suede finger holder; metal interior; beveled mirror; France; 2" dia. $400.00 – 450.00.

Left – Henriette ball-shaped goldtone "Loves Me Loves Me Not" compact; Yes-No-Maybe printed around daisy petals; rolling ball selector; all enclosed under plastic dome; metal interior; Patent #2138514; 2" dia. $150.00 – 225.00.

Center – Wadsworth goldtone "Ball & Chain" compact; goldtone lipstick tube attached by chain to round compact; plastic interior; 2" dia. $150.00 – 175.00.

Right – Green iridescent ball-shaped Christmas ornament compact; exterior highlighted with red and white stripes; plastic interior; also comes in solid iridescent colors of red or green and in a striped red iridescent color; 2" dia. $150.00 – 250.00.

Left – Kigu goldtone ball-shaped world globe compact; plastic interior; 1940s – 1950s; England; 2⅛" dia. $150.00 – 200.00.

Center – Kigu goldtone and silvertone ball-shaped world globe compact; continents in goldtone; oceans in silvertone; plastic interior; 1940s – 1950s; England; 2⅛" dia. $200.00 – 250.00.

Right – Pygmalion goldtone ball-shaped compact; exterior engraved with beautiful floral design; plastic interior; 2⅛" dia. $150.00 – 200.00.

Left – Rust-colored leather mini ball-shaped compact with goldtone bands around flip-over closure; leather lined swinging beveled mirror; France; 1⅞". $150.00 – 250.00.

Center – Majestic goldtone egg-shaped compact; metal interior; 2" x 3". $80.00 – 100.00.

Right – Multicolored fabric mini ball-shaped compact with goldtone bands around flip-over closure; leather lined; interior mirror; 1¾". $150.00 – 250.00.

Sterling silver mini ball-shaped pendant compact; engraved exterior; 1" dia. $200.00 – 250.00.

Left – K & K brass-colored basket-shaped compact; engine tooled; satin-finish lid; embossed swinging handle; metal interior; 2⅛" dia. x 1¼". $80.00 – 120.00.

Center – Henriette black enamel basket-shaped compact without handle; goldtone trim; metal interior; Patent #2138514; 2" dia. x 1¼". $80.00 – 100.00.

Right – Kigu "Bouquet" goldtone basket-shaped compact; embossed with swing handle; plastic interior; England; 2" dia. x 1⅛". $100.00 – 150.00.

Revlon adorable round blue plastic "Love Pat" composition compact, lid decorated with white daisies and a girl with a blonde bouffant hairdo, 4¼" dia. $35.00 – 45.00.

Round black composition compact with applied white faux ivory fan on lid, 4½" dia. $35.00 – 45.00.

Two round Estee Lauder watch fob compacts. Lower left: Goldtone "Golden Tracery," compact elaborately engraved, attached blue silk tassel, 1963, reissued in 1971 as "Filigree Watch" compact; upper right: silvertone "Silver Hours," compact, 1997. Interior of both reveals mirror, puff, and powder well, 1⅞" dia. $45.00 – 65.00 each.

Round red plastic compact with the embossed white "Stork Club" logo applied to lid; flanked by two white plastic lipsticks with a black Stork Club logo and the names Jacqueline and Shermaine imprinted on them; Stork Club match book and postcards; many of these items were given away as promotional gifts by Sherman Billingsley, 4½" dia. x ¾". $120.00 – 150.00.

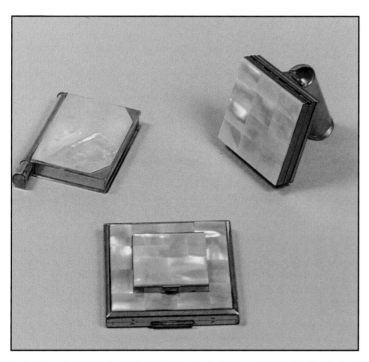

Left – Goldtone mother-of-pearl vanity designed to resemble book; lipstick tube slides out from spine; interior reveals beveled mirror, powder, and rouge compartments; 2" x 2½" x ½". $60.00 – 100.00.

Right – Mother-of-pearl compact with swing-out lipstick on back lid; interior mirror; exterior mirror on back lid beveled; 2" x 2" x ½". $60.00 – 80.00.

Center – Elgin American mother-of-pearl vanity; rouge compartment with mother-of-pearl lid centered on compact lid; 2¾" x 2¾". $60.00 – 100.00.

Left – Polished goldtone compact with lock motif; 2½" dia. $80.00 – 100.00.

Top – Zell goldtone heart-shaped compact; embossed key with red enameling applied to lid; slit on top of applied key comes complete with cardboard key and red tassel; the cardboard key is meant to be replaced with an actual key; 2¾" x 2¾" x ½". $125.00 – 200.00.

Right – Zell Fifth Avenue goldtone compact with lock motif; outer lid decorated with ring of rhinestones; inner circle has clock face centered with a rotating dial; 2½" dia. $175.00 – 225.00.

Bottom – Hingeco sterling silver heart-shaped compact; interior reveals heart-shaped puff, screen, and mirror; cartouche on lid monogrammed with initials R.G.; 2½" x 2½". $125.00 – 175.00.

 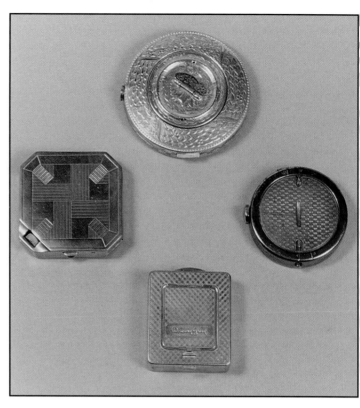

Reverse sides of compacts described below.

Left – *S.G.D.G. silvertone powder-grinder vanity; interior (shown below) reveals metal mirror which separates powder and rouge compartments; interior powder well lifts up to reveal solid powder grinder; France; 2" x 2". $70.00 – 90.00.*

Top – *Elizabeth Arden engraved silvertone powder sifter compact; top unscrews (shown below) to reveal powder sifter; Switzerland; 2½" dia. $60.00 – 100.00.*

Right – *Montre A. Poudre round goldtone powder-grider; back unscrews (shown below) to reveal powder grinder; France; 2" dia. $60.00 – 100.00.*

Bottom – *Dorothy Gray silvertone vanity powder-grinder; lid decorated with four shades of blue enamel; interior (shown below) reveals metal mirror which separates powder, rouge, and lipstick compartments; back lid lifts off to reveal powder grinder; 1¾" x 2". $45.00 – 65.00.*

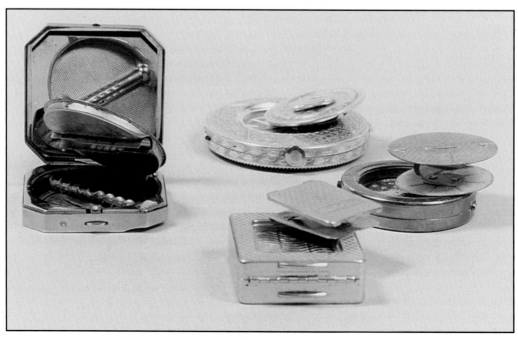

Left – Petit point compact/cigarette case combination with lip-lock lipstick; front lid decorated with floral petit point; opens to reveal powder compartment; back lid brushed goldtone opens to reveal cigarette compartment; Patent #2060466; 3½" x 2½" x ¾". $125.00 – 175.00.

Center – Petit point compact in fitted B. Altman Co. presentation box; front lid decorated with scene of man and woman walking hand-in-hand; back lid is black faille; 3¼" x 3¼" x ⅜". $175.00 – 225.00.

Right – Elgin American petit point compact; lid decorated with petit point city scene bordered by floral petit point; back lid brushed goldtone; 3⅓" x 3". $80.00 – 120.00.

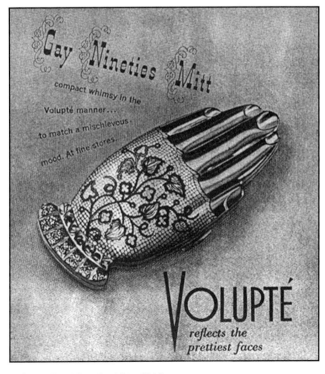

Volupté Gay Nineties Mitt, 1948.

Left – Volupté goldtone hand-shaped compact; lid decorated with enameled white lace mitt; multicolored enamel bracelet; Des. Patent #120,347; 4½" x 2". $250.00 – 350.00.

Center – Volupté goldtone hand-shaped compact; lid decorated with enameled black lace mitt; faux diamond engagement ring; faux diamond bracelet; 4½" x 2". $450.00 – 550.00.

Right – Volupté goldtone hand-shaped compact; front and back lids personalized with engraved bracelet and monograms; 4½" x 2". $125.00 – 175.00.

99

Lower left – German silver engraved compact/music box combination designed to resemble hand mirror; interior beveled mirror; lipstick in handle; Germany; 2½" dia. x 5¼". $150.00 – 225.00.

Upper left – Wan damascene compact/music box combination with side clip for lipstick; interior beveled mirror; 2" x 3¾". $125.00 – 175.00.

Top center – Marquis wedge-shaped engraved goldtone compact/music box combination; lid decorated with two cornucopias set on black disc; 2¾" x 3½". $125.00 – 175.00.

Upper right – Clover goldtone compact/music box combination; lid decorated with Asian scene; 3½" x 2¼". $125.00 – 175.00.

Lower right – Goldtone version of compact at lower left.

Lower center – Elgin American brushed goldtone compact/music box combination; lid engraved with polished goldtone instruments; lyre-shaped closure; 2¾" x 1¾". $125.00 – 150.00.

Center – Black enamel and goldtone compact/music box combination; enamel lid decorated with music notes set with green stones and G clef; 3¼" x 2½". $150.00 – 175.00.

Left – Volupté brushed goldtone "Lucky Purse" compact "With Captive Lipstick;" polished goldtone flap opens to reveal opening for picture or rouge; tango chain lipstick tube suspended by two chains; sticker on mirror reads "Genuine Collectors Item by Volupté;" 3½" x 2¾". $135.00 – 160.00.

Top – Volupté brushed silvertone "Lucky Purse" compact; polished silvertone flap; sticker on mirror reads "Genuine Collectors Item by Volupté;" 3½" x 2¾". $80.00 – 100.00.

Right – Volupté polished goldtone "Lucky Purse" compact "With Captive Lipstick;" hammered goldtone flap decorated with multicolored stones; tango chain lipstick tube suspended by two chains; sticker on mirror reads "Genuine Collectors Item by Volupté;" 3½" x 2¾". $150.00 – 200.00.

Bottom – Volupté brushed goldtone "Lucky Purse" compact; polished goldtone flap; sticker on mirror reads "Genuine Collectors Item by Volupté;" 3½" x 2¾". $80.00 – 100.00.

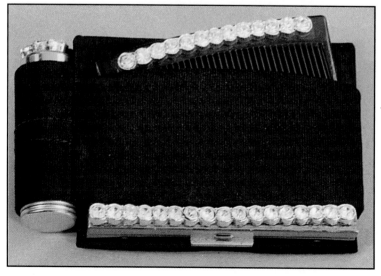

Volupté oblong goldtone compact, comb, and lipstick, enhanced with crystals, complete with carrying case, 3⅛" x 2¼". $95.00 – 115.00. Insert reads, "Volupté reflects the prettiest faces. This Volupté compact has been designed by skilled artists, and created with the greatest possible care on hand-tended machines. See how precisely it closes, how perfectly the hinges, spring-catch, and leakproof powder door work. It will give you long and faithful service. CARE OF YOUR COMPACT. This Volupté compact is specially lacquered to retain its jewel-like beauty. Clean with soft cloth only, never with polish. Avoid spilling perfume or alcohol on it, or sliding it across hard surfaces. Always carry the compact in its cover."

Sterling Siamese octagon compact belt buckle combination; three silver elephants decorate black compact lid; reverse side reveals belt loop and hook; 2¾" x 2¾". $350.00 – 450.00.

Underside of compact at left, revealing belt loop and hook.

Silver compact designed as hand gun, shown open above left, closed above right; complete exterior beautifully hand engraved; back end of barrel of gun contains lipstick tube which slides out; front end of barrel contains perfume atomizer which releases perfume when trigger is pulled; front lid opens to reveal powder well and beveled mirror; bottom of powder well reads "Weihnachten 1928;" 3" x 2½". $800.00 – 1,200.00.

Gilt-inlaid vanity case; lid decorated with Asian scene; interior reveals compartments for powder, rouge, framed mirror, and cigarettes; carrying chain with finger ring; 3½" x 2¾". $225.00 – 275.00.

Winnie Winkle silvertone mini bolster-shaped vanity; beautiful engine-turned case; mirror on outside of bottom cap; bottom cap contains rouge compartment and puff; upper compartment contains puff and powder compartment; wrist chain attached to top lid; 1920s; 1" dia x 1¾". Vanity shown open below. $250.00 – 300.00.

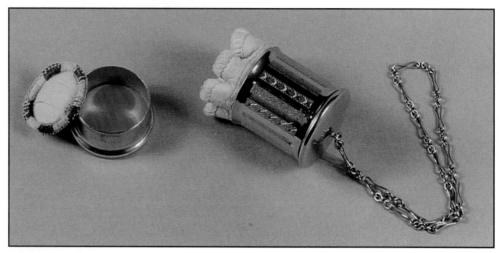

Left – Red, white, and blue round compact designed to resemble telephone dial with campaign slogan "We Need Stevenson" imprinted on lid; red map of the United States centered on lid; 3½" dia. $200.00 – 250.00.

Top right – Red, white, and blue round compact with campaign slogan "We Want Willkie" imprinted on lid; 2¾" dia. $175.00 – 225.00.

Bottom right – Copper compact/coin holder combination; front lid decorated with raised elephant; slots for coins on front lid; back lid contains exterior mirror; interior reveals metal powder sifter and puff; 2⅛". $150.00 – 200.00.

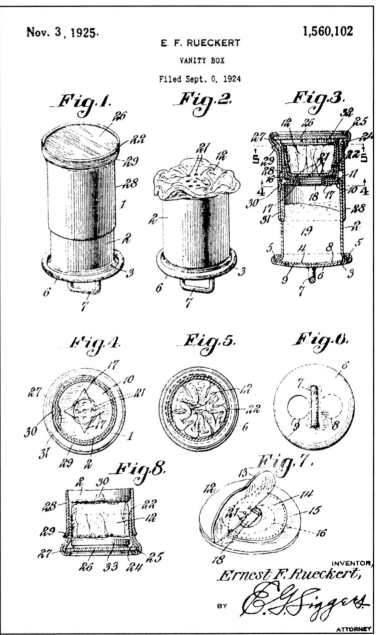

Patent drawing.

Winnie Winkle Vanitie ad, October 1926.

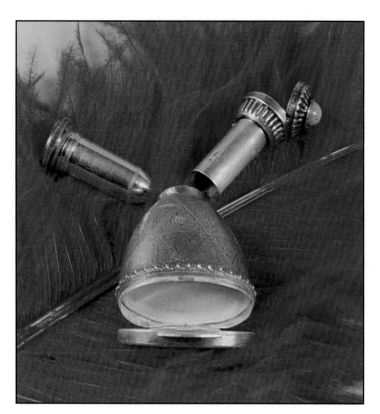

Silver vanity designed to resemble bottle; exterior bottom lid contains mirror; bottom lid opens to reveal powder compartment; upper lid decorated with cabochon turquoise stone which pulls out to reveal rouge compartment with lipstick tube underneath; second tube under top tube unscrews to reveal perfume container; 2" x 3". $800.00 – 1,000.00

Vanity at left opened to show parts.

Three Coty compacts, lids decorated with the white and gold Coty trademark: stylized puffs on an orange background. Left: Square compact, 1¾" sq. $15.00 – 25.00; top: round with thin goldtone frame, 2½" dia., $20.00 – 30.00; bottom: round with wide goldtone frame, 2¾" dia., $25.00 – 35.00.

Coty "Air-Spun" box of powder with plastic Coty "Parisienne Vanity" attached by plastic band; vanity insert reads "Cream Powder Patty" and "Sub-Deb" lipstick sold only attached to "Air-Spun Face Powder" "NOT FOR SALE SEPARATELY;" 2¼" x 4½", box 3½" dia. $60.00 – 100.00.

Left – Schildkraut round cloisonné enamel goldtone compact; lid decorated with French scene; 2½" dia. $50.00 – 70.00.

Right – Schildkraut oblong cloisonné enamel goldtone compact; lid decorated with French scene; 2¾" x 2½". $50.00 – 70.00.

Frosted milk glass compact designed as clam shell; goldtone interior; hallmarked with a hammer and sickle; Russia; 2½" x 3". $225.00 – 250.00.

Left – Textured goldtone compact formed in the shape of an owl; faux emerald and diamond eyes; beveled interior mirror; Italy; 2¾" x 2". $350.00 – 450.00.

Right – Textured goldtone compact formed in the shape of a fox; faux diamond eyes; framed interior mirror; Italy; 2¾" x 2". $350.00 – 450.00.

Center – Textured goldtone compact formed in the shape of a cat; faux sapphire, emerald, and diamond eyes; interior beveled framed mirror; Italy; $350.00 – 450.00.

Wooden carved tortoise compact, opens to reveal mirror and fitted sifter covering powder well, $175.00 – 225.00.

Polly Bergen round silvertone compact, lid designed to resemble shell of a turtle, 1½" dia. $35.00 – 55.00.

Unusual rare Napier silvertone compact designed to resemble an apple with goldtone stem and leaves, interior reveals mirror, sifter, and puff, 2" dia. $350.00 – 450.00.

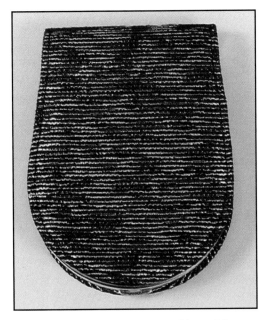

Purple and black saddle bag-shaped lamé fabric vanity case; opens to reveal attached compact, sleeve with lipstick tube, and pocket with comb; closed 3¼" x 4"; open 3¼" x 8¾". Shown open at right. $125.00 – 175.00.

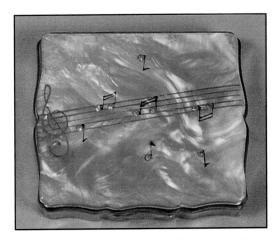

Top – Hand-painted enamel compact; lid decorated with Japanese scene; 2¾" x 2½". $50.00 – 75.00.

Bottom – Hand-painted enamel compact; lid decorated with Japanese scene; 2½" x 2". $50.00 – 75.00.

Stratton compact/music box combination; mother-of-pearl lid decorated with notes and G clef; 3¼" x 2¾" x ¾". $150.00 – 175.00.

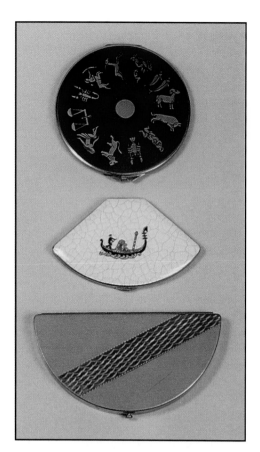

Top – Round blue enamel compact; border of lid decorated with goldtone astrological signs; 3¾" dia. $80.00 – 125.00.

Center – Melissa inverted fan-shaped compact; enamel gondola centered on white cracked eggshell lid; England; 4¼" x 2½". $80.00 – 125.00.

Bottom – Rex half-moon-shaped compact; blue enamel lid decorated with goldtone band; 5¼" x 2½". $60.00 – 100.00.

Left – Volupté mink covered compact; 3" x 3". $75.00 – 100.00.

Top – Tan snakeskin compact; enamel decorated strips flank compact on two sides; 3" x 3". $75.00 – 100.00.

Right – Crystal gray snakeskin compact; back lid brushed goldtone; 3" x 3". $40.00 – 60.00.

Bottom – Red lizard saddle bag-shaped vanity; interior contains beveled mirror; pull-out lipstick tube on one side of top; perfume container on other side of top; 2½" x 3½". $100.00 – 125.00.

Top – Dorset round brushed goldtone compact; lid decorated with polished goldtone heart and arrow and "I Love You" printed around lid; 2½ " dia. $60.00 – 80.00.

Center – Schildkraut goldtone compact; lids decorated with "I love you" hand-painted in different languages and colors; applied pen point; 2¾" x 2¼" x ½". $60.00 – 100.00.

Bottom – Elgin American brushed goldtone stylized heart-shaped compact; lid decorated with polished goldtone cupid, hearts, and "I love you" in several languages; 3¼" x 3¼". $60.00 – 100.00.

Left – Dunhill "Clearview" blue leather compact; interior reveals mirror windshield wiper; attached sleeve for lipstick; 2½" x 3½". $150.00 – 175.00.

Top – Majestic unique green leather compact/note pad combination; first opening reveals mirror and powder compartment; second opening reveals blue paper note pad; sleeve for pencil on outer lid; 2¾" x 2¾". $175.00 – 225.00.

Right – Red leather compact; attached sleeve for lipstick; pull-out mirror; 3" x 3½". $125.00 – 150.00.

Bottom – Lampl black enamel vanity; top lid has slide out comb; interior has mirror, rouge, lipstick, powder sifter, and powder compartments; 3" x 3". $150.00 – 175.00.

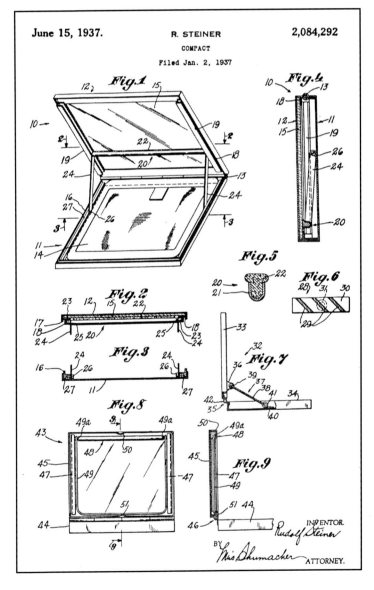

Sterling hallmarked pendant compact; black onyx lid with silver cartouche center; silver tassel; 1½" dia. x 3". $250.00 – 350.00.

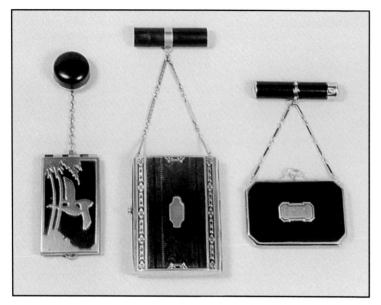

Left – Vashe black and silvertone fob compact; lid decorated with silvertone scene; fob cream lip and cheek rouge attached by chain; 1½" x 2½", fob 1" dia. $80.00 – 125.00.

Center – Terri black and silvertone tango chain vanity; silvertone cartouche centered on lid; lipstick tube attached by two chains; interior reveals mirror which separates powder and rouge compartments from cigarette compartment; 2½" x 3" x 6½". $125.00 – 175.00.

Right – E.A.M. black enamel and silvertone tango chain vanity; monogrammed silver cartouche centered on lid; interior reveals mirror, powder, and rouge compartments; lipstick attached by enamel link chain; 2½" x 1¾" x 4½". $125.00 – 175.00.

Toilet Requisites, *September, 1927.*

Volupté brushed silvertone necessaire; interior reveals metal mirror which encloses cigarette compartment; center panel conceals slim removeable vanity case; compartment on other side of vanity for small necessities; removeable silvertone vanity has compartments for powder, lip, and cheek rouge, metal mirror, and compartment for comb; metal carrying chain; 2" dia. x 4¼". $250.00 – 350.00.

Minaudière described at right.

Square brushed goldtone minaudière with cut-off corners; brown suede interior reveals mirror, compartments for powder and other small necessities; lid centered with polished goldtone stylized flower; mesh carrying handle; 5" x 5". $200.00 – 250.00.

Goldtone pearl and rhinestone compact/perfume/lipstick combination; lipstick tube attached to side of mini-compact and mini-perfume holder; compact and perfume holder are attached back-to-back; mirror on exterior of perfume holder; exterior decorated with pearls and rhinestones; 2" x 2½" x 1¼". $100.00 – 150.00.

Black suede and brass cone-shaped vanity purse; opens to reveal compact; second opening reveals purse; pull-out lipstick on bottom of bag; carrying chain; France; 3½" dia. x 6½". $300.00 – 400.00.

Black suede and brass heart-shaped vanity purse decorated with brass bow; top opens to reveal compact; front opens to reveal purse; carrying chain; France; 3¼" x 5½" x 2¼". $300.00 – 400.00.

Vanuette round lavender enamel sterling silver compact/vinaigrette pendant combination; first opening reveals convex mirror and powder lid covering powder well; second opening reveals vinaigrette compartment; perforations around rim of vinaigrette section; sterling longnette neck chain; 1" dia. $275.00 – 375.00.

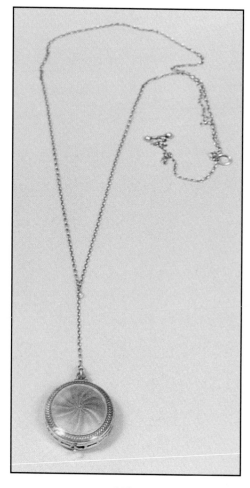

Left – Elgin American hammered goldtone square compact; lid centered with rhinestone Christmas bell; red stone moveable clapper; 2¾" x 2¾". $60.00 – 100.00.

Top – Faberge gold and silver-plated basket weave design triangle compact; one side silvertone, other side goldtone; packet of powder refill; 3" each side of triangle. $65.00 – 80.00.

Right – Henriette copper-colored "Jack-in-the-Box" compact; lid decorated with rhinestone and green-colored stones; center rhinestone motif, hearts, diamonds, spades, and clubs; bellow sides allow for expansion when filled with powder; 3" x 3". $125.00 – 175.00.

Bottom – Elgin American brushed goldtone compact; the endearment "Mother" and leaves in polished goldtone decorate lid; 3" x 2¼". $60.00 – 100.00.

Center – Volupté brushed goldtone square compact with dime centered on lid; 2½" x 2½". $40.00 – 60.00.

Left – Round silvertone compact with large pink cabochon stone centered on lid; plastic interior; mirror; 3" dia. Contemporary compact from Poland. $45.00 – 60.00.

Right – White plastic compact with black etched balcony scene on lid; interior mirror and sponge powder puff; 2¾" x 2¾". Contemporary compact from Poland. $45.00 – 60.00.

Center – Woven green, brown, and gold fabric compact; zippered closing; plastic interior; mirror; 2½" dia. Contemporary compact from Poland. $45.00 – 60.00.

Left – Beauty Mate mini black enamel compact; lid decorated with enameled hummingbird and flowers; pull-out compact with pop-up mirror and powder compartment; 1" x 1¾". $25.00 – 50.00.

Top center – Green plastic compact; enameled disc with "American Red Cross Volunteer" encircling the Red Cross insignia centered on lid; 2¾" x 2¾". $60.00 – 80.00.

Right – Compact on left shown closed.

Bottom center – Round silvertone compact with plastic discs on either side; discs depict musicians in relief playing instruments, 2¼" dia. $50.00 – 75.00.

Dermay gold-plate mini-carryall; textured polished goldtone lid decorated with bands of black enamel and black cartouche; gilded interior (shown at right) reveals powder and rouge compartments and well with mini-perfume bottle; center mirror flanked by two lipstick tubes; cigarette compartment behind mirror; mesh carrying chain; 2¾" x 4". $175.00 – 250.00.

Three sterling silver charms. Left: Hammered silver compact charm; interior mirror and powder well; ⅝" dia. Center: Engine-turned silver vanity tango chain charm; interior reveals mirror, rouge, and powder compartments; lipstick attached to compact by chain; ⁷⁄₁₆" dia., lipstick ¾". Right: Basket weave silver compact charm; interior mirror and powder well; ½". $25.00 – 50.00 each.

Round celluloid compact; lid decorated with a painted three-dimensional face of Pierrot, a French pantomime; interior contains mirror and puff; Austria; 2¼" dia. $250.00 – 400.00.

Round plastic compact; Lucite lid encloses painted picture of lady on a swing; marbleized iridescent background; France; 2½" dia. $150.00 – 225.00.

Platé "Trio-ettes;" green, tortoise, white, pink, and blue plastic vanities shaped like hand mirrors; open on both sides; one side, mirror and powder compartment with puff; other side contains rouge compartment with puff; exterior mirror on rouge lid; lipstick slides out of handle; also available in other colors; 2¾" dia. x 4¼". All things being equal, prices vary according to color — blue, pink, and green command higher prices. $125.00 – 250.00

Black composition Platé Trio-ette compact with hang-tag, decorated with hand-painted pink enamel rose on lid and pink enamel on end of lipstick tube, reverse side reveals beveled mirror, interior reveals mirror, powder well, and puff, lipstick tube pulls out from the bottom, 4½" x 2¾" dia. $225.00 – 275.00.

Black composition Platé Trio-ette compact decorated with crystals around outer rim on front and reverse side, hang-tag on lipstick reads "Twist to Tighten," 4½" x 2¾" dia. $225.00 – 275.00.

House & Garden, *June, 1946.*

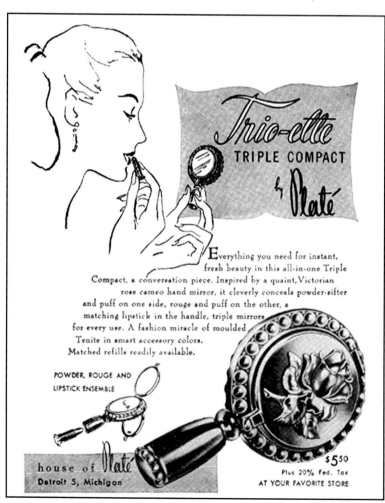

Trio-ette
TRIPLE COMPACT
by Platé

Everything you need for instant, fresh beauty in this all-in-one Triple Compact, a conversation piece. Inspired by a quaint, Victorian rose cameo hand mirror, it cleverly conceals powder-sifter and puff on one side, rouge and puff on the other, a matching lipstick in the handle, triple mirrors for every use. A fashion miracle of moulded Tenite in smart accessory colors. Matched refills readily available.

POWDER, ROUGE AND LIPSTICK ENSEMBLE

house of Platé
Detroit 5, Michigan

$5.50
Plus 20% Fed. Tax
AT YOUR FAVORITE STORE

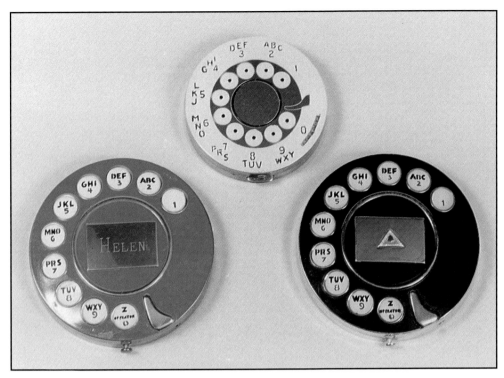

Left – Green-enameled compact; lid designed to resemble telephone dial; red numbers and black letters imprinted on white enameled goldtone framed circles; center goldtone cartouche engraved with the name "Helen," 3½" dia. $150.00 – 200.00.

Center – Pink-enameled goldtone compact; lid designed to resemble telephone dial; numbers and letters around lid; 2¾" dia. $100.00 – 125.00.

Right – Black-enameled compact; same as compact on left; logo "Telephone Pioneers of America" centered on cartouche. $150.00 – 200.00.

Lest you forget your telephone number (we must admit we do), this clever compact acts as a reminder. Black enamel cover, a facsimile of an actual phone dial, is engraved with your name and number. 3½" in diameter, with powder sifter, velour puff and full mirror, $2.25

Redbook, 1954.

Top – *Dorothy Gray oval brushed goldtone Savoir Faire compact; black raised enameled harlequin mask centered on lid; lid enhanced with rhinestones and incised ribbons; 3¾" x 3".* $125.00 – 150.00.

Center – *Elgin American goldtone compact; textured lid decorated with polished goldtone harlequin masks; 2¾" x ¾".* $40.00 – 60.00.

Bottom – *Elizabeth Arden polished goldtone mask-shaped compact; 3" x 1⅝".* $125.00 – 175.00.

Vogue, *1949.*

THE DOROTHY GRAY GALLERY OF FASCINATING WOMEN — ONE OF A SERIES

"Savoir Faire"

unique beauty creams...
fragrance ... make-up ...
sumptuously presented

"Savoir Faire"—*know-how.* So very expressive of these beautiful new cosmetics. *Know-how* in that the fine creams contain protective ingredients exclusive with "Savoir Faire." *Know-how* in that the Eau de Parfum possesses a fragrance of great style and originality. *Know-how* in that the make-up accessories are so decorative as to be conversation pieces!

Mrs. John J. Astor of New York City, the former Gertrude Gretsch. Portrait by the celebrated painter, Walter Klett.

Illustrated: Dusting Powder, $5; Compact, $10; Night Cream, $5; Eau de Parfum $12 . . . Also available: Perfume, $25 and $5; Cleansing Cream and Face Powder, each $5; Lipstick, $3. (*Plus tax.*)

Dorothy Gray

THE DOROTHY GRAY SALON · 445 PARK AVE, NEW YORK

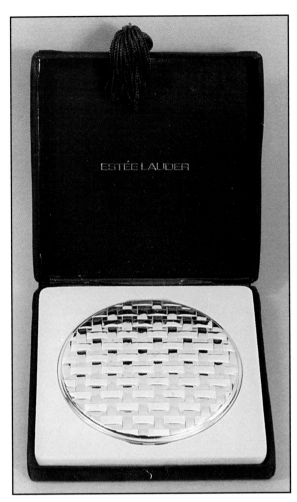

Estee Lauder round antique goldtone "Watchfob" compact, 1965, lid decorated with simulated mother-of-pearl, lid centered with goldtone design, complete with black tassel, 2¼" dia. Re-issued in 1999 as the "Golden Classic compact." $25.00 – 55.00.

Estee Lauder 1969 round goldtone and silvertone basket weave design "Big Weave" compact; interior reveals mirror and powder well; in original beautiful blue presentation box with tassel; 4" dia. $175.00 – 225.00.

Reverse side showing relief eagle.

Round goldtone Elgin American coin compact with helmeted profile in relief on front lid, reverse side has an eagle in relief, 3" dia. $65.00 – 85.00.

Square Volupté brushed goldtone compact lid centered with penny, 2½" sq. $40.00 – 60.00.

Round silvertone compact, lid decorated with goldtone, silvertone, and bronze neo-classical high relief profile discs, 4" dia. $125.00 – 175.00.

Two round mini compacts, front view of the goldtone on left has profile of Napoleon's head, silvertone on right shows reverse side of compact, NAPOLEON and EMP ET ROI appear on the front lids framed by a rope design, interior reveals mirror, powder well, puff, and sifter, 1½" dia. $65.00 – 85.00 each.

Goldtone compact in the shape of a change purse, lid decorated with basket weave pattern, complete with ball-twist closure, beveled mirror, sifter, powder well, and puff, 2¼" x 3½". $65.00 – 80.00.

Round goldtone Kigu compact/locket combination, highly engraved lid centered with opening for photos, interior of compact reveals puff, mirror, and powder well, complete with signed brown carrying sleeve, 3¼" dia., Directions for inserting pictures on card in locket read: "To fit a photo, lift this cover with nail file under the arrow. Then put photo in place of this card and slide lugs of transparent cover into slots on both sides." $125.00 – 175.00.

Kigu compact/locket shown open.

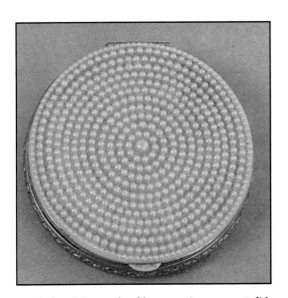

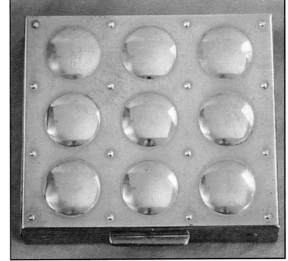

Round Max Factor Golden Zodiac watch fob compact, zodiac symbols in relief decorate front lid of compact, complete with hook and push-button stem, 2" dia. $45.00 – 65.00.

La Mode mini round goldtone vanity compact, lid decorated with faux mini seed pearls, metal mirror separated powder compartment from rouge compartment, yellow enamel reverse lid, 1½" dia. $35.00 – 45.00.

Rectangular polished and brushed compact, brushed goldtone lid decorated with polished goldtone raised circles, interior reveals mirror and powder well, 2½" x 2¾". $25.00 – 35.00.

Volupté square goldtone compact with swivel exterior mirror, when compact is opened, exterior mirror swings around, 3" sq. $45.00 – 65.00.

Volupté compact shown open.

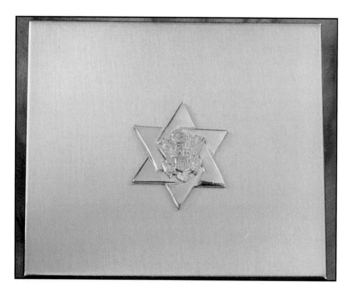

Brushed goldtone compact, lid decorated with service emblem centered on the Star of David, interior mirror, puff, and powder compartment, 2¼" x 2¾". $55.00 – 75.00.

Round goldtone compact, lid decorated with engine-turned design, tassel centered on top lid, powder well and mirror, 2¼" dia. $45.00 – 55.00.

Left – Red reptile skin Kamra-Pak compact/music box/cigarette case combination; top front lid incorporates music box; lower portion contains powder compartment; sliding lipstick; back contains cigarette case; 2" x 3⅞". $175.00 – 225.00.

Center top and bottom – Multicolored Persian design embossed leather Kamra-Pak compact/cigarette case combination; powder compartment on front lid; sliding lipstick; cigarette case on reverse side; matching cigarette lighter; 2" x 3⅞". $175.00 – 225.00.

Right – Marbleized tortoise shell-colored Kamra-Pak compact/cigarette case combination; front lid decorated with petit point; powder compartment; sliding lipstick; reverse side reveals cigarette compartment; Germany; 2" x 3⅞". $175.00 – 225.00.

Left – Goldtone compact designed to resemble a Postal Telegraph message; white lid decorated with Postal Telegraph heading and the name "Virginia Zenour;" interior powder well inscribed with the name "Andre Duval;" 3¼" x 2". $125.00 – 200.00.

Top center – Volupté goldtone compact; lid designed to resemble gift package; raised gift card and bow decorate lid; 3" x 3". $50.00 – 75.00.

Right – Goldtone vanity designed to resemble Air Express delivery; blue lid decorated with "Air Express, RUSH Railway Express Agency" and destination labels; raised goldtone cord; interior reveals mirror, powder, and rouge compartments; Patent #1883793; 3⅛" x 2⅛". $125.00 – 200.00.

Bottom center – Coty goldtone and green enamel vanity designed to resemble gift package; lid decorated with raised goldtone bow; interior reveals mirror, powder, and rouge compartments; 3" x 1⅞". $80.00 – 120.00.

Bottom left – Stratton goldtone compact with lipstick incorporated in lid; front lid decorated with troubadour transfer scene; Stratton hand logo on interior powder well; label on mirror reads "To open inner door: press mirror-lid gently back; door springs open—To shut bring mirror lid forward and press door down;" England; 3¼" x 2¾". $60.00 – 80.00.

Upper left – Stratton round goldtone compact; lid decorated with drinking toasts in different languages; Stratton hand logo on interior powder well; inner powder door release; England; 3" dia. $40.00 – 60.00.

Top center – Kigu round goldtone compact; white enameled lid decorated with simulated clock, pictures, and suggestions not to waste time; England; 3¼" dia. $40.00 – 60.00.

Upper right – Stratton round goldtone compact; white lid decorated with windmill scene; Stratton written on inner powder lid; England; 2¾". $30.00 – 50.00.

Lower right – Same as troubadour compact to left, lid decorated with all-over black and gold design.

Center – Round black plastic commemorative compact; lid decorated with coronation picture of King George VI and Queen Elizabeth, 1937; 3" dia. $60.00 – 100.00.

Round goldtone compact lid decorated with enamel Asian scene, powder well, puff, and mirror, 3½" dia. $45.00 – 65.00.

Round goldtone Queen Star compact, black suede lid with mother-of-pearl Asian good luck symbol, 3" dia. $75.00 – 85.00.

Round cobalt blue enamel stacked compact/music box, top contains music box, lower portion contains powder well, mirror, and puff, 3¼" dia. x ¾" h. $150.00 – 175.00.

Lucien Lelong round polished goldtone compact designed to resemble tambourine; lid decorated with incised birds, disc with Lucien Lelong logo and eight moveable rings on outer rim of compact, interior mirror, powder compartment and puff, 2½" dia., $175.00 – 275.00.

Large round silvertone and red enamel compact, white enamel lover's sentiment decorates lid, 4". $150.00 – 175.00.

Round hallmarked engraved silver compact, lid centered with composition disc enhanced with a man on horse in high relief, 2½" dia. $150.00 – 175.00.

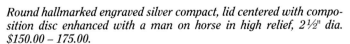

Round pewtertone compact, lid decorated with hand-painted enamel girl and Asian lettering, interior mirror and powder well, 2¾" dia. $35.00 – 45.00.

Hand-crafted oblong signed compact, purple lid centered with hand-painted picture of a girl wearing a red hat, interior contains mirror and powder well, signed "Gemma, Mexico," 2" x 2½". $20.00 – 30.00.

Round goldtone Miref compact, lid decorated with painted courting scene, signed "I. Peynet," beveled glass bottom, interior reveals beveled mirror and puff, 2¾" dia. $125.00 – 140.00.

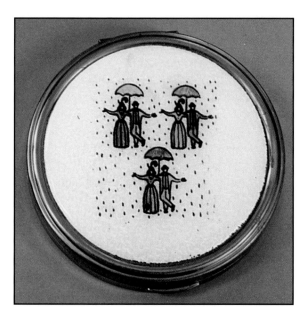

Round goldtone compact decorated with three couples in the rain underneath umbrellas on a white enamel disc centered on top lid, 3⅛" dia. $55.00 – 75.00.

Round Stratton compact, blue iridescent enamel lid decorated with two white swans, interior reveals framed mirror, powder well, sifter, and puff, 3" dia. Label on mirror reads, "To open inner door, press mirror lid gently back, door springs open. To shut bring mirror lid forward, and press door down." $45.00 – 65.00.

Estee Lauder 1973 hexagonal goldtone "Royal Enamel" portrait compact, 1¾". Insert reads: "A Gift for You from Mr. and Mrs. Joseph H. Lauder." $75.00 – 90.00.

Miref round goldtone compact, glass bottom, revealed underneath domed glass top lid are colorful horses and riders, centered under dome is a black spinning arrow indicator, 2¾" dia. $125.00 – 150.00.

Chez Re Lew round silvertone vanity compact, lid decorated with hand-painted girl, interior reveals mirror, lower part of mirror contains a section for rouge, opposite side contains powder well, puff, and powder, 2" dia. $15.00 – 25.00.

Estee Lauder 1973 goldtone and cobalt blue enamel hexagon-shaped "Royal Enamel" compact, 2" x 2½". $50.00 – 75.00.

Octagonal green enamel compact, hand-painted scene on front lid, interior reveals mirror and rotating perforated powder well, 2¼" x 2¼". $150.00 – 200.00.

Melissa round goldtone compact, enameled goldfish underneath plastic domed lid, 2¾", England. $65.00 – 75.00.

Left – Silvertone framed black silk vanity bag; oval frame heavily embossed; silver carrying chain; pink silk interior contains mirror, pocket for puff, and second pocket with change purse; 3¾" x 5½". $175.00 – 250.00.

Right – Trinity Platé goldtone vanity bag; petit point front lid opens to reveal beautifully framed beveled mirror and green silk pocket for puff; second opening reveals green silk lining with shirred pockets on either side; top of frame enhanced with red enameled flowers and colored stones; carrying chain interspersed with red beads; metal tassel; 2¾" x 5". $225.00 – 325.00.

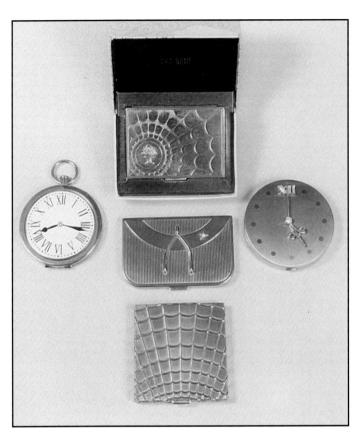

Left – Wadsworth round goldtone compact designed to resemble train conductor's pocket watch; lid decorated with paper transfer of watch face with Roman numerals; back lid decorated with old-fashioned steam locomotive; 2¾" dia. $40.00 – 60.00.

Top center – Cara Noma, Langlois goldtone vanity; lid decorated with flower basket centered in incised web; interior reveals mirror, powder, and rouge compartments; 3¼" x 2¼". $60.00 – 85.00.

Right – Round brushed goldtone compact; lid decorated as watch; hands decorated with rhinestones; 3" dia. $40.00 – 60.00.

Bottom center – Volupté goldtone compact designed to resemble spider web; lid decorated with raised web; 3" x 3". $50.00 – 75.00.

Center – Coty goldtone vanity; lid decorated with wishbone and star set with rhinestone; interior reveals rouge and powder compartments; 3¾" x 2¼". $80.00 – 100.00.

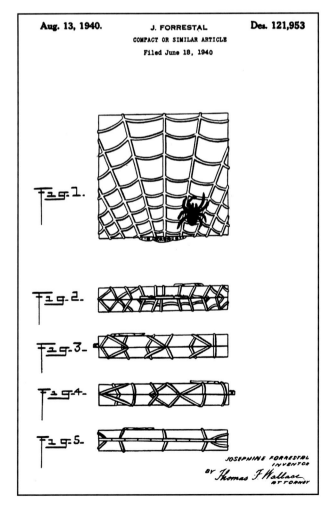

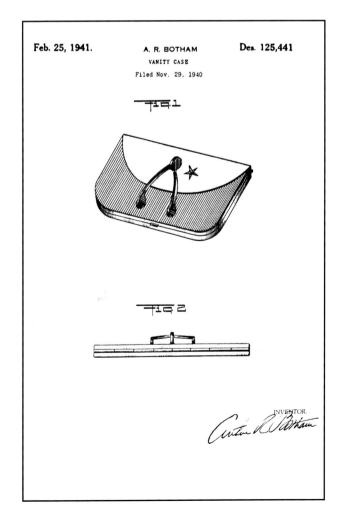

129

Vanity, round red floral fabric and metal compact; interior reveals powder well; outer rim of compact black enamel and goldtone; front and back lids fabric; bow on front lid contains sleeve for lipstick tube; comb slides in behind top of bow; carrying handle; 3¼" dia. x 7" long. $150.00 – 175.00.

Left – Triangle-shaped red velvet cardboard compact; interior reveals mirror and powder compartment; exterior red velvet lid decorated with miniature applied raised Egyptian face framed by black rings; two additional white rings decorate lid; metal tassel; carrying cord with wooden handle; 2⅛" x 2⅛". $120.00 – 200.00.

Right – Blue silk cardboard vanity case; interior reveals mirror, powder, rouge, and lipstick compartments; blue silk lid decorated with metallic cord and miniature fabric flowers; wooden tassel; metallic carrying cord; 3" x 4". $150.00 – 250.00.

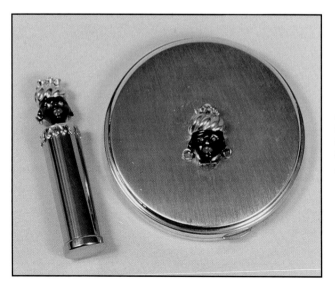

Round brushed goldtone compact with matching lipstick; compact lid and lipstick tube decorated with a raised applied blackamoor head; head decorated with a pearl and rhinestone turban, green stone eyes, red enamel lips, and moveable goldtone hoop earrings; 3½" dia. $225.00 – 300.00 set.

Lower left – Raquel embossed leather vanity designed to resemble book; multicolored leather lids; interior reveals metal-framed mirror, powder, and rouge compartments; 2" x 3". $80.00 – 125.00.

Upper left – Raquel compact, green and gold embossed leather.

Top center – Raquel compact, red and gold embossed leather (shown open).

Upper right – Raquel compact, tan and gold embossed leather.

Lower right – Raquel compact, multicolored leather lids.

Center – Mondaine embossed multicolored leather vanity; interior reveals beveled mirror; compartments for powder and rouge; 1⅞" x 2¾". $80.00 – 125.00.

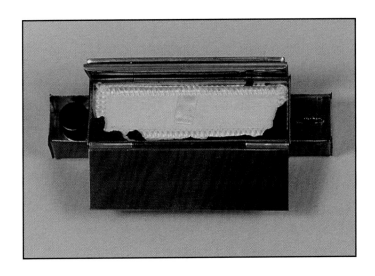

Quinto goldtone vanity, closed at left, open at right; raised squares enhanced with rhinestones applied to lid; interior reveals powder well and puff; sides contain slide-out lipstick and perfume bottle; 3" x 1¼" x 1". $75.00 – 125.00.

131

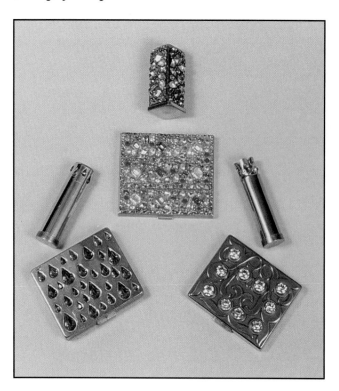

Left – *Flato goldtone compact with matching lipstick; compact lid and lipstick tube decorated with green pear-shaped stones; interior reveals powder well, puff, and mirror; 2⅛" x 2⅛". $150.00 – 200.00.*

Center – *Schildkraut goldtone compact with matching lipstick; compact lid and lipstick tube decorated with beautiful bezel set multicolored, various shaped stones; 2¾" x 2½". $125.00 – 175.00.*

Right – *Flato goldtone compact with matching lipstick; compact lid has applied cut-out design enhanced with bezel set turquoise stones; lipstick tube decorated with turquoise stones; 2½" x 2¼". $150.00 – 225.00.*

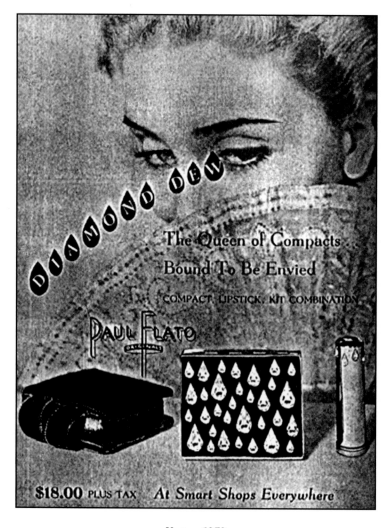

Vogue, *1950.*

Brass compact on black velvet display stand; exterior mirror framed with beautiful cut-out brass design; deeply beveled interior mirror; France; 3¼" x 4". $150.00 – 200.00.

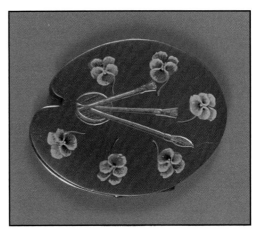

Henry A. La Pensee handmade coppertone compact designed to resemble an artist's palette; lid decorated with engraved brushes and colorful enamel flowers; Paris; 3" x 2¼". $275.00 – 325.00.

Platé silver bullet-shaped vanity; engine-turned exterior; cartouche on side; interior reveals framed mirror that separates powder compartment from second compartment; finger ring carrying chain; 1" dia. x 3½". $150.00 – 250.00.

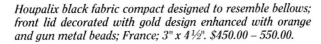

Houpalix black fabric compact designed to resemble bellows; front lid decorated with gold design enhanced with orange and gun metal beads; France; 3" x 4½". $450.00 – 550.00.

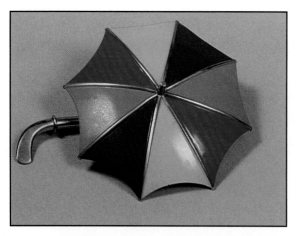

Goldtone compact designed to resemble beach umbrella; lid decorated with brightly colored green, yellow, blue, and red panels; interior reveals mirror; handle folds flat against back of compact, pulls away, and acts as handle while using compact; 2¾" closed, 3½" upright. NPA.

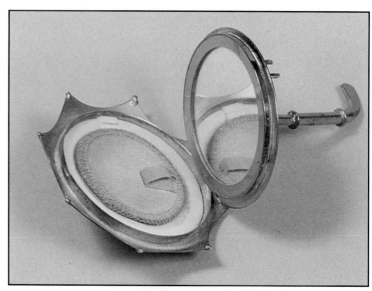

Umbrella compact open.

"Merry-Go-Round" goldtone compact designed to resemble carousel; colorful red, white, and blue horses decorate the outer rim; goldtone and white carousel lid top; 2½" dia. $350.00 – 450.00.

Wadsworth compact designed to resemble shirt; raised gray collar extends above lid; interior mirror reads "A Madison Creation;" 3" x 3¼". NPA.

Miref "Mirador" round goldtone compact; incised rings around compact; slide-out lipstick; top and bottom exterior beveled mirrors; interior reveals beveled mirror and powder compartment; Paris; 2" dia. $125.00 – 175.00.

134

Left – Round fabric powder case; top lid decorated with flapper girl; black lace around exterior rim; ribbon on front lid lifts to reveal puff attached to lid, and powder compartment; exterior mirror on reverse side; 4" dia. $30.00 – 60.00.

Top and bottom – Two black silk paddles on black sticks; composition female faces decorated with string of pearls and blonde hair applied to lid; marabou feathers around outer rims of paddles; reverse side of one reveals puff, other reveals mirror; 3" dia. x 9". $35.00 – 70.00.

Right – Miniature puff concealed in yellow dress of doll; flapper doll wears lace and silk hat; yellow skirt snaps open to reveal puff; 3" x 2¾". $15.00 – 30.00.

Round goldtone compact; lid has picture of a female flamenco dancer with an applied lace skirt protected by beveled glass dome; beveled glass bottom lid; 2¾" dia. $80.00 – 100.00.

Red faux leather compact designed to resemble hat box; snaps open and shut; faux zipper; interior reveals mirror and puff; carrying handle; 3" x 2¾". $75.00 – 125.00.

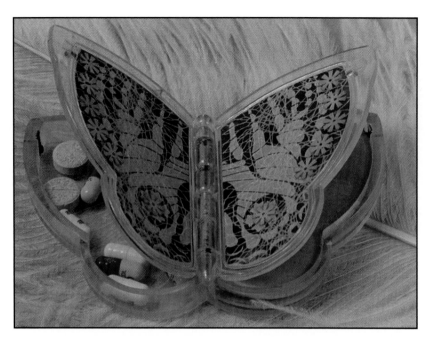

Wadsworth "Crystelle" butterfly compact; black, blue, and silver design on lid; mirrors on interiors of both wings; puff and powder compartment on one side; other side for pills; 4¼" x 2¾". $225.00 – 325.00.

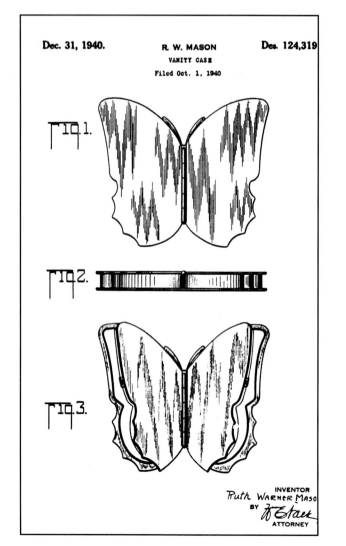

Dec. 31, 1940.   R. W. MASON   Des. 124,319

VANITY CASE

Filed Oct. 1, 1940

Fig.1.

Fig.2.

Fig.3.

INVENTOR

Ruth Warner Maso

BY

ATTORNEY

new "Crystelle" compacts

Wadsworth's Luminous Lightweights

If you're tired of toting a heavy handbag, you'll applaud these luminous lovelies that help to lighten that load. Such light, and such bright! ways to beauty—sequin spangled, color lined. Look for Wadsworth's new "Crystelle" compacts . . . at all fine stores.

SOCIAL BUTTERFLY, sequin-spangled. One wing holds powder, the other pills. $7.95

PARQUET, underlaid with sequins. $7.95

AMOURETTE, crowned with golden cupid. $7.95

1952

Wadsworth COMPACTS

Wadsworth Compact ad, 1952.

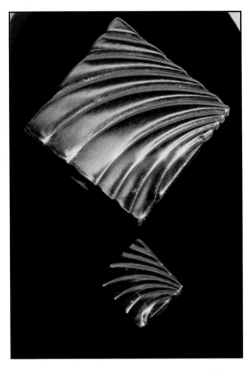

Volupté matching "Mother-Daughter" goldtone compacts; lids decorated with raised swirls; interiors reveal mirror and puff; daughter's, 1¼" x 1⅛"; mother's 3" square. $175.00 – 200.00 set.

Ladies' Home Journal, *December 1947.*

Left – Evans round blue enamel mesh vanity pouch; light blue mesh bottom; interior reveals powder well; metal mirror opens to reveal rouge compartment; 2¼" dia. $40.00 – 60.00.

Right – Large round blue enamel mesh vanity pouch; silvertone mesh bottom; interior reveals mirror and powder compartment; 4" dia. $60.00 – 80.00.

Hallmarked silver compact/brush combination; compact centered on elegantly engine-turned top of hair brush; side pull-out comb; interior of compact (shown on right) reveals mirror and puff; 3¾" x 2¾". $350.00 – 450.00.

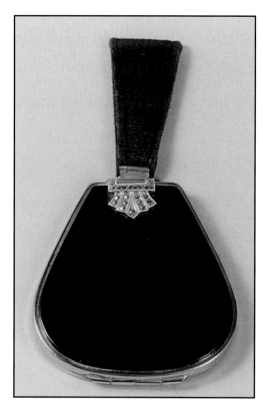

Black enamel and goldtone saddle bag-shaped compact; lid decorated with marcasites; interior reveals powder compartment and beveled mirror; suede finger carrying handle; West Germany; 2¾" x 5". $150.00 – 225.00.

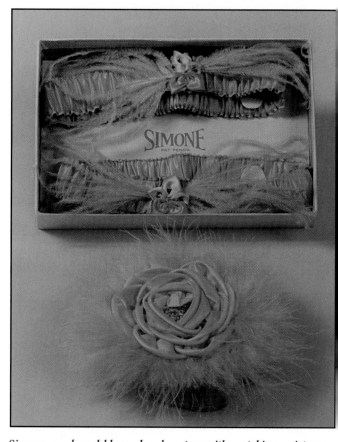

Simone peach and blue colored garters with matching wrist compact; garters decorated with peach-colored marabou feathers and blue silk flowers; wrist compact decorated with blue silk flower and blue maribou feathers; reverse side reveals wrist band and purse; purse interior has attached mirror and drawstring puff; France. $125.00 – 175.00.

Top – Richard Hudnut "le Début" octagon-shaped light blue enameled tango chain finger ring vanity; fitted presentation box; light blue and white enamel decorate lid and lipstick tube; interior reveals powder and rouge compartments separated by mirror; 2" dia. $175.00 – 250.00.

Bottom – Richard Hudnut "le Début" octagon-shaped light blue vanity case; interior reveals powder and rouge compartments separated by mirror; 2" dia. $50.00 – 75.00.

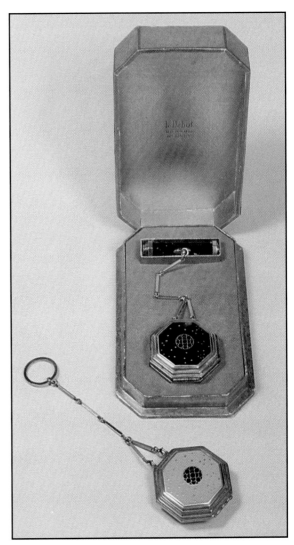

Top – Marbleized metal compact; lid decorated with transfer of period portrait; interior reveals mirror and powder well; 2¾" x 2¾". $40.00 – 60.00.

Center – Round goldtone compact; lid decorated with painted silhouette; interior reveals mirror and powder well; 2½" dia. $40.00 – 60.00.

Bottom – Square black enamel vanity with rounded sides; lid decorated with signed hand-painted period portrait; interior reveals powder compartment; metal mirror concealing rouge compartment, powder puffs; 2" x 2". $60.00 – 90.00.

Top – Richard Hudnut "le Début" octagon-shaped dark blue-enameled tango chain vanity; fitted presentation box; dark blue and gold enamel decorate lid and lipstick tube; interior reveals powder and rouge compartments separated by mirror; 2" dia. $175.00 – 250.00.

Bottom – Richard Hudnut "le Début" octagon-shaped green-enameled finger ring vanity; green and gold enamel decorate lid; interior reveals powder and rouge compartments separated by mirror; 2" dia. $150.00 – 225.00.

Top – Zell tan leather oval compact designed to resemble football; impressed simulated laces on front lid; coppertone interior reveals mirror and powder compartment; 4½" x 3½". $60.00 – 100.00.

Center – Round white enamel compact designed to resemble baseball; team name "Giants" centered on front lid; lid also decorated with blue and white painted stitching; interior reveals mirror and powder compartment; 3" dia. $60.00 – 100.00.

Bottom – De Corday "Silver Queen" round white compact designed to resemble golf ball; textured lids slightly domed; interior reveals mirror and powder well; 2" dia. $25.00 – 50.00.

Silver Queen Golf Ball Compact ad, May, 1928.

"Right on the Nose!"

The New Sports Compact "Silver Queen"

The golf ball is the inspiration for this newest of toilet accessories.
Very thin, very smart, very practical.
Single or Double. Poudre: 4 shades (Naturelle, Rachel, Blanche, Tan). Rouge: 2 shades.
Perfumed with "Blanchette" an enticing odor by

CORDAY, 15 Rue de la Paix. Paris

Round white enamel metal compact, the word "Orioles," a baseball, bats, and an Oriole bird decorate the lid, 3" dia. $65.00 – 85.00.

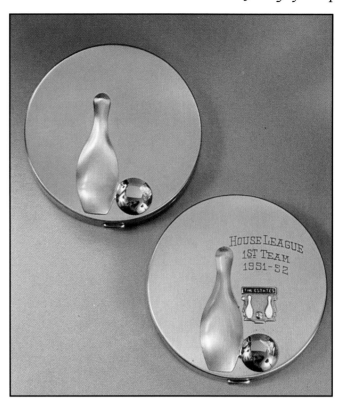

Two round brushed goldtone compacts, lids decorated with applied bowling pin and ball, inscribed on lower left compact "House League 1st Team, 1951 – 1952" with an applied disc reading "The Estates," beveled mirror, 3" dia. $55.00 – 75.00 each.

Oblong goldtone compact, inlaid wooden lid decorated with a bowling ball and pins, 3½" x 2¼". $40.00 – 60.00.

Elgin American brown leather oval compact designed to resemble football, 3" x 2". $55.00 – 75.00.

Round J.D. Creation round black compact designed to resemble a record complete with grooves and red center label which reads "Melody, J.D. Creation;" interior reveals beveled mirror, puff, sifter, and powder well. Also available with blue, green or cream-colored center labels. Made for the foreign market, available in the U.S. under the Columbia Records label, 3¾" dia., complete with original box. $350.00 – 450.00.

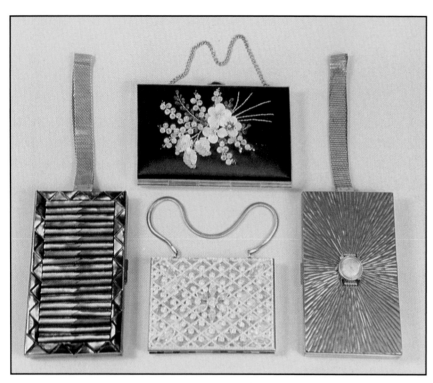

Left – Dual opening goldtone carryall; lids beautifully inlaid with fluted lavender and purple shaded mother-of-pearl; mesh carrying chain; one opening reveals lipstick tube, mirror, money clip, and powder compartment; second opening, cigarette case; 3¼" x 5½". $250.00 – 300.00.

Top – Black silk and goldtone vanity bag; lid lavishly decorated with beads, pearls, mother-of-pearl, and embroidery; top closure decorated with rhinestones; interior contains beveled mirror, powder, and rouge sleeves; link carrying chain; imprinted in gold on interior lining "Made in France for The French Bazaar, Colon-Panama;" 5½" x 3¾". $225.00 – 275.00.

Right – Evans dual opening goldtone carryall; watch centered on embossed sunburst lid; interior contains powder compartment, mirror, and coin, lipstick and comb holders; cigarette case on other side; mesh carrying chain; 3¼" x 5½". $250.00 – 325.00.

Bottom – Mini-goldtone carryall; lid enhanced with bezel set Aurora Borealis rhinestones; interior contains powder compartment, lipstick tube, comb pouch, swinging mirror concealing cigarette compartment; snake carrying chain; 4¼" x 3". $175.00 – 225.00.

Ciner black enamel and gilt egg-shaped minaudière; stripes of black enamel and gilt decorate exterior; interior reveals center framed mirror separating powder compartment from second compartment; black enameled finger ring carrying chain; 2" dia x 3". $250.00 – 350.00.

1⅝" round compact/dress clip combinations; riding crop applied to brown-enameled compact; navy insignia applied to blue compact; flag applied to black compact; Scottie dog transfer applied to silvertone compact; compact with carved orange Bakelite lid; compact with marcasite lid; and lower center, 1½" x 2" brown compact has transfer portrait on lid; upper center compact shown open. $100.00 – 150.00.

Silvertone vanity; lids beautifully engine turned; enamel flowered disc centered on lid; interior reveals mirror, powder, rouge, and lipstick compartments; metal carrying chain; 2⅞" x 1¾". This compact was the start of my collection, purchased on July 4, 1976. $125.00 – 200.00.

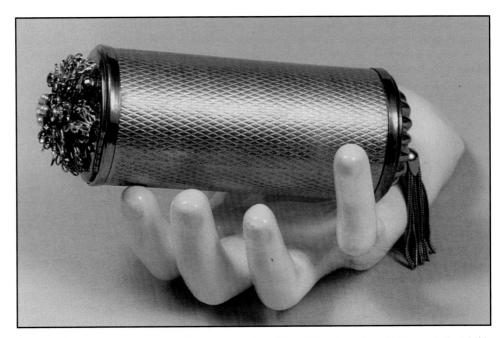

Wadsworth "Bon Bon" textured goldtone necessaire with goldtone tassel; top lid decorated with filigree leaves, pearls, rhinestones, and colored stones; top opens to reveal mirror and powder well; bottom pulls out to reveal tube for cigarettes or other small items; 1¾" x 4¾". $150.00 – 175.00.

Dorset Fifth Avenue incised goldtone bolster-shaped compact, green cabochon stones on either end of compact, twisted goldtone handle, interior reveals mirror, puff, and powder well, 2¼" x 1½" dia. $65.00 – 75.00.

Polished goldtone bolster-shaped necessaire, with tango goldtone lipstick, white enamel top lid of necessaire enhanced with enameled pink roses, the name "Joan" inscribed on reverse lid, top lid opens to reveal mirror, powder sifter, and puff, lower lid reveals mirror and large cavity for other necessities, 3¼ x 1½" dia. $145.00 – 175.00.

La Pomponette goldtone bolster-shaped pli, interior of hinged top reveals mirror and puff, reverse end screws off revealing metal sifter and powder well, France, 2⅞" x 1" dia. $100.00 – 125.00.

La Pomponette pli shown closed.

144

Mini brushed goldtone necessaire, complete with adjustable wrist chain, lid enhanced with seven small garnets, top lid opens to reveal beveled mirror and puff, second opening reveals perfume bottle surrounded by a row of pins around bottle, bottom opening reveals coin holder, England, 2½" x 1⅛" dia. $500.00 – $600.00.

Top two sections of necessaire at left, shown open.

Lower coin section of necessaire above.

All three sections of necessaire shown open.

Black enamel goldtone bolster-shaped vanity, decorated with applied goldtone leaves, opens to reveal powder well and pill compartment, compartment for cigarettes behind swinging center mirror, rigid handle, 3½" long x 1¾". $125.00 – 150.00.

Top – Calvaire round brass compact; lid decorated with faceted oval-shaped colored stones; interior mirror and powder compartment; 2½" dia. $75.00 – 150.00.

Center – Round goldtone compact; lid set with multi-shaped, multicolored stones; interior powder well and mirror; 2½" dia. $50.00 – 80.00.

Bottom – Pilcher round goldtone compact; prong set emerald cut and round rhinestones decorate lid; interior mirror and powder well; 3½" dia. $75.00 – 150.00.

Black enamel egg-shaped compact with sterling chain; rhinestones encircle circumference of compact, top and lower portion of compact decorated with onyx stones and rhinestones; compact opens to reveal beveled mirror and powder well; 1¾" dia. x 2½". $450.00 – 550.00.

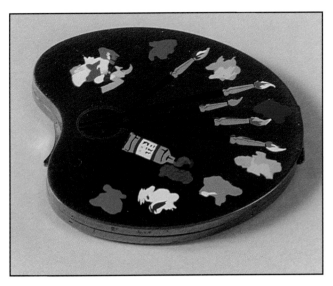

Volupté brushed goldtone compact designed to resemble artist's palette; lid decorated with paint tube, paint brushes, and colors; interior mirror and powder compartment; 3" x 2¾". $125.00 – 175.00.

J.M. Fisher silvertone vanity; lid decorated with colorful enamel scene of Robin Hood in Sherwood Forest; interior contains mirror, two lipstick tubes, powder, and rouge compartments; link carrying chain; 3" x 2¼". $350.00 – 450.00.

Wadsworth square goldtone compact; colorful enameled picture of Madam DuBarry centered on lid; outer rim of lid reads "QUITE A GAL WAS MADAM DUBARRY — WAS SHE A LADY? — WELL NOT VERY;" interior mirror and powder compartment; 3" x 3". $125.00 – 150.00.

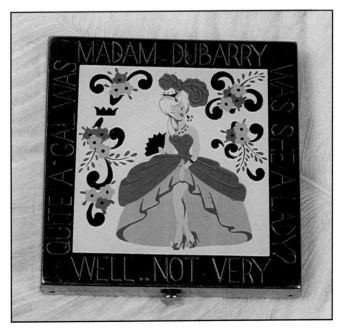

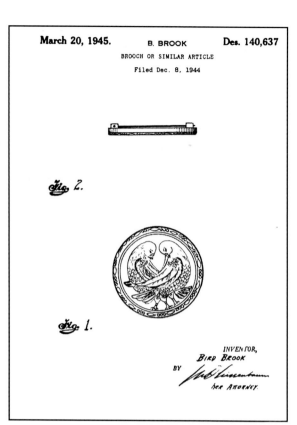

March 20, 1945.   B. BROOK   Des. 140,637

BROOCH OR SIMILAR ARTICLE

Filed Dec. 8, 1944

Fig. 2.

Fig. 1.

INVENTOR,
BIRD BROOK

BY

her ATTORNEY.

Left – Round polished goldtone compact; two repoussé doves centered on lid; interior reveals mirror and powder compartment; 2⅞" dia. $80.00 – 120.00.

Right – Clear square Lucite compact; sterling repoussé medallion of two doves centered on lid; 2⅞" x 2⅞". $150.00 – 175.00.

Stratton Wedgwood Jasperware convertible goldtone compact; lid inset with cameo of the "Three Graces," Aglair, Euprosyne, and Thalia, Greek mythological companions of Venus who endow mortals with beauty, wisdom, and charm; blue label on interior beveled mirror reads, "The cameo on this Stratton product is made by Josiah Wedgwood & Sons, Ltd.;" 3¼" dia. $50.00 – 75.00.

Left – Round goldtone compact; textured silvertone lid decorated with applied enameled charms, heart, cap, wishbone, etc.; black enameled reverse lid; interior mirror and powder compartment; 2" dia. $150.00 – 175.00.

Right – Square brushed goldtone compact; lid decorated with applied enameled charms, suitcase, monkey organ grinder, duck, etc.; interior mirror and powder compartment; 2¼" x 2¼". $150.00 – 175.00.

Left – Volupté polished goldtone compact designed to resemble apple; engraved lines radiate from top; stem opens compact; interior mirror and powder well; 3" x 3". $125.00 – 185.00.

Right – Volupté red enameled compact designed to resemble apple minus stem; interior mirror and powder well; 3" x 3". $150.00 – 225.00.

Super-sized round bi-colored goldtone compact; polished goldtone lid decorated with raised, polished pink goldtone leaping gazelles; pink goldtone scalloped design at top and bottom of front lid; deeply beveled interior mirror, puff, and powder compartment; 5⅞" dia. x ⅝". $300.00 – 350.00.

Elgin American polished goldtone compact; lid decorated with crown set with five red stones, lady sitting on chair, banner underneath chair reads "Queen for a Day;" beveled mirror and powder compartment; 3½" x 2¾". $100.00 – 150.00.

Coty "Memo" goldtone compact with matching lipstick/perfume combination; compact designed to resemble book; embossed basket weave design on lid; cartouche on polished goldtone spine; lipstick/perfume combination designed to resemble pencil; one side of tube contains creamy lipstick, other side contains small bottle of Chypre perfume; 3½" x 2¼"; lipstick, 3½". $175.00 – 225.00.

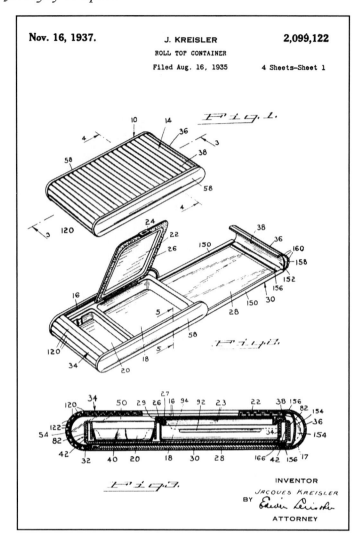

Nov. 16, 1937.   J. KREISLER   2,099,122
                    ROLL TOP CONTAINER
              Filed Aug. 16, 1935   4 Sheets—Sheet 1

INVENTOR
JACQUES KREISLER
BY
ATTORNEY

Mini roll-top vanity; coppertone roll-top, red-enameled side pieces; interior mirror, powder, and rouge compartments; 2" x 3". $125.00 – 175.00.

Left – Volupté square goldtone compact in black moire "Whisk-er Brush" slip case containing outside sleeve for lipstick tube; 3" x 4". $50.00 – 100.00.

Right – Volupté square goldtone compact in black moire "Whisk-er Brush" slip case; 3" x 4". $25.00 – 75.00.

Square ivorene compact/easel; centered on lid of compact is round picture of man and woman in goldtone embossed frame; easel is made in same design as outer rim of compact; back of picture reads "La Musette" (Boucher); 3⅛" x 1¾". NPA.

Mini round compact/key chain combination; snakeskin lids; interior metal mirror, swansdown puff, and powder compartment; key chain attached to side rim of compact; Italy; 1½" dia. $80.00 – 100.00.

Schuco miniature Teddy Bear compact; opens to reveal powder compartment; head lifts off to reveal lipstick tube; Patent #1,693,563; 3¾". $700.00 – 900.00.

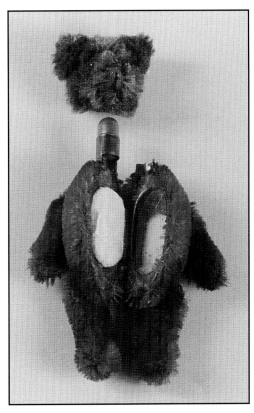

Schuco compact open.

Rare Schuco velvet and felt compact designed to resemble a penguin with a pink ribbon, interior reveals mirror, powder well, and puff, signed Schuco under powder well, 1920s, 2" dia. x 3". $800.00 – 1,000.00.

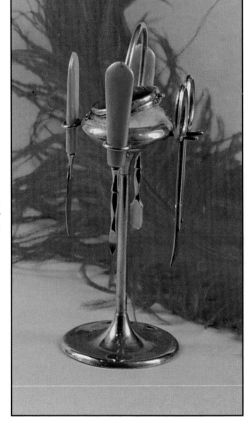

Dresser vanity/manicure combination; round compact centered on top of silvertone stand; blue butterfly wings under glass decorate compact lid; rings around outer rim secure manicure implements; carrying handle; Germany; 2¼" x 6¼". $275.00 – 350.00.

Red leather-rimmed compact designed as tambourine; red and yellow chenille ball fringe; hand-painted scene of bullfighter on front lid; "Mallorca" written on top of front lid; interior mirror and powder compartment; 4" dia. x ⅞". $225.00 – 325.00.

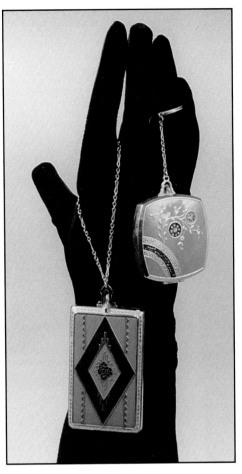

Shari "Langlois" round goldtone vanity; lid decorated with beautiful Asian scene; unusual fitted silk octagonal presentation box has identical scene executed in color on the lid; interior of compact reveals metal mirror separating rouge and powder compartments; compact 2¼" dia.; box 3". $150.00 – 225.00.

Left – Evans silvertone vanity case; lid decorated with purple, lavender, and silvertone designs; interior reveals mirror, powder and rouge compartments, and two coin holders; carrying chain. 2" x 3½". $175.00 – 225.00.

Right – Evans silvertone vanity case; lid decorated with purple, lavender, and silvertone designs; interior reveals mirror, powder, and rouge compartments; finger ring chain; 2" x 2". $125.00 – 150.00.

Mini-goldtone compact designed to resemble fan; exterior lid decorated with yellow, pink, silvertone, and goldtone flowers; pearl twist lock; interior mirror and powder well; 2½" x 1½". $25.00 – 50.00.

Left – Evans silvertone vanity with through handle; black enamel disc with scene of bird and flowers centered on engine-turned vanity lid; interior reveals mirror, powder, rouge, and lipstick compartments; 3" x 3½". $125.00 – 175.00.

Right – Evans silvertone vanity with through handle; black enamel disc with scene of bird and flowers centered on engine-turned vanity lid; interior reveals mirror, powder, and rouge compartments; 2" x 3¼". $75.00 – 100.00.

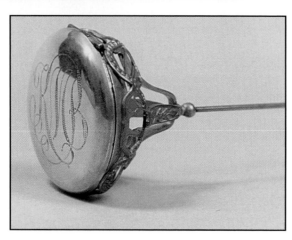

Goldtone compact/hatpin combination; silvertone compact lid monogrammed; interior reveals mirror and puff; decorative Art Nouveau goldtone mounting; 12" shank; compact 1½" dia. $800.00 – 1,200.00.

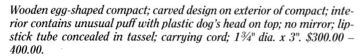

Wooden egg-shaped compact; carved design on exterior of compact; interior contains unusual puff with plastic dog's head on top; no mirror; lipstick tube concealed in tassel; carrying cord; 1¾" dia. x 3". $300.00 – 400.00.

Round bone-colored plastic compact/perfume combination; screw-off bottom lid decorated with black painted ruffles; man with pilgrim hat centered on top lid; hat screws off to reveal perfume bottle; interior reveals powder well and puff, mirror missing; 1½" dia. x 3". $200.00 – 275.00.

Pilgrim man compact, closed

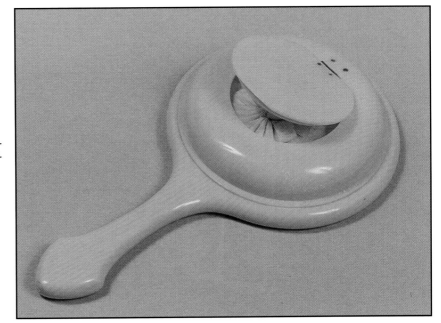

Ivory celluloid compact designed as hand mirror; exterior mirror; top lid opens to reveal powder compartment; 2¾" dia. x 5". $100.00 – 125.00.

Round silvertone vanity; painted flapper celluloid domed disc applied to lid; eyes inset with blue faceted stones; rhinestones decorate hair; interior mirror, rouge, and powder compartments; 1⅞" x ½". $225.00 – 275.00.

Richard Hudnut Deauville Dusting Powder Box.

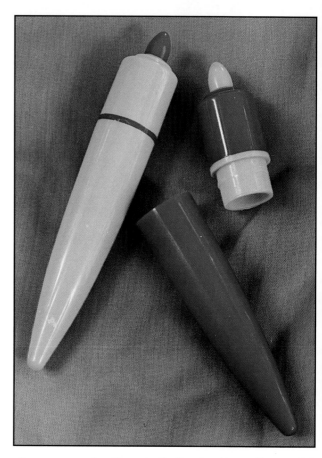

Two green and yellow plastic Powderettes, yellow on left shown closed, green on right shown open. To use: unscrew top and fill cavity with powder and screw top back on; to release powder, press point on top against powder puff, complete with instructions, 4" x ⅝" dia. $10.00 – 15.00.

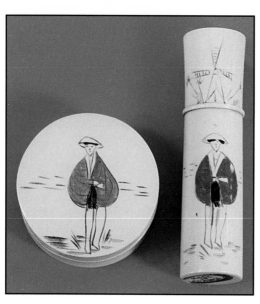

Mini cream-colored Bakelite compact complete with mirror, puff, and powder, and matching perfume tube, compact and perfume both decorated with hand-painted Asian woman and with screwtop lids, compact 1½" dia., perfume tube 2½" x" dia., France. $100.00 – 125.00 set.

How to fill . . .
Powderette

1. Unlock your Powderette.
2. Fill top of container out of powder box.
3. Hold top in upright position after filling, insert base and lock.
4. Try point to assure free flow of powder.

Powderette instructions.

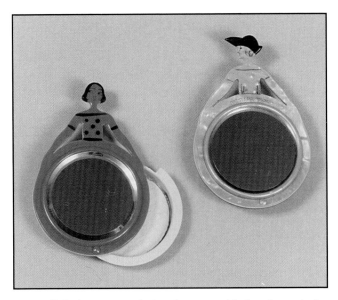

Two celluloid compacts designed to resemble females; exterior swinging beveled mirrors incorporated as part of skirt. Left: front of dress orange accented with black dots; interior powder well showing; right: front of dress marbleized pink, black hat, shown with mirror in closed position; imprinted above mirrors "Pat'd Apr 28 – 25." $200.00 – 300.00.

Reverse sides of compacts at left: back of dress caramel-colored, black hat; right: back of dress white with red and black decorations.

Enamel and sterling dresser vanity designed as period piece, lady in a ball gown; ivorene female figure dressed in light blue and lavender cloisonné enameled ball gown; gilded lower interior section reveals mirror and powder well; exterior bottom lid reads "Déposé;" inner rim of compact reads "Sterling" and "Germany;" 2½" dia. x 3". NPA.

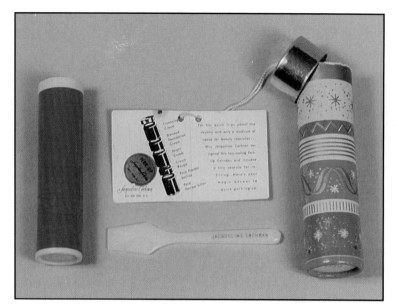

Jacqueline Cochran make-up kit; red and white plastic tubular container with compartments for cleansing cream, blended foundation cream, night cream, cream rouge, face powder section, face powder sifter; plastic cream applicator; 1" dia. x 4". $60.00 – 80.00.

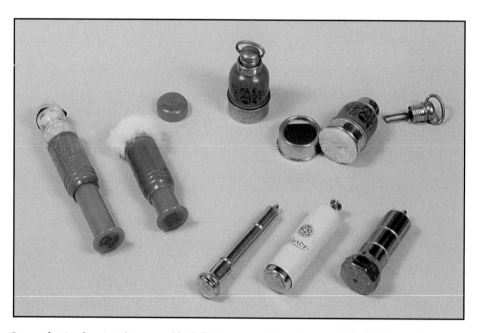

Left 1 – Green plastic pli painted to resemble doll; tri-cornered hat; France; 4¼". $150.00 – 200.00.

Left 2 – S.G.D.G. green plastic pli; powder well in bottom; puff pushes out on top; France; $60.00 – 100.00.

Top 1 – Red enamel and silvertone canister-type powder container; outside bottom lid contains mirror; bottom lid reveals powder puff; top unscrews to reveal powder scoop; France; 1" dia. x 2¼". $75.00 – 125.00.

Top 2 - Blue canister-type powder container open.

Bottom 1 – Princess Pat goldtone powderette lipstick; lipstick concealed under upper lid; ¾" dia. x 2½". $75.00 – 125.00.

Bottom 2 – Luxor cream-colored enamel powderette; powder releases when top is pushed down; Luxor logo on lid; premium gift, "Compliments of Luxor" written on bottom lid; Patent #1872836; ⅝" x 2½". $40.00 – 60.00.

Bottom 3 – Princess Pat silvertone powderette lipstick; lipstick concealed under upper lid; ½" dia. x 3". $50.00 – 75.00.

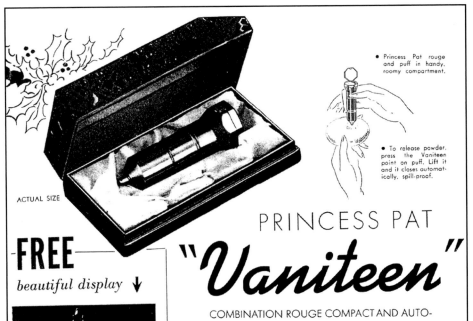

ACTUAL SIZE

- Princess Pat rouge and puff in handy, roomy compartment.

- To release powder, press the Vaniteen point on puff. Lift it and it closes automatically, spill-proof.

PRINCESS PAT

"Vaniteen"

COMBINATION ROUGE COMPACT AND AUTO-MATIC LOOSE POWDER HOLDER—**RETAIL $1**

This Princess Pat Vaniteen solves that knotty problem—the low-price gift that makes an instant hit. Vaniteen has class and distinction, yet its price of one dollar makes it a fast, easy seller. Very handsomely finished in the color of gold and richly embossed, the Vaniteen looks right at home in the proudest purse. If ever an idea held allure for the gift-seeking eye, this one is well-nigh irresistible. It's the kind of item each Christmas shopper will buy *several* of and it's just the thing all the year round for that adorable bridge prize, hostess gift or birthday token. It supplies that search for something really different and clever.

Real Holiday Helps—You can have Vaniteens on the handsome silver-crystal display tree, each vanity in a transparent package (see illustration at left) or, if preferred, we will package them individually in beautiful Christmas holly-and-snowflake boxes, satin lined, as pictured above. Please indicate your choice when ordering. Minimum fair trade retail price of this Vaniteen is $1 subject to regular trade discount.

FREE
beautiful display ↓

...rilliant silvery display tree, mounted in crystal-cut glass base.

A sales-inspiring decoration in your holiday scheme—exceptionally attractive and very, very smart. 20 inches high, displays a dozen Vaniteens and is pilfer-proof.

Princess Pat ad, September 1940.

Instructions for use of Houppette "Pli."

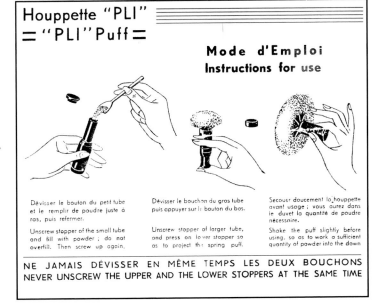

Houppette "PLI" = "PLI" Puff =

Mode d'Emploi
Instructions for use

Dévisser le bouton du petit tube et le remplir de poudre juste à ras, puis refermer.

Unscrew stopper of the small tube and fill with powder ; do not overfill. Then screw up again.

Dévisser le bouchon du gros tube puis appuyer sur le bouton du bas.

Unscrew stopper of larger tube, and press on lower stopper so as to project the spring puff.

Secouer doucement la houppette avant usage ; vous aurez dans le duvet la quantité de poudre nécessaire.

Shake the puff slightly before using, so as to work a sufficient quantity of powder into the down

NE JAMAIS DÉVISSER EN MÊME TEMPS LES DEUX BOUCHONS
NEVER UNSCREW THE UPPER AND THE LOWER STOPPERS AT THE SAME TIME

Hallmarked sterling compact/cane combination; cane handle is compact; interior contains framed mirror and powder compartment; compact lid decorated with black island scene; "Erica" engraved on the collar of the cane; dark brown wood shaft designed to resemble bamboo; metal ferrule protector at end of stick; wrist cord under compact handle; 1¾" dia. x ½". $375.00 – 500.00.

Hallmarked sterling compact/cane combination; cane handle is compact; gilded interior contains framed mirror and powder compartment; textured lid and collar; slightly domed lid centered with round polished cartouche; tan wood shaft designed to resemble bamboo; metal ferrule protector at end of stick; 2" dia. x ⅜". $325.00 – 400.00.

Hallmarked sterling compact/cane combination; cane handle is compact; gilded interior contains framed mirror and powder compartment; blue cloisonné enameled lid; incised flower on collar; black wood shaft; metal ferrule protector at end of stick; 1⅞" dia. x ½". $650.00 – 950.00.

Hallmarked sterling compact/cane combination; cane handle is a compact; gilded interior contains framed mirror and powder compartment; lid decorated with black Siamese scene; mahogany wood shaft; metal ferrule protector at end of stick; 2⅛" dia. x ½". $375.00 – 500.00.

Ivorene lipstick tube holder/cane combination; disc with painted cat's head on lid of handle; handle unscrews to reveal well with removeable sterling lipstick tube; brown wood shaft; metal ferrule protector at end of stick; 1½" dia. x 2¾". $275.00 – 375.00.

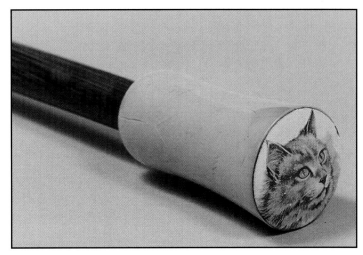

Ivorene cane showing lipstick tube.

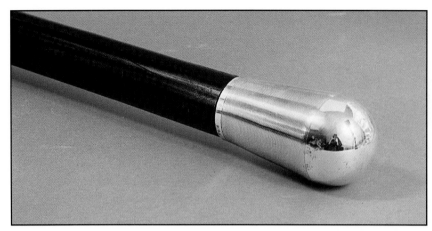

Hallmarked sterling silver pli/cane combination, cane knob unscrews to reveal well with removable hallmarked sterling pli, black wood shaft, ivory ferrule protector at end of stick, 2¼" x 1". $750.00 – 950.00.

Pli/cane above, open.

Lucille Buhl "Vaniti-Bank" square compact/bank combination; textured goldtone lid highlighted with blue enamel acorns; logo "The Broadway National Bank of Paterson" imprinted on dime bank; reverse side reads "A.R. Martine Co. Inc., 2 Wall St., New York;" interior reveals mirror, bank, and powder compartment; 2¼" x 2¼" x ¾". $125.00 – 175.00.

Lucille Buhl/compact/bank, open.

Flamand-Fladium Oar goldtone compact cuff bracelet; medallions on compact lid and side pieces decorated with a griffin; red enameled flowers applied to lattice work on side pieces; beveled mirror and puff; Paris; 2¼" round x 1¾". $250.00 – 350.00.

Silver compact/parasol combination; knob-shaped handle contains compact; elaborate engravings and repoussé work decorate knob compact and collar; gilded interior contains framed mirror, puff, and powder well; braided wrist cord under compact; black silk ruffled parasol (replaced); black wooden shaft; metal ferrule protector at end of parasol; 1½" dia. $450.00 – 550.00.

Round goldtone compact/bank combination; textured lid slightly dome-shaped; opening for coin near top hinge on back lid; bank on back lid opens with key for removal of coins; interior mirror and powder compartment; 1⅞" dia. $125.00 – 175.00.

Round goldtone compact/pendant, lid decorated with colorful hand-painted ballerina, framed by a goldtone twisted rope, opens from the back to reveal metal mirror, powder sifter, powder well, and puff, 1½" dia. $100.00 – 125.00.

Coppertone compact/pendant designed to resemble a mini apple, complete with goldtone leaf and chain, interior reveals mirror and puff, 1⅛" dia. $250.00 – 300.00.

Apple compact/pendant, open.

Oval compact/cameo pendant combination; shell cameo bezel set in sterling Art Nouveau ribbon filigree frame; female profile carved in relief, mounted on lid; interior reveals mirror on one side, fitted metal powder sifter and fitted puff on other side; sterling filigree neck chain; 1½" x 2". $900.00 – 1,200.00.

Round antique goldtone compact/pendant decorated with scroll work, turquoise stones and pearls, interior mirror framed by metal braid, complete with beautiful matching chain, France, 2" dia. $225.00 – 285.00.

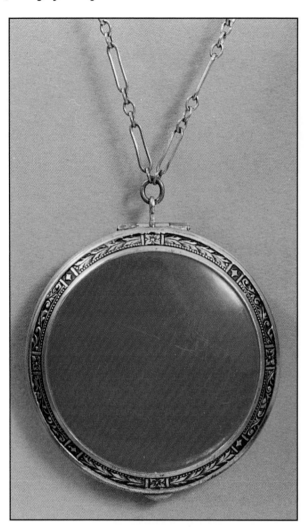

Oblong silvertone compact/pendant, cut-off corners, white enamel lid decorated with black silhouette of a period lady, back opens to reveal metal mirror and powder well, complete with chain, 1¾" x 1½". $95.00 – 125.00.

Round red enamel silvertone compact/pendant complete with chain, interior reveals framed mirror and rotating perforated powder well and puff, 2¼" dia. $45.00 – 55.00.

Left – Le Rage goldtone compact/bracelet designed to resemble wrist watch; hours on the lid of compact set with green and clear stones; moveable hands; bubble link chain; interior reveals mirror and puff; England; 1½" dia., 7" long. $400.00 – 500.00.

Right – Round goldtone compact/bracelet combination; multi-colored stones centered on lid of compact; interior reveals mirror and puff; 1½" dia., 7" long. $300.00 – 400.00.

Black enamel Popaea compact/bracelet, lid decorated with black and goldtone enamel stripes, interior reveals beveled mirror, sifter, and puff, Germany, compact 1¼" x 1". $400.00 – 475.00.

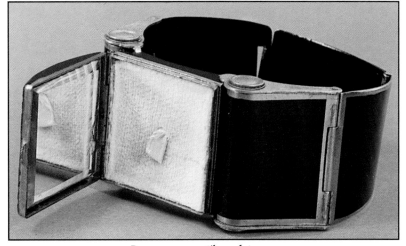

Popaea compact/bracelet, open.

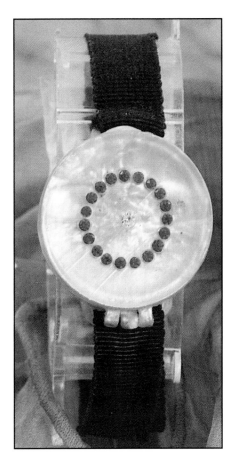

Round white marbleized composition compact/bracelet, lid decorated with circle of red faceted stones, interior reveals mirror and powder well, adjustable grosgrain band, 1" dia. $125.00 – 175.00.

Sene silvertone compact/bracelet, engine-turned lid bordered with green enamel, center cartouche, interior reveals metal mirror which separates the powder/puff well and the rouge and lipstick compartments, grosgrain band, Paris, France, 1¼" x 1". $300.00 – 350.00.

Hammered silvertone compact/bracelet with cartouche in corner, grosgrain band, interior reveals mirror and powder well, 1¼" x ⅞". $200.00 – 250.00.

Silvertone compact/bracelet with rigid engine-turned design wrist band, lid decorated with embossed design, cartouche centered on lid, interior reveals mirror and powder well, compact, 1⅛" x ⅞", $250.00 – 300.00.

Marques de Elorza silvertone/goldtone compact/bracelet, design in relief decorates silvertone lid of goldtone compact, adjustable mesh band, interior reveals metal mirror which separates the powder/puff well and rouge and lipstick compartments, 1½" x 1⅛", Paris, France. $400.00 – 500.00.

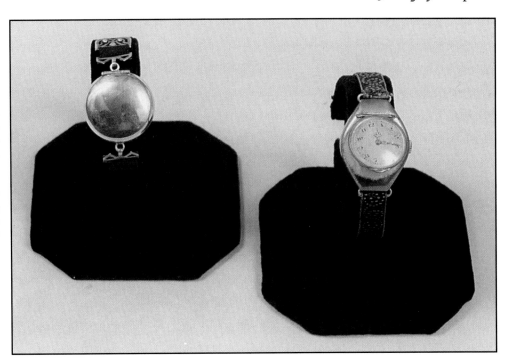

Left – Round polished silvertone compact/bracelet; grosgrain band with silver buckle closure; reverse side of compact reads "Junior Prom, 1923;" interior reveals convex mirror; 1" dia. $100.00 – 125.00.

Right – Goldtone compact/bracelet designed to resemble wrist watch; watch face under glass crystal on lid; faux winder; interior reveals convex mirror; black and gold grosgrain band; 1" x 1¼". $225.00 – 350.00.

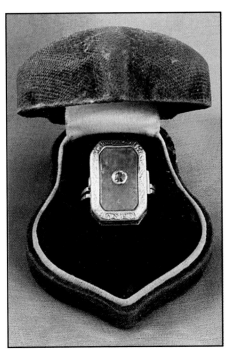

Oblong convertible vanity ring with rounded corners, lid centered with a crystal, gift with purchase of a two-year subscription ($1.00.) to Woman's World *magazine, 1925, double shank opens for use as a bracelet or pendant, ¾" x ½", $225.00 – 275.00. Shown closed in original presentation box.*

Convertible vanity ring pendant on silk cord.

Convertible vanity ring as bracelet with grosgrain wrist band.

Left – K & K polished satin-finish compact/bracelet combination; hinged bracelet; shown open; 2" x 1½". $200.00 – 250.00.

Right – K & K polished satin finish compact/bracelet combination; lid of compact set with red and clear crystal stones; 2" x 1½". $250.00 – 300.00.

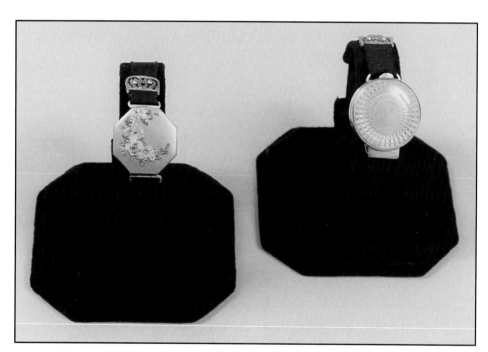

Left – Octagon-shaped enamel compact/bracelet combination; pearlized pink enamel lid decorated with raised flowers; interior reveals mirror and puff; grosgrain band with silver catches; 1" x 1". $275.00 – 325.00.

Right – Round sterling silver compact/bracelet combination; pink cloisonné enamel lid; interior reveals mirror; grosgrain band with silver catches; 1" dia. $300.00 – 350.00.

Flamand-Fladium goldtone compact/bracelet combination; compact lid decorated with goldtone stars on onyx disc; cut-outs of stars surround cuff bracelet; signed by Claudine Cereola; France; 1½" dia. $275.00 – 375.00.

Antique goldtone compact/bracelet, highly embossed lid decorated with turquoise, coral stones, and yellow enamel, interior reveals mirror and sifter, adjustable grosgrain band, 2" x 1". $150.00 – 200.00.

Round red enamel compact/bracelet cuff, "A Century of Progress 1934" silvertone disc centered on lid, silvertone bracelet, interior reveals metal mirror, puff, and swivel powder well, 1¾" dia. $175.00 – 200.00.

Unmarked round goldtone compact bracelet with stretch band, monogrammed lid framed by crystals, compact ⅞". $225.00 – 275.00.

K & K goldtone compact/bracelet cuff, lid beautifully decorated with goldtone Asian man pulling a goldtone rickshaw, 1⅞" x 1¼". $275.00 – 375.00.

Beautiful goldtone cut-out cuff bracelet compact, lid decorated with colorful enamel coat-of-arms, interior reveals beveled mirror, puff, and sifter, 2¾" dia. x 1¾", France, $350.00 – 450.00.

Vanitie round goldtone compact bracelet, orange cabochon stone centered on repoussé lid, 1¼" dia. $275.00 – 325.00.

Forerunner to the "Fanny-Pak," brown lizard skin Rex vanity case with brown lizard skin belt looped through back of vanity-case, opens to reveal mini goldtone compact, comb, and lipstick, 3¼" x 2¼", $75.00 – 100.00.

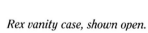

Rex vanity case, shown open.

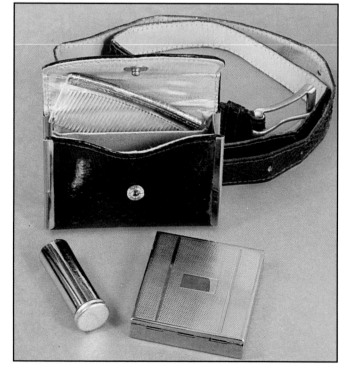

Left – F.J. Co. antique goldtone compact/bracelet combination; lid set with black onyx; marcasite flowers centered on onyx; flowers on hinged band; 1⅞" dia. $300.00 – 400.00.

Right – F.J. Co. antique goldtone compact/bracelet combination; compact lid decorated with filigree; flowers on hinged band; 1⅞" dia. $350.00 – 450.00.

Silvertone compact/bracelet combination; bracelet designed to resemble belt and buckle; applied goldtone insignia; bracelet opens to reveal powder well, metal mirror, puff, and powder well cover; 2¼" dia. $275.00 – 375.00.

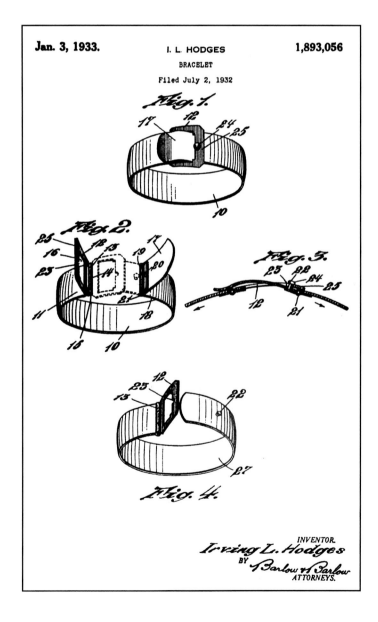

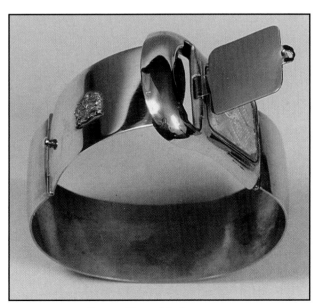

Compact/bracelet above, open.

Zama polished goldtone compact/bracelet combination; one side of hinged cuff bracelet opens to reveal mirror, powder and rouge compartments, and compartment with lipstick tube; other side of hinged cuff bracelet opens to reveal comb; France; 1½" x 2¾" dia. $450.00 – 550.00.

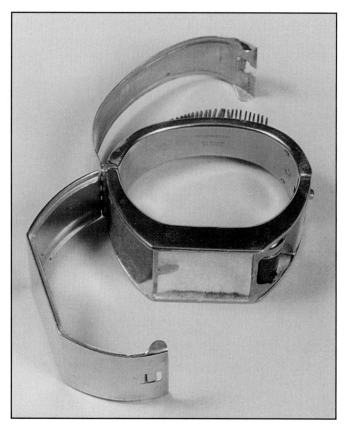

Zama compact/bracelet, open.

Flamand gold and silvertone compact/bracelet combination; lipstick separates the two Bakelite discs on the cuff bracelet; one side has compact centered on disc, other side has mirror centered on disc; goldtone bands decorate discs; rumor has it that this was one of the compact bracelets that Josephine Baker commissioned to be made for her to give as gifts to her friends; 1¾" x 2¼" dia. $450.00 – 550.00.

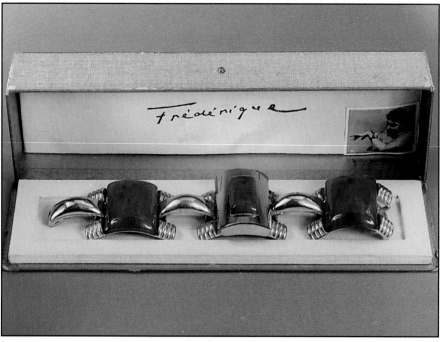

Frederique rare, coveted goldtone link compact/bracelet combination, tortoise colored Bakelite centered on compact lid and on two links on either side of compact, interior reveals beveled mirror, sifter, and puff, comes complete with original presentation box with photograph of Josephine Baker looking at a compact/bracelet that she is wearing, compact, 1⅝" x 1⅛", Paris, France. $550.00 – 750.00.

Week-End goldtone compact/cuff bracelet combination, center compact lid decorated with tortoise-colored Bakelite, lipstick tubes on either side of compact, tortoise Bakelite flanks lipsticks, Paris, France, 2¾" x 2¼" including lipsticks and Bakelite. $450.00 – 550.00.

Princess Eve goldtone cosmetic bracelet combination; four cosmetic tubes suspended from link chain; tubes contain eye make-up, lipstick, wick (possibly for scent), collapsible plastic cigarette holder; bracelet 7"; tubes 1¼". $60.00 – 90.00.

Round yellow celluloid fob vanity/compact, black enamel lid, "F.C. – '36" inscribed on lower lid, interior reveals metal mirror separating powder and rouge compartments, mirror on reverse side, complete with leather fob, 2½" dia. $125.00 – 150.00.

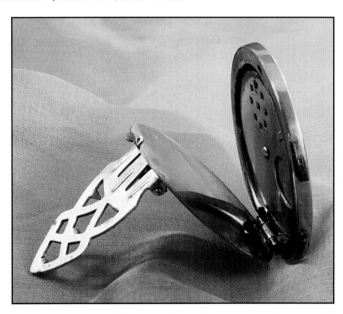

Round black enamel silvertone dress clip/compact combination, lid centered with white profile silhouette of a woman's face (see below), interior reveals metal mirror and perforated rotating powder well, 1⅝" dia. $100.00 – 150.00.

Dress clip/compact, closed.

Three Marlowe Co. "Parisienne" plastic compact/bracelet combinations; decorative metal band slides to reveal two mirrors and five cosmetic compartments; green and butterscotch shown closed; burgundy shown open; also available in other colors; ¾" deep. $225.00 – 325.00 each.

Antique silvertone dresser powder box; exterior heavily embossed; interior reveals mirror; Greece; 5" x 5". $75.00 – 125.00.

Town & Country, *September 1942.*

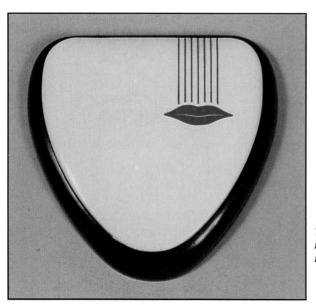

Tangee dresser/vanity; white-enameled top lid decorated with stylized red lips; blue bottom lid; interior reveals wells for lipstick, powder, and rouge cases; Patent #D-128-188; 5" x 5". $75.00 – 125.00.

W.B. Manufacturing Co. stylized silvertone triangular dresser vanity; lid decorated with elephant; interior reveals fitted wells for powder, rouge, and lipstick cases; Pat. 7-22-30; 4½" x 3½" x 3½". $125.00 – 175.00.

Dresser Vanity ad, 1931.

177

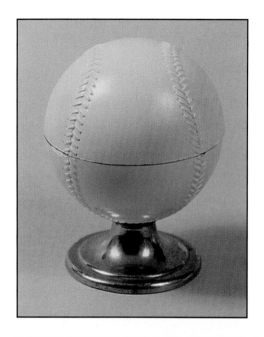

White metal baseball dresser vanity; raised stitches on seams; set on gold-tone pedestal; goldtone interior reveals beveled mirror, puff, and powder well; Germany; 2½" dia. $150.00 – 250.00.

"Victory Vanity" amber glass Army hat dresser vanity; exterior beveled mirror; raised army insignia on crown; interior reveals powder compartment; 4¾" dia. x 2". $50.00 – 125.00.

Evans gray suede fitted presentation boxed set; lipstick tube, cigarette case, compact, and cigarette lighter; white enamel decorated with hand-painted roses; 9½ " x 4" x 1½". $125.00 – 175.00.

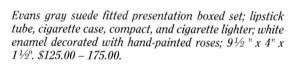

Avon black faille fitted presentation boxed set; matching goldtone lipstick tube, perfume bottle, compact and rouge case; interior white satin; enclosed card reads "In addition to the pleasure and satisfaction the lovely contents of this Avon Set will give you, the box itself can be used as a jewel case for your Dressing Table. Just remove the puffed satin platform and you will have a lovely, smooth satin lined case for this purpose." Compact 2¾" x 2¾"; box 8" x 4" x 1¾". $100.00 – 125.00.

Left – Kreisler brown suede fitted presentation boxed set; brushed goldtone with silvertone flap envelope style vanity; matching cigarette lighter; compact interior contains mirror and powder and rouge compartments; Patent #1987533; compact 3" x 2", box 6" x 4¼" x ¾". $100.00 – 125.00.

Center – Evans tan suede fitted presentation boxed set; matching goldtone compact and cigarette lighter; compact and lighter decorated with scenic transfer; compact tap-sift model; compact 2" dia., box 5" x 3" x 1½". $60.00 – 100.00.

Right – Lentheric holiday wrapped presentation boxed set; black and goldtone matching vanity and lipstick; interior reveals metal mirror that separates powder and rouge compartments; Patent #1987533, Des Patent #96680; compact 2¾" x 2¼"; box 4¼" x 4". $50.00 – 75.00.

Left – Green leather envelope-style presentation case; interior includes matching green and black compact, lipstick tube, and comb all in designated fitted slots; compact 2½" dia., case 5" x 3". $125.00 – 150.00.

Right – B.B. & Co. red leather envelope-style presentation case; interior contains matching sterling silver compact, lipstick tube, perfume flacon, and comb; all pieces are green cloisonné decorated with hand-painted pink flowers; compact 2" x 2", case 5½" x 3". $275.00 – 300.00.

Left – La Mode red velvet fitted presentation boxed set; contains matching mother-of-pearl vanity and locket with chain; interior of compact reveals metal mirror that separates powder and rouge compartments; compact 2¼" dia., box 4¾" x 3¾" x 1". $100.00 – 125.00.

Right – La Mode matching compact and locket set; green enamel compact and matching locket decorated with hearts; interior of compact reveals metal mirror that separates powder and rouge compartments; 2¼" x 2¼". $250.00 – 350.00.

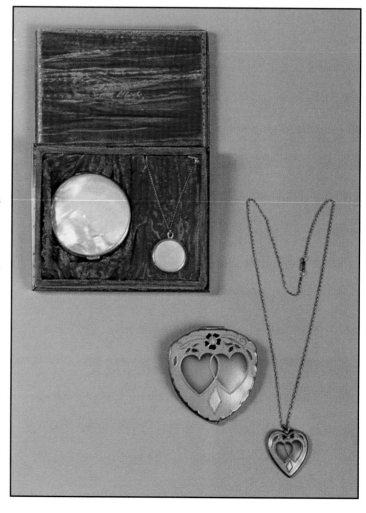

Left – La Mode fitted red suede presentation boxed set; goldtone heart-shaped compact with matching heart-shaped expansion bracelet; heart-shaped cartouche on pink and yellow goldtone decorates lid of compact and bracelet; compact 2½" x 2¼", box 7" x 3¾" x 1½". $175.00 – 250.00.

Right – Henriette maroon velvet fitted presentation boxed set; brushed and satin goldtone decorated compact with Air Force insignia centered on lid and on matching bracelet; braided goldtone mesh bracelet band with tassel; gift boxed by Hilborn-Hamburger, Inc, Military Jewelers, N.Y.; compact 2½" x 2½", box 7" x 4" x 1". $175.00 – 225.00.

Coral, green, and white Bakelite compact, rouge pot, perfume container, and sewing container in original fitted presentation box; rouge pot ⅞"; compact has mirror and puff, 1½" dia.; perfume bottle in Bakelite tube, 2¼"; sewing tube contains needles, thread, and pins, top is a thimble, 2¼"; all have green and white engraved decorations enhanced with rhinestones. $175.00 – 225.00.

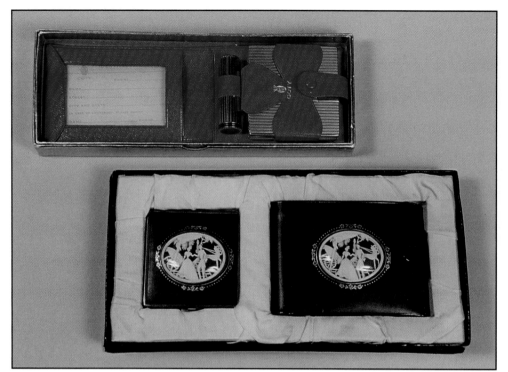

Top – Coty red leather billfold; interior of billfold contains sleeves with matching Coty compact and lipstick tube; 2¾" x 2¾". $80.00 – 100.00.

Bottom – Daniel black leather compact with matching billfold; centered on compact lid and billfold is an ivorene three-dimensional cut-out scene of a man and woman encased under a plastic dome; 2¾" x 2¾". $150.00 – 175.00.

Sterling round blue enamel compact/perfume combination; lid of compact decorated with goldtone decoration; top cap unscrews to reveal perfume well; Austria; 2½" dia. $450.00 – 500.00.

Turquoise enamel and goldtone clover-shaped purse-motif compact; interior reveals framed beveled mirror and powder compartment; matching brooch and clip-on earrings; Italy; 2¾" x 2½". $250.00 – 300.00.

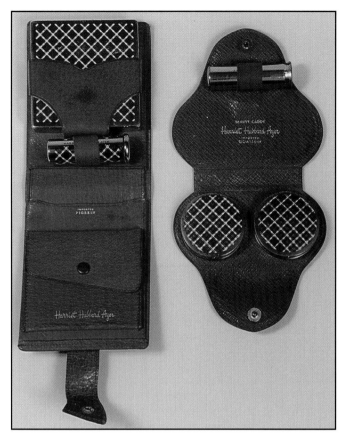

Left – Harriet Hubbard Ayer green pigskin compact/billfold combination; opened billfold has sleeves for H.H.A. compact and matching lipstick tube; closed 4" x 3", open 8½" long. $100.00 – 125.00.

Right – Harriet Hubbard Ayer clover-shaped red goatskin "Beauty Caddy;" opened caddy reveals sleeve for lipstick holder and permanent powder and rouge cases; 3¾" x 3¾", open 7½" long. $125.00 – 150.00.

Harriet Hubbard Ayer ad, 1951.

AND ONE TO CARRY =

MERRY CHRISTMAS

■ Good-looking carry-alls that also contain what-keeps-her-beautiful

... what more flattering way could you gift a lady?

Harriet Hubbard Ayer designs in leather and satin,

at better department stores.

BEAUTY WALLET—uncommon-carrier... holds compact, lipstick and her money. Navy leather and colors, 12.00

BEAUTY CADDY – new palm-size leather kit holds pressed powder, dry rouge, lipstick. Natural and colors, 5.00

SATIN COSMETIC CASE – shining evening companion, contains compact and lipstick. Aqua, green or rose, 6.25

LEATHER FEEDBAG—over-shoulder or in-hand, an eye-catcher! Fitted with compact and lipstick. Red and colors, 18.50

HARRIET HUBBARD AYER
505 PARK AVENUE, NEW YORK 22

all prices plus tax

HAL PHYFE

gala holiday Ayer 1951

183

Ferrieres green snakeskin oval-shaped bolster, dual openings, top opening reveals beveled mirror and puff, second opening reveals deep compartment which contains a matching green snakeskin envelope-style currency holder, green snakeskin adjustable handle, lipstick concealed in fancy green silk tassel, ca. 1924, 3½" long 2" x 1½". $550.00 – 650.00.

Ferrieres bolster, closed.

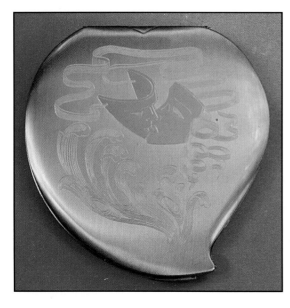

Elgin American brushed goldtone stylized heart compact, lid decorated with polished goldtone Comedy and Tragedy masks, 2½" x 2¾". $35.00 – 55.00.

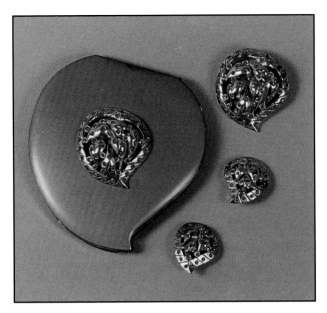

Elgin American polished goldtone compact, earrings, and pin set; stylized heart shape; center of compact set with applied heart enhanced with red stones; matching earrings and pin; 3¼" x 3¼". $150.00 – 225.00.

Vanity-Kid silvertone engine-turned vanity, front lid opens to reveal compact; lipstick tube on right side of compact; perfume tube on left side of compact; France; 2¼" x 2¼". $150.00 – 175.00.

Elgin American Catalog, 1949.

6062/037—Set consists of compact, brooch and matching earrings. Compact has an applied heart-shaped ornament set with imitation rubies on a gold Roman finish. Brooch matches compact ornament. Set is supplied with a heart-shaped red velvet covered, satin lined display and gift box. Subject to federal excise tax.

600/001—Set consists of heart-shaped brooch set with imitation rubies, matching earrings. Gift box 42. Subject to federal excise tax.

Gift Box No. 40. Special book style box, covered with red velvet and trimmed with white satin. Sold individually to dealer for $1.00.

Blue enamel compact centered on multi-sided cut crystal perfume bottle; etched flowers on perfume bottle surround compact; blue enamel perfume cap; 2½" dia. Shown closed and open. $500.00 – 600.00.

Black enamel oval compact/perfume combination; compact suspended by two ornate filigree chains from a finger ring; lid centered with oval floral silver cut-out disc; silver perfume screw-top; gilt interior with powder compartment; mirror framed in gilt braid; Austria; 1½" x 2½". $400.00 – 450.00.

Square silvertone compact/perfume combination; lid decorated with painted scene on enamel; shown with perfume wand extended; wrist carrying chain; 2¾" x 2¾". $250.00 – 300.00.

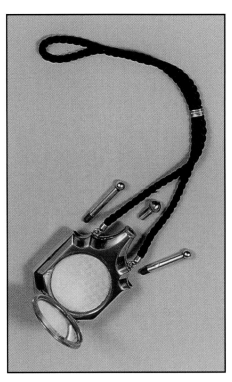

Dual opening brass vanity; powder compartment and mirror on one side; rouge compartment and mirror on other side; two pull-out lip rouge sticks; top center unscrews to reveal perfume compartment; silk braid carrying cord; 2" x 2¾". Shown closed and open. $300.00 – 400.00.

R. & G. Co. gold and silvertone compact/perfume combination; screw-top perfume closure on top complete with perfume wand; engine-turned lid decorated with blue flag with the letter M; front lid opens to reveal powder well and mirror; 1¾" x 2". $100.00 – 150.00.

Light blue oval hallmarked sterling cloisonné enamel compact/perfume combination; gilded interior reveals mirror and powder well; perfume knob unscrews to reveal perfume compartment; carrying chain; 1½" x 2½". $350.00 – 450.00.

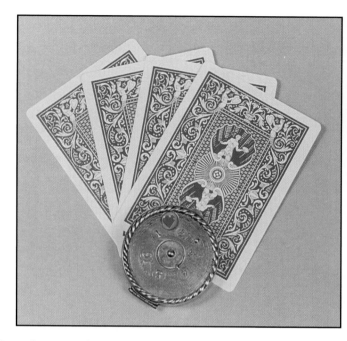

H.W.K. Co. round silvertone compact/bridge indicator combination; enameled blue and white front lid; reverse side reveals center dial indicating raised numbers 1, 2, 3, 4, 5, or 6; spinning selector displays heart, diamond, spade, club, or NT; suits in black or red enamel; interior reveals mirror and powder well; 1¾" dia. $325.00 – 425.00.

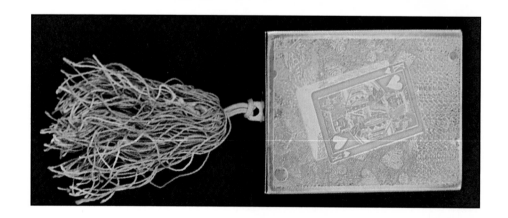

Oblong brass compact, lid decorated with engraved King of Hearts, when drawer tassel is pulled, beveled mirror pops up, revealing powder well and metal sifter, Japan, 1⅝" x 2⅞". Shown closed at left, open below. $125.00 – 155.00.

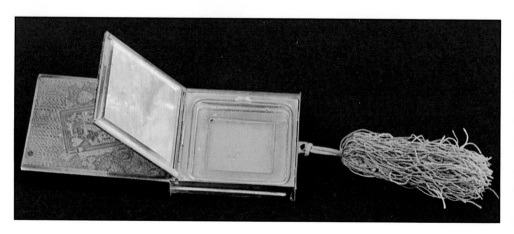

Round Wadsworth goldtone compact, lid decorated with enamel hearts, spades, diamonds, and clubs, 2¾" dia. $45.00 – 55.00.

Oblong black enamel vanity/compact, lid decorated with colorful round cards, slide-open lid reveals mirror, powder, and rouge compartments, 2" x 2½", $55.00 – 65.00.

Black enamel compact above, partially open.

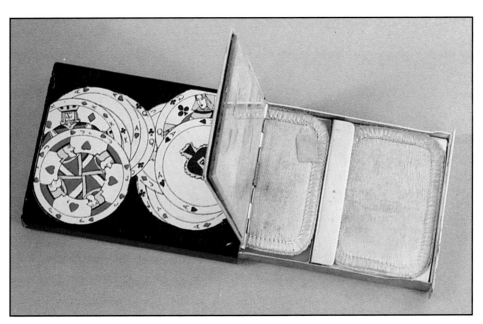

Same compact, fully open.

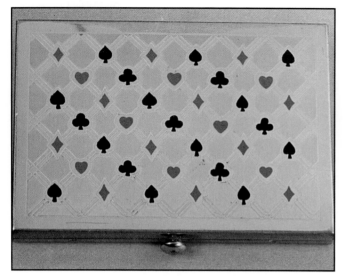

Wadsworth Parker Pen oblong goldtone compact, lid decorated with red and black card suits, interior reveals powder well and mirror, 2" x 3", $55.00 – 65.00.

Square goldtone compact, stippled lid decorated with four mini enameled cards, interior reveals beveled framed mirror, puff, and powder well, 2¼" sq. $55.00 – 65.00.

Elgin American square brushed and polished goldtone compact, brushed goldtone lid decorated with polished goldtone dice, unique feature, above the thumbpiece is a pair of dice in a cage, pull cage down to gain access to the dice, 2¾" sq. $145.00 – 175.00.

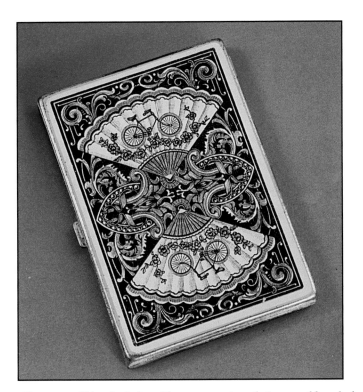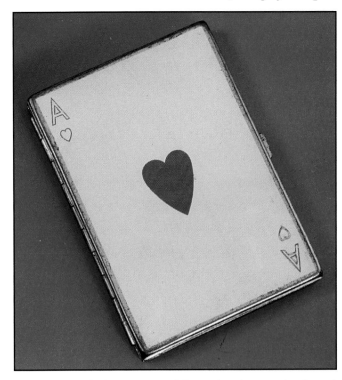

Blue enamel bicycle design oblong compact made to resemble a deck of cards, reverse side shows an Ace of Hearts, interior contains framed mirror, puff, and powder well, 2" x 3". $150.00 – 175.00.

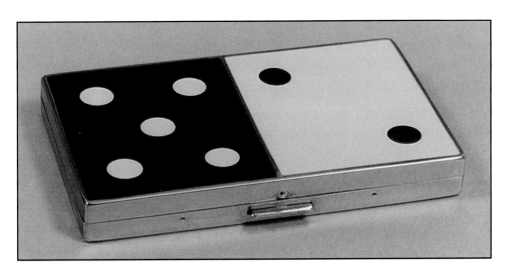

Coty "Come Eleven" goldtone vanity divided into two sections, one white enamel, one black enamel, designed to resemble a pair of dice, interior reveals mirror, powder and rouge compartments, and puffs, sometimes referred to as the domino compact, 3¾" x 2¾". $150.00 – 250.00.

191

Left – Illinois Watch Case Co. brushed goldtone vanity watch combination; interior reveals powder and rouge compartments; 2¾" x 2¾". $100.00 – 125.00.

Right – Evans compact-watch-music box combination; watch centered on embossed sunburst design lid; interior reveals powder well and music box; 3" x 2 ". $175.00 – 250.00.

Bottom – Evans compact watch combination; beautiful white cloisonné enhanced with hand-painted roses decorate lid; interior metal swinging mirror conceals watch; 2½" x 2½₂". $150.00 – 200.00.

Sterling red enamel side-by-side compact/watch combination; one side opens to reveal powder compartment, puff, and mirror (left photo); other side reveals watch (right photo); pull-out lipstick; Germany; 1" x 3 ". $550.00 – 650.00.

Musical vanity compacts at left shown open.

Two musical vanity compacts. Top: oblong goldtone vanity/compact lid decorated with Asian lady, interior reveals music box, metal powder container, metal rouge and lipstick containers, and perfume bottle, 2¾" x 5½", $45.00 – 55.00. Bottom: Silvia red plastic Dandy-Mate powder vanity/compact, yellow plastic interior reveals powder well, puff, and place on the opposite interior lid for cigarettes, 4" x 2½". $25.00 – 35.00.

Plastic Art Deco compact/flashlight combination; interior contains metal mirror which conceals battery; flashlight above mirror; powder compartment; black and white shown open; purple shown closed; 1⅜" x 3¼". $80.00 – 150.00 each.

HOW TO FILL APPLICATORS

Unscrew the cap from the PERFUME Applicator, pour in the perfume, replace the cap. NEXT, remove the cap from the POWDER applicator and fill with powder, immediately replacing the cap. Use the LOTION applicator the same way, remove cap, fill, re-cap. This procedure will insure each applicator being filled with the proper cosmetic.

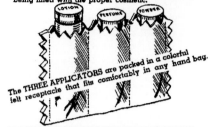

The THREE APPLICATORS are packed in a colorful felt receptacle that fits comfortably in any hand bag.

CAUTION. Fill and recap each applicator, one at a time as suggested, and you'll not mix them. Each is made for a specific cosmetic and can not be interchanged without dissatisfaction.

THE LADY ACME APPLICATOR
For Cosmetics

LADY ACME APPLICATORS are Made in California, where the cosmetic business is acknowledged one of world-wide dominance and where every care is exercised to insure the maintenance of a high standard in everything relating to cosmetics.

Made of lightweight metal and will last indefinitely,

ACME PRODUCTS, Manufacturers, 7725 Santa Fe Ave.Los Angeles, Calif.

Lady ACME Applicator for Cosmetics.

The THREE LADY ACME Applicators

Illustrated below are the THREE cosmetic applicators. one each for PERFUME, POWDER and LOTION. They are not interchangeable, and emphasis must be placed on this statement. Each of the applicators is carefully machined to accomodate the three different items, and to attempt to use them except for the specific cosmetic as indicated on top of the screw cap is to cause dissatisfaction. Fill them one at a time, don't get the caps mixed and you'll be delighted for years to come with the LADY ACME APPLICATORS.

No. 1. The LADY ACME Applicator. To use it, place the forefinger on the plunger. press down, and the proper amount of perfume will emerge on your finger, after which the odor may be transferred to the back of the ear, to the garment, to your kerchief. This manner of applying conserves the perfume supply.

No. 2. The LADY ACME POWDER Applicator. To properly apply the powder, it is recommended that the applicator be used as shown above. It is depressed so as to release the powder, on the puff, on the hand or wherever desired. Powder will appear as little rings around the plunger and on the pad. After which distribution is easily made.

No. 3. The LADY ACME LOTION Applicator. Like all applicators, it is leakproof. To get the best results, apply as shown in the picture above, either to the back of the hand or in the palm, and then the proper distribution may be made, just as you distribute it when applying lotion direct from the bottle.

Lower left – Green enamel goldtone compact with interior light; wedge-shaped; 2¾" x 3¼". Shown closed. $80.00 – 100.00.

Upper left – Black enamel compact like above, shown open.

Upper right – Venus-Ray goldtone compact with interior light; engraved compact lid; one side of compact contains lipstick tube; small perfume container and opening for battery on other side; 3½" x 2¾". $125.00 – 175.00.

Lower right – Venus-Ray compact closed.

Bottom – White enamel compact/flashlight combination; lid decorated with a firefly; exterior flashlight activated when button is pushed on outer lid; 3½" x 3". $125.00 – 150.00.

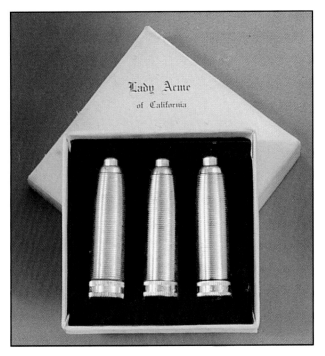

Three bullet-shaped white metal Lady Acme Applicators for Cosmetics, one for powder, one for lotion, and one for perfume, complete with red flannel protective/carrying case, each 2¼" x ½" dia. $75.00 – 125.00.

Two Darnee "Colleen Moore" silvertone vanity cases, one open, one closed, lids centered with painting of a castle framed by an engraved silvertone border, interior contains mirror, metal mirror divides compartments for rouge and rouge puff from the powder compartment. 1¾" x 2". $45.00 – 55.00 each.

Vanity/binoculars with powder pli and lipstick tube removed.

Black plastic faux vanity/binoculars complete with fitted black silk case; lipstick tube and powder pli slide out from top eye pieces; mirrors on bottom lens; case lined, with interior mirror on lid; 3" x 2½". $450.00 – 550.00.

Colmont "Pomponnette" opera glasses/compact; goldtone opera glasses covered in green leather, white pearlized lens dial rims; compact set in center; white pearlized lid which opens to reveal beveled mirror and powder (above right); puff attached to powder well lid; Paris; 3½" x 2" x 1". $800.00 – 1,000.00.

Vogue, *1950.*

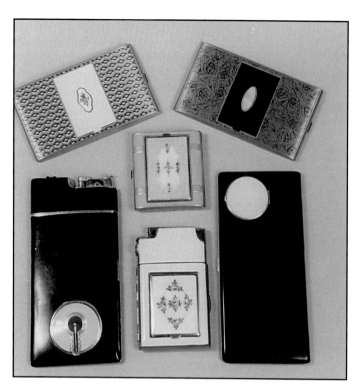

Lower left – Evans compact/cigarette case/lighter combination; black enamel case has white enamel compact enhanced with Art Deco motif on lid; Patent #1624874 and 1869983; 3¼" x 6¾". $175.00 – 200.00.

Upper left – Brushed goldtone vanity cigarette case combination; lid decorated with black enamel design; white enamel vanity decorated with white flower cloisonné disk on lid; interior vanity reveals powder and rouge compartments; Licensed Patent #1869983; 3" x 5". $150.00 – 175.00.

Upper right – Brushed goldtone vanity cigarette case combination; lid decorated with black enamel design; black enamel vanity decorated with mother-of-pearl disc on lid; interior vanity reveals powder and rouge compartments; Licensed Patent #1869993; 3" x 5". $150.00 – 175.00.

Lower right – La Mode black enamel vanity cigarette case combination; white enamel vanity on lid; interior vanity reveals metal mirror with powder and rouge compartments; 3" x 7". $150.00 – 175.00.

Lower center – Marathon white enamel goldtone combination compact/lighter/cigarette case; white enamel lid of compact decorated with enamel flowers; Patent #2053455 and 2071601; 2½" x 4¼". $150.00 – 175.00.

Center – La Mode green enamel vanity cigarette combination; green enamel lid of vanity decorated with flowers; vanity reveals powder and rouge compartments; 2½" x 2¾". $50.00 – 75.00.

Left – Black enamel vanity cigarette case combination; white enamel disc with pink flowers centered on vanity lid; Army Air Force insignia applied to center of cigarette case; Licensed Patent #1869983; 3" x 4". $100.00 – 125.00.

Top – Lampl goldtone compact/cigarette case/watch combination; compact in center flanked by compartment for cigarettes; watch set on front lid; Patent #2085502; 5½" x 3". $175.00 – 250.00.

Right – Richard Hudnut goldtone vanity/cigarette case combination; white enamel lids decorated with purple enamel orchids; vanity interior reveals compartments for powder, rouge, and lipstick tube; 3" x 4½". $150.00 – 175.00.

Bottom – Brushed goldtone side-by-side bolster compact/cigarette combination; 5" x 1¾". $60.00 – 80.00.

Center – Girey red enamel vanity cigarette combination case; black enamel vanity lid; interior contains rouge and powder compartments; 3¼" x 3½". "$100.00 – 125.00.

Gorgeous, unusual round goldtone sliding compact and beveled mirror, each suspended from beautifully engraved golden arm set with cabochon turquoise stones, swinging compact lid enhanced with applied filigree design centered with turquoise cabochon stone, top center has loop, mirror swings behind compact when not in use, compact 1¾", mirror 1½", France. $600.00 – 700.00.

Beautiful goldtone "Horn of Plenty" shaped compact, decorated with leaves in high relief, interior reveals beveled mirror, sifter, and puff, 2" x 4½". $400.00 – 450.00.

Left – Alfred Dunhill sterling engine-turned vanity designed to resemble cigarette lighter; front opens to reveal beveled mirror, powder, and rouge compartments; top lifts to reveal sliding lipstick; Patent No. 1639628; 1⅞" x 1⅞". $225.00 – 300.00.

Right – Alfred Dunhill goldtone vanity designed to resemble cigarette lighter; front lifts up and reveals beveled mirror, powder, and rouge compartments; sliding lipstick on one side of vanity; phial for perfume on other side of vanity; pencil on top behind vanity; Reg. No. 737179; 2¼" x 2¼". Similar item (enameled) sold at auction, Phillips, London, March 8, 1990, for $510.00. $650.00 – 750.00.

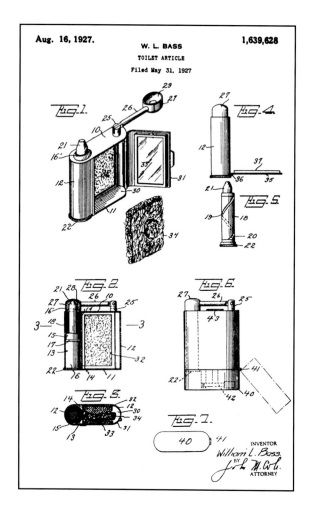

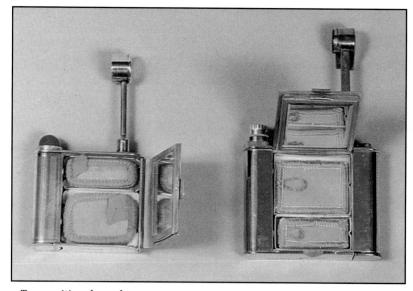

Two vanities above shown open.

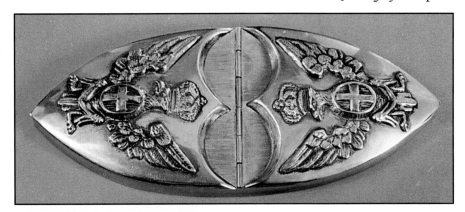

Unusual brass dual opening compact, lid decorated with coats-of-arms in high relief, one side opens to reveal framed mirror, powder well, and hinged metal powder sifter, opposite side opens to reveal framed mirror and two compartments with lids, 2¼" x 8¾". $250.00 – 350.00.

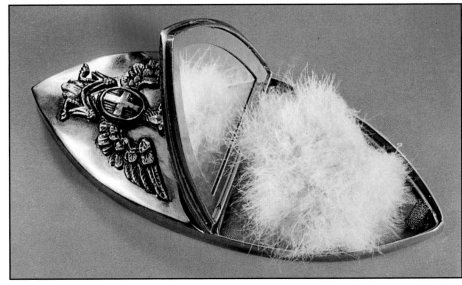

Powder well open.

Compartment side open.

Unusual brushed goldtone unmarked mini bolster-shaped compact set on two moving wheels, rhinestones centered on wheels, complete with steering post, interior reveals beveled mirror, sifter, and puff, 2" x 1¼" x 1¼". NPA.

La Brise tortoise shell compact/fan combination; exterior mirror on compact lid; lid opens to reveal powder compartment and puff; reverse side has three blades; pressure of thumb on metal plunger activates blades which creates a breeze; England; Patent: #21777-13; blade span 5¼", compact 1¾" dia. $175.00 – 275.00.

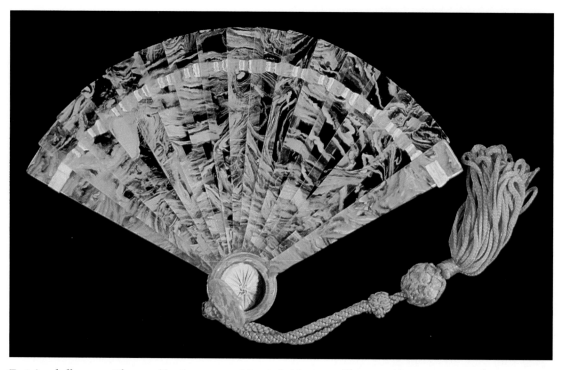

Tortoise shell compact/fan combination; compact located at bottom of fan; one side opens to reveal compartment for powder and puff; reverse side of compact has exterior mirror; matching silk braided carrying cord; span of fan when opened 6½" x 6¼". $400.00 – 600.00.

Lower left – White enamel compact shaped like hand mirror; hand-painted flowers on lid; 2" x 5". $100.00 – 125.00.

Center left – Volupté goldtone "Demitasee" compact formed as hand mirror; black enamel lid decorated with goldtone dots; lipstick in handle; 2" x 4½". $75.00 – 125.00.

Upper left – Petit point goldtone compact shaped as hand mirror; filigree handle; Austria; 2¾" dia. x 4". $60.00 – 80.00.

Top – Art Deco style miniature compact shaped as hand mirror; lid decorated with rhinestones and purple and lavender colored stones; interior mirror and exterior mirror on back lid; 2" x 3½". $75.00 – 100.00.

Upper right – Round black enamel compact shaped as hand mirror; lid decorated with floral disc; interior and exterior mirrors; 1½" dia. x 3½". $60.00 – 80.00.

Center right – Miref "Mirador" gilt compact formed as hand mirror; lipstick in handle; interior and exterior beveled mirrors on both outer lids; 2" dia. x 4¼". $125.00 – 150.00.

Lower right – Black and goldtone compact shaped as hand mirror; lid decorated in black and gold swirls; lipstick in handle; interior and exterior beveled mirrors; 2½" x 5¼". $150.00 – 175.00.

Lower left – Silver mini compact shaped as hand mirror; brushed silver lid decorated with scattered engraved flowers; lipstick in handle; Italy; 1¼" x 3¾". $125.00 – 175.00.

Upper left – Sterling compact formed as hand mirror; exterior beveled mirror; interior ivory writing slate; 1½" x 2" x 4½". $350.00 – 450.00.

Top – Silver compact shaped as hand mirror; exterior of lid engraved; lipstick in handle; interior and exterior mirrors; scalloped frame around exterior mirror; 2" x 5". $200.00 – 250.00.

Upper right – D.R.G.M. silvertone vanity shaped as hand mirror; compartments on both sides, one for powder, one for rouge; both lids engraved; interior mirrors; top cap opens for perfume; German; 1½" x 3½". $150.00 – 175.00.

Lower right – Silver mini compact shaped as hand mirror; heavily engraved; lipstick in handle; blue cabochon thumbpiece; Italy; 1½" x 3¾". $150.00 – 200.00.

Bottom – International Sterling octagonal vanity with handle; cartouche on lid; interior reveals rouge and powder compartments; 2" x 3". $80.00 – 100.00.

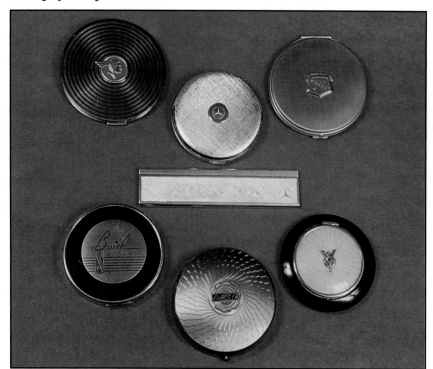

Lower left – Round silvertone and maroon compact with "Buick Eight" logo applied to lid; 3" dia. $70.00 – 85.00.

Upper left – Round goldtone compact with "Pontiac" logo applied to lid; 3¼" dia. $50.00 – 65.00.

Upper right – Round brushed goldtone compact with "Buick" logo applied to lid; 3" dia. $50.00 – 65.00.

Lower right – Round black plastic compact with "Ford" logo centered on pearlized plastic; framed by silvertone rim; 3" dia. $70.00 – 85.00.

Lower center – Round goldtone compact with "Chrysler" logo applied to lid; 3" dia. $50.00 – 65.00.

Center – Brushed silver compact and matching comb/case with "Mercedes Benz" logo; Germany; 2¾" dia. $75.00 – 150.00.

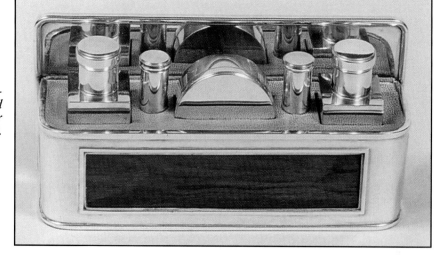

Chrome and leather car vanity/bar accessory; bar contains chrome compact, two chrome lipstick tubes, and two chrome metal containers; vanity bar affixed either to dashboard or side panel of luxury car; 6½" x 3¼". $250.00 – 350.00.

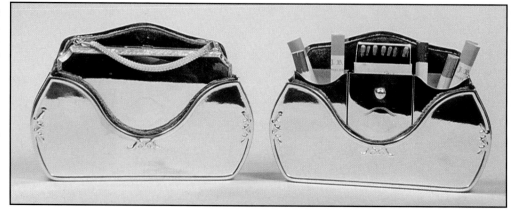

Elgin Vanity silvertone car/vanity and Elgin Smoker cigarette/match stick caddy vanity contains removeable Elgin American vanity case; interior reveals covered powder and rouge cases, covered cold cream case, two lipstick tubes, and mirror; mesh carrying chain; smoker contains removeable match stick holder flanked by two removeable cigarette holders on either side; vanity and smoker affixed to side panels of luxury car; 5½" x 3¾". $350.00 – 500.00.

New Ensemble Sets

Now, Ternstedt provides sets of vanity and smoking cases, *especially designed for each particular car.* Look for these Ensemble Sets on the finer cars—and note how exactly they harmonize with the interior. ¶ Not only is the "theme" design wrought into the metal but the exterior panelling of the cases is in perfect harmony with the car's interior color scheme and appointments. ¶ Ternstedt designers and silversmiths are keenly aware of the public's ever growing appreciation of quality and beauty, in automobile fittings. The new Ensemble Sets are certain to further increase that appreciation, for they surpass even the rich and beautiful craftsmanship which has won for Ternstedt recognition as the leader in its field. ¶ The significance of "Fittings by Ternstedt" in a motor car—the fact that they actually are indicative of a higher degree of quality—is at once made evident to anyone who contrasts the Ternstedt-equipped car in any given price field with any other car in that field which lacks the advantage of Ternstedt equipment.

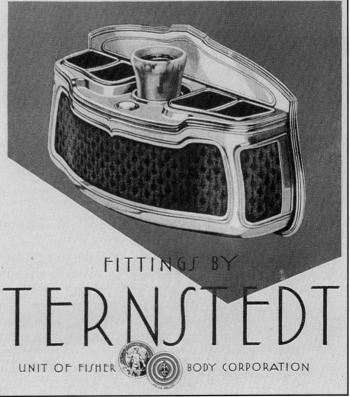

FITTINGS BY

TERNSTEDT

UNIT OF FISHER BODY CORPORATION

The Saturday Evening Post, *September 28, 1929.*

Evans engine-turned silvertone miniature vanity designed to resemble cigarette lighter; top opens to reveal powder compartment; lipstick tube slides out of bottom; 1½" x 1⅞". $125.00 – 150.00.

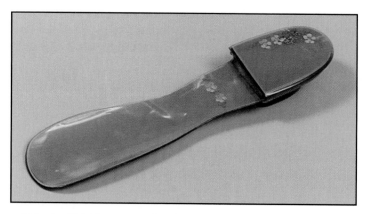

Green marbleized celluloid compact/shoe horn combination; top of shoe horn decorated with painted flowers; reverse side butterscotch colored; heel lifts to reveal framed mirror, puff, and deep powder compartment; 1¾" x 6" x 1". $275.00 – 350.00.

Gallery of Vogue Compacts

There are very few manufacturers of contemporary collectible compacts. As most compact collectors know, Estee Lauder has been manufacturing compacts, consistently for over 30 years. Today they are the most prolific manufacturers of desirable contemporary compacts, creating well over 25 new exciting designs each year. Originally their compacts were made in beautiful goldtone classic styles which they retain in their line. Over the last decade, Estee Lauder has created compacts in different shapes and styles. Their current compacts are made in the shapes of animals, fruits, and zodiac figurals in colorful enamels and are often beautifully encrusted with a spectrum of Austrian crystals.

A sampling of other manufacturers of collectible contemporary compacts are also included in the following pages: Debbie J. Palmer, Katherine Baumann, Madelin Beth, 1928 Gift Accessory Co., Masque, Versace, Elizabeth Arden, Gucci, Stratton, Paloma Picasso, Elsa-Peretti, Princess Marcella Borghese, Yves St. Laurent, and Halston. Many of these manufacturers use the shape of a heart, and some produce lids in the shape of a lock with a small key attached. There are also compacts decorated with colorful enamel paints and tassels. These other manufacturers create very few compacts, many producing one a year. All these affordable contemporary compacts are very desirable collectibles, attracting enthusiastic collectors around the world.

About 14 years ago when *Powder Puff*, the Compact Collectors Chronicle, was started, one of our charter members was Deborah Krulewitch. Deborah was and still is an avid collector of ladies' compacts. We corresponded quite frequently, discussing compacts. One day her letter arrived on Estee Lauder letterhead. When I asked her about that, she told me that she worked at the Estee Lauder corporate headquarters. Over the years we developed a warm relationship, and Deborah became one of my very dear friends. It was quite a while before I learned that Deborah was the Vice President of Corporate Administration.

Once I knew the prestigious position that Deborah held at Estee Lauder, I did not hesitate to enlist her help in sharing information about the new Estee Lauder compacts coming out each year so that this information could be shared with our collectors via *Powder Puff*. Her help has been indispensable to compact collectors. Deborah takes time out from her very busy schedule to respond to our requests. As an avid collector herself, she appreciates our obsession, and is very gracious with her time and compact information. At our annual Compact Collectors convention in May, 1999, at Cape May, Deborah honored us by attending and being our keynote speaker. I share the following speech that she gave at that convention.

Deborah Krulewitch – Keynote Speech – May 1999

I am so delighted to be with all of you, such wonderful, friendly people and passionate collectors. On behalf of Mrs. Estee Lauder, Leonard Lauder, chairman and CEO of the Estee Lauder companies, and his wife, Evelyn Lauder, who is senior corporate vice president, I would like to thank the compact collectors club for your wonderful loyalty to Estee Lauder, and the enthusiastic responses we receive from your members to our every compact launch, even our special launches in Europe and Australia. It's always thrilling for us to see our compacts highlighted in most every issue of your *Powder Puff* newsletter —your last newsletter was too fabulous!

Those of you who had the opportunity to tune into A&E's "Biography" segment this past Monday, (June 7, 1999) were, I'm sure, fascinated by Mrs. Estee Lauder's life story, which was featured that evening. As vice president of corporate administration, working closely with the Lauder family, it has been one of my greatest privileges to become acquainted with Mrs. Estee Lauder, this completely captivating and remarkable lady, whom *Time*

magazine recently included in their list of the 100 most remarkable people of the century. I thought you would enjoy hearing some of my personal anecdotes, and learning more about Mrs. Lauder's unique personal philosophy and style, and how she built from the ground up a global business that owns 45% of the prestige cosmetics market in U.S. department stores.

Mrs. Estee Lauder was born in Corona, Queens, New York, of eastern European ancestry. Even as a child, she always had a passion for beauty and a commitment to excellence. She began her company with four products: Estee Lauder creme pack, Estee Lauder cleansing oil, Estee Lauder all-purpose creme and skin lotion. Initially, she sold her products to small hair salons in New York City where she immediately discovered their popularity and touched so many customers, to make them beautiful. Our corporate vision statement is "bringing the best to everyone we touch," and this was Mrs. Lauder's basic philosophy. Mrs. Lauder proudly established her first retail account at Saks Fifth Avenue in New York City in

1948; in 1960, Estee Lauder products became available at Harrods in London.

In the early days of her business, Mrs. Lauder realized she did not have the money for an advertising budget. One of her mottoes was "tell-a-phone, tell-a-graph, tell-a-woman." Her products quickly became known for their exceptional quality and, as Mrs. Lauder knew, once a woman tried the product, she liked it and told her friends.

One of the world's best salespeople, Mrs. Lauder spent a great deal of time behind the counter during the many years she was actively involved in the business. "Know your customer, understand their needs, and surpass their expectations" was Mrs. Lauder's guiding philosophy.

Mrs. Lauder's philosophy and vision are clearly brought to life in the fabulous fragrance compacts she began producing in 1968, when she introduced the gorgeous Youth Dew golden rope solid perfume compact with a faux turquoise stone in the center. Mrs. Lauder always claimed that she could see a fragrance, as well as smell it, and with the solid perfume compacts she proved to the world the truth of her claim. This resulted in an Estee Lauder tradition of creating beautiful, luxurious compacts that women and men love — and love to collect. Actually, Mrs. Lauder's love of beauty first married successfully with her genius for scent and marketing in 1953, with the creation of Youth Dew, which in that year alone did an astounding $50,000 worth of business.

In 1984, that figure had jumped to over $150 million dollars. In 1953, Youth Dew had created a mini-revolution; Dolores Del Rio announced in public that year that her secret to "driving men ga-ga was wearing one's hair in an upsweep that has been brushed with Youth Dew." Similarly, Joan Crawford once gave an interview in which she said that she'd enticed her husbands by dabbing a bit of Youth Dew in her hair. "I can't stop dancing with you," said Mr. Pepsi Cola to Ms. Crawford, "You smell so exquisite."

1953 was the year that Mrs. Lauder found out what being a nose really meant. In the world of perfume, a nose is a rare person, one who possesses a special olfactory sense and who can identify exactly what components make up a fragrance.

A nose can differentiate between a great and irresistible scent and a mediocre one. The greatest perfumes in the world have been noses. At a perfumery conference in France held several years ago, the chief perfumer of international flavors and fragrances, announced that "in America, there is only one true nose and it belongs to Estee Lauder." This was an extraordinary statement, especially when one considers that up until then the traditional world of perfumes had been strictly male dominated.

Mrs. Estee Lauder remains an inspiration to all of us. "I didn't get there by wishing for it or hoping for it, but by working for it," she often reminded her sales force. Attention to even the minutest details, an emphasis on the highest possible quality standards, and an amazing, intuitive sense of the consumer, and a passion for excellence enabled Mrs. Lauder to create one of the world's best companies.

From the beginning, family has been as important to Mrs. Lauder as business, and family and business are closely united in her company. Her son Leonard is chairman of the Estee Lauder companies, and son Ronald is chairman of Clinique and Estee Lauder International; both have been involved since their youth, and today, the third generation of Lauders is also active in the business.

Leonard's son, William Lauder, is president of Clinique, and Ronald's daughter, Aerin Lauder, is executive director of product development for Estee Lauder, while her younger sister, Jane Lauder, is director of make-up marketing & new concepts for Clinique.

The Estee Lauder companies include Estee Lauder, Aramis, Clinique, Prescriptive, Origins, Bobbi Brown Essentials, Mac, Jane, Aveda, and licensing agreements with Tommy Hilfiger toiletries and Donna Karan cosmetics. Products are available in more than 100 countries and territories worldwide, and the company employs approximately 15,000 people.

This year we will have achieved almost $4 billion in sales. This is a remarkable result of the vision and drive of one very special and inspiring woman . . . Mrs. Estee Lauder.

And talk about a woman of passion! It has been my pleasure to get to know Roz Gerson over the last five years. Roz has been your most ardent advocate to obtain all the latest news on Estee Lauder Compacts and solids. Roz often knows about a particular solid perfume before I do. She is the most dedicated person, and so generous of spirit in sharing her ideas. Roz and I hit it off immediately because she and I both love people of passion and commitment. She cares deeply about her family, doing good deeds for others, paying attention to detail, and giving of herself. Roz is a staunch advocate for all of you, providing you with the best, most up-to-date and interesting information that she can scope out. If Roz cannot get it, no one else will. I want to thank Roz for her tremendous personal interest in Estee Lauder, as well as thank all of you for your interest, and for helping Estee Lauder build an incredible business in solid perfumes and compacts. Through your enthusiasm Roz, Estee Lauder has been inspired to establish an archive collection, and although there are a few missing pieces, the Estee Lauder Companies now have a special treasure that will keep these beautiful pieces and the company's legacy in the public eye forever.

I think that collecting must be in the genes. I am a collector, and I know that is why I bonded so well with Roz and the Compact Collectors Club. I collect state memorabilia — glasses, plates, and handkerchiefs, and now Roz has gotten me started on Christmas ornaments related to beauty themes. My husband collects antique cars, and my son started a collection of light bulbs when he was one year old — he was obsessed until he discovered Mickey Mouse. We love our collections, and I know I share with all of you the thrill of the hunt, whether it be at a flea market, garage sale, antique store, or eBay, the fun of bringing it home, adding it to your display, and thinking about the history of the object purchased. And for the Compact Collectors Club members, there is the added thrill of the wonderful camaraderie of your group, and the ability to share your passion with others. I think this is an insightful quote about a collection: "It is a message of hope, a proof that the past is in all of us and we will be in all that comes after us."

Paloma Picasso silver and goldtone round compact; dome-shaped lid; interior mirror set at angle; red faceted stone and signature on inside gilded lid; 2½" x ¾". $125.00 – 175.00.

Estee Lauder 1994 round brushed goldtone "Starry Nights" compact, cobalt blue enamel lid enhanced with rhinestone stars and cosmic band, 2¼" dia. $125.00 – 175.00.

1928 Gift Accessory Co., 1998 round goldtone compact, lid decorated with open work and band of black enamel, clear crystal centered on lid, interior reveals mirror, puff, and powder well, 2¼" dia. $60.00 – 70.00.

Estee Lauder, 1998 round "Holiday Lights" mini compact, lid completely covered with red and clear crystals in a checkerboard design, 1¾" dia. $125.00 – 150.00.

Estee Lauder 1999 round goldtone "Good Fortune" red enamel compact, lid decorated with goldtone Chinese good luck symbols, red tassel, inspired by Mrs. Evelyn Lauder's design concept, 2¼" dia. $50.00 – 75.00.

Stunning goldtone and black enamel Estee Lauder 1999 "Grand Piano" compact, highlighted with crystals, 2⅓" x 2½". $125.00 – 150.00.

Estee Lauder 1999 round brushed goldtone "Golden Millennium" compact, lid enhanced with stylized hourglass filled with crystals and imprinted with the year 2000, 2¼" dia. Legend: "GOLDEN MILLENNI-UM, For all time. For all women. This timeless collectible compact symbolizes all your golden moments ... past, present, and future. The sands of time continuously move forward; live in anticipation of the delightful surprises your future holds. Here's to a golden millennium." Estee Lauder. $50.00 – 75.00.

Three round goldtone Gucci compacts, dyed lizard lids, interiors reveal beveled mirror, puff, sifter, and powder well; Left: Red lizard, 3" dia; right: green lizard, 3" dia.; $45.00 – 55.00 each; bottom: black lizard 2½" dia., $35.00 – 45.00.

Estee Lauder 1994 polished and brushed goldtone "Ladybug" compact, brushed goldtone compact lid designed to resemble a leaf with a red and black enamel ladybug, 2¾" x 2¼". $65.00 – 75.00.

Estee Lauder 1995 brushed goldtone "Prince Charming" compact, brushed goldtone lid designed to resemble lily pad, green enamel frog rests on the lily pad, green enamel thumb-piece, 2" dia. $75.00 – 95.00.

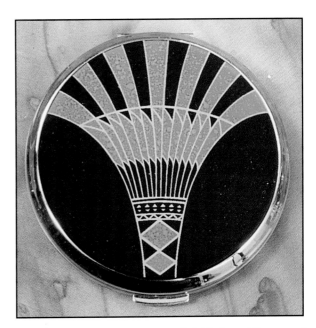

Round Stratton compact, enameled black, goldtone, and orange Art Deco design on lid, interior reveals framed mirror and puff, 3" dia. $35.00 – 45.00.

Left – Halston Elsa Peretti-designed silver-plated heart-shaped compact; #56620 incised on bottom of powder well; interior mirror; 3" x ¾". $150.00 – 200.00.

Right – Halston Elsa Peretti-designed goldtone heart-shaped compact; label on reverse side reads "Not for individual sale," sold boxed in conjunction with Halston fragrance; interior mirror, pressed powder, and puff; 2" x ½". $125.00 – 175.00.

Two goldtone heart-shaped Estee Lauder Pink Ribbon breast cancer awareness ribbon design compacts. Top left: Decorated with enamel pink ribbon, 1996, 2" x 2", $29.50; bottom: enhanced with pink crystals, 1998, 2" x 2". $35.00.

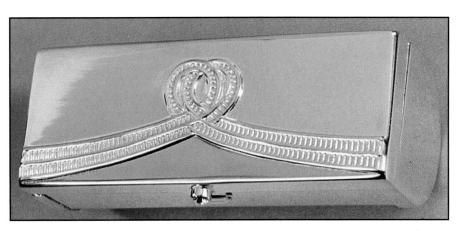

Goldtone Estee Lauder Pink Ribbon Lipstick Case, decorated with pink enamel ribbon, interior reveals mirror, velvet lined, 1998, 3¼" x 1¼". Inserts: Thank you for your purchase of the Estee Lauder Pink Ribbon Compact, Charm, and Lipstick Case. All Estee Lauder Inc., net proceeds from their sales will be donated to The Breast Cancer Research Foundation to fund clinical research in the causes and treatment of breast cancer at leading medical institutions nationwide. With your help, we are making a difference! Evelyn A. Lauder. $10.00.

Estee Lauder Pink Ribbon Charm Pin, enhanced with dazzling pink crystals, crystal ribbon can be detached from bar brooch and used as a charm, 1½" x ¾", 1999. $15.00.

Estee Lauder, 1997 October Angel round brushed goldtone compact, lid decorated with angel holding crystal studded mirror, crystal thumbpiece, one of a series of 12 birth month angel compacts, 2½" dia. $55.00 – 75.00.

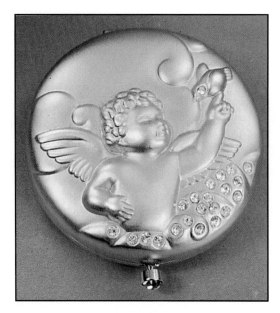

Estee Lauder 1997 March Angel brushed goldtone compact, lid has an angel in high relief enhanced with crystals, one of a series of 12 birth month angel compacts, 2¼" dia. $55.00 – 75.00.

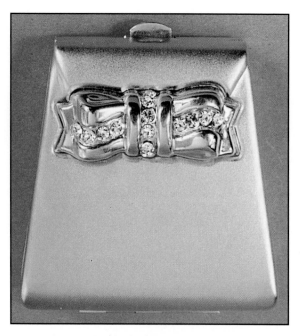

Estee Lauder 1995 brushed goldtone "Minaudiere" compact in the shape of a miniature handbag, lid decorated with polished bow and crystals, 2" x 2". $75.00 – 100.00.

Estee Lauder 1994 oblong brushed goldtone "Golden Age" compact, lid exquisitely decorated with repoussé Art Deco lady, 2¾" x 2¼". $60.00 – 80.00.

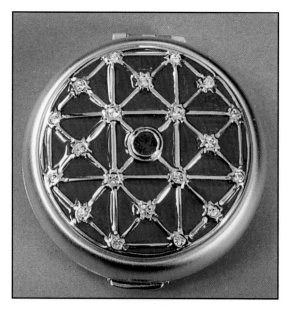

Estee Lauder 1996 round goldtone "Collector's" compact, red enamel lid decorated with goldtone criss-cross enhanced with crystals, centered with red stone, 3¼" dia. $70.00 – 80.00.

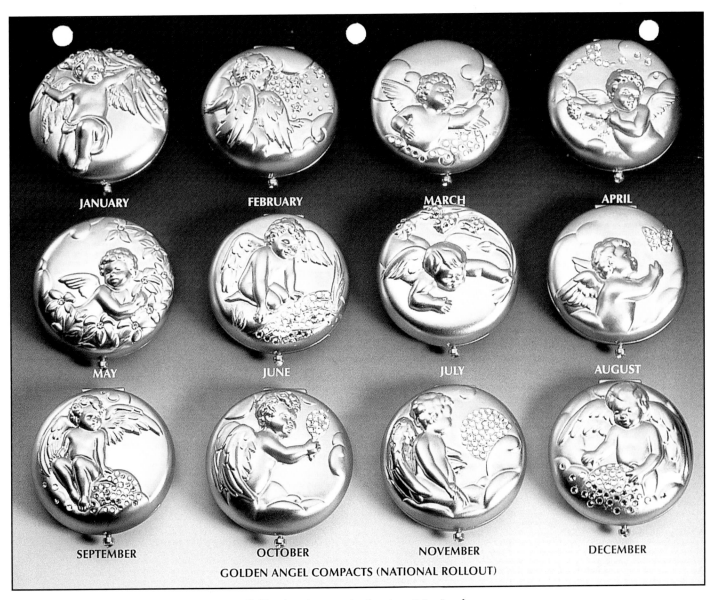

Golden Angel compacts. Courtesy Estee Lauder.

On the next pages are twelve brushed goldtone Estee Lauder 1996 "Zodiac" compacts, lids decorated with appropriate zodiac symbol enhanced with crystals. $70.00 – 100.00 each.

Top: Golden Aquarius compact. Legend: AQUARIUS, January 21 – February 19. Yours is a friendly spirit. Open-minded. Original. Altruistic. You believe in the power of ideas. You want to change lives. And change the world. You see the big picture. Your color is blue, like the limitless sky.

Bottom: Golden Pisces compact. Legend: PISCES, February 20 – March 20. You are a dreamer. Mysterious. Intuitive. Emotional. You're creative and imaginative. Always a good listener with a sensitive soul and understanding nature. Your colors are turquoise and green, like the sea.

Top: Golden Aries compact. Legend: ARIES, March 21 – April 20. Yours is a courageous spirit. Energetic. Exciting. Spontaneous. You're a positive thinker. Gifted with the capacity to dream and to fall in love at first sight. You make things happen. Yours is the color of passion, red.

Bottom: Golden Cancer compact. Legend: CANCER, June 22 – July 23. Yours is a sympathetic soul. Perceptive. Sensitive. Loyal. You know exactly who you are. And you're intuitive about others. When you love, you love completely. Your home is a place of peace. Your colors are sea green and silver moon.

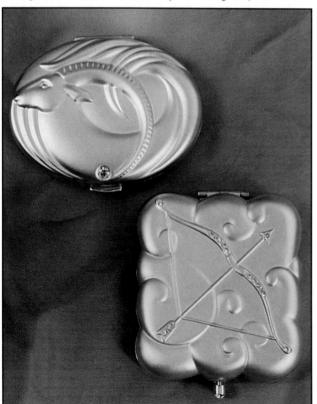

Top: Golden Capricorn compact. Legend: CAPRICORN, December 22 – January 20. Yours is a confident spirit. Ambitious. Patient. Loyal. You have a strong sense of purpose. And a belief in your own abilities. You can be elusive yet your feelings run deep. Your colors are dark green, brown, and gray, the colors of nature.

Bottom: Golden Sagittarius compact. Legend: SAGITTARIUS, November 23 – December 21. Yours is an optimistic spirit. Independent. Adventurous. Free. You are direct, open, and impetuous. Thriving on changes and challenges. You have a sense of humor and your spirit is absolutely irascible. Your color is purple, the color of royalty.

Top: Golden Scorpio compact. Legend: SCORPIO, October 24 – November 22. You're a passionate idealist. Intense. Emotional. Magnetic. You seek to live life fully. And you understand the depths of the heart. You are tempestuous in love. Disarmingly unpredictable. Your colors are crimson and burgundy, the colors of excitement.

Bottom: Golden Libra compact. Legend: LIBRA, September 24 – October 23. You have an effortless charm. Warm-hearted. Sentimental. Optimistic. You appreciate beauty in every form. And people are irresistibly drawn to you. You're a peacemaker striving for balance. Your colors are lavender and blue, the colors of harmony.

Top: Golden Leo compact. Legend: LEO, July 24 – August 23. You are the essence of exuberance. Enthusiastic. Extravagant. Expansive. You're flamboyant. Lavish with your affections. Generous with gifts. You love to be the center of attention. Your colors are gold and orange, magnetic as the sun.

Bottom: Golden Virgo compact. Legend: VIRGO, August 24 – September 23. Yours is an intelligent mind. Truthful. Conscientious. Inquisitive. You thrive on challenges. A perfectionist bringing order out of chaos. And known for your crystal-clear thinking. Your colors are navy blue and gray, the colors of style and refinement.

Top: Golden Gemini compact. Legend: GEMINI, May 22 – June 21. You are curious about everything. Outgoing. Imaginative. And bright. You love the excitement of change. Encountering new ideas. Making new friends. Traveling to new places. Your color is yellow, the color of novelty.

Bottom: Golden Taurus compact. Legend: TAURUS, April 21 – May 21. Yours is a devoted heart. Strong. Steadfast. And true. You enjoy all the finer things. The luxuries of life. And the warmth of love and home. Your colors are pale blue and mauve, the colors of tenderness.

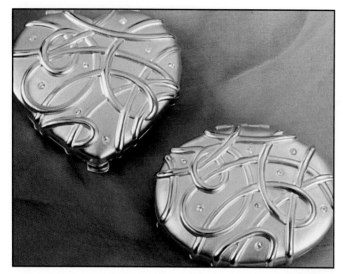

Four brushed goldtone Estee Lauder 1999. "True Expressions" compacts, lids enhanced with crystals, interior reveals mirror, puff, and powder well, reflected in mirrors are expressions imprinted on inner lower lid above thumbpiece. $55.00 each.

Top: Heart-shaped "Love Compact," interior imprinted with "You're In My Heart."

Bottom: Oval-shaped "Mother Compact," interior imprinted with "Thanks Mom."

Love and Mother compacts, open.

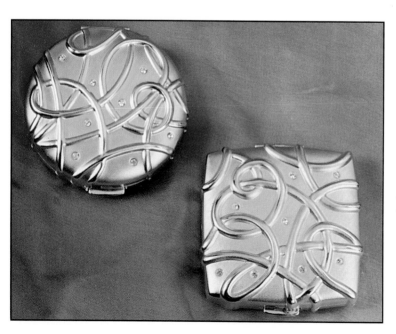

Top: Round-shaped "Friend Compact," interior imprinted with "Friends Forever."

Bottom: Square-shaped "Inspiration Compact," interior imprinted with "Live! Love! Laugh!"

Friend and Inspiration compacts, open.

Following are nine brushed goldtone Estee Lauder 1998/1999. "Animal Attraction" compacts, lids enhanced with an animal in high relief. $50.00 – $70.00 each.

"Golden Leopard" compact. Legend: The leopard, brave and mysterious, is a messenger of the gods. Known as the Great Watcher, her luminous eyes open into the spirit world, revealing truth to all who humbly seek it.

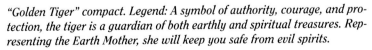

"Golden Tiger" compact. Legend: A symbol of authority, courage, and protection, the tiger is a guardian of both earthly and spiritual treasures. Representing the Earth Mother, she will keep you safe from evil spirits.

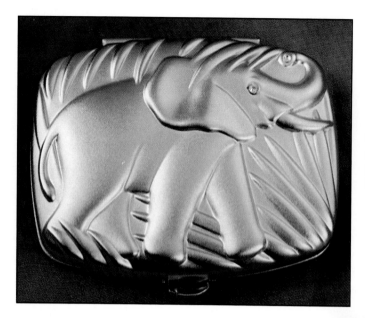

"Golden Elephant" compact. Legend: The elephant represents the sacred wisdom of the gods, combining patience and love with power and strength. Her noble presence confers status and dignity on all around her.

"Mystical Monkeys" compact. Legend: See no evil, hear no evil, speak no evil — these wise monkeys remind us always to strive for virtue. With their intelligence, cunning, and strength of character, they help keep evil influences at bay.

"Golden Dolphins" compact. Legend: Symbol of Happiness. Playful and clever, dolphins leave every care behind as they leap and spin for the sheer fun of it. Let this dancing duo share their high spirits as they remind you of life's many joys.

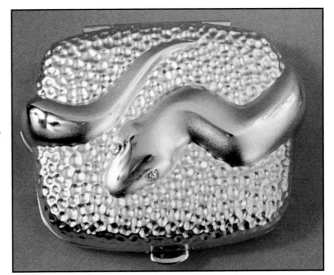

"Golden Serpent" compact. Legend: Representing the dual nature of the universe, the all-seeing serpent embodies the mystical opposites: male and female, body and soul, destruction and creation.

"Golden Stallion" compact. Legend: Symbol of Freedom. Swift, strong, and self-assured, the horse has always held a special place in our hearts. Let this free-spirited charger remind you to think for yourself and to follow your dreams wherever they lead.

"Gentle Giraffe" compact. Legend: Symbol of Grace. Elegant, serene, and singularly graceful, giraffes rise above life's daily squabbles. Follow the lead of this golden pair and remember to hold your head high, never letting the little things get you down.

"Golden Dragon" compact. Legend: Symbol of Good Fortune. Noble, wise, and virtuous, the dragon brings celestial harmony into the world. This mythical beast will watch over you, keeping dark spirits away and bringing luck and prosperity to your family.

Below are four goldtone Estee Lauder 1999 "Enchanted Faerie" compacts, lids enhanced with crystals. $55.00 each.

Top: "Spirit of Air" compact. Legend: The Air Signs are Gemini, Libra, Aquarius. You are intelligent and verbal, quickly grasping ideas and expressing them with ease. You have the rare ability to make your dreams come true.

Bottom: "Spirit of Earth" compact. Legend: The Earth Signs are Taurus, Virgo, Capricorn. You are practical and patient. Industrious. Strong-willed. You value commitment and security. You are tender and loving, with a generous heart.

Top: "Spirit of Fire" compact. Legend: The Fire Signs are Aries, Leo, Sagittarius. You are full of energy and enthusiasm. Impulsive, flamboyant, expansive. You are an extrovert at heart, and you have a passionate soul.

Bottom: "Spirit of Water" compact. Legend: The Water Signs are Cancer, Scorpio, Pisces. You are intuitive and empathetic. Creative. Imaginative. Sensitive to your surroundings and to other people. You have hidden depths.

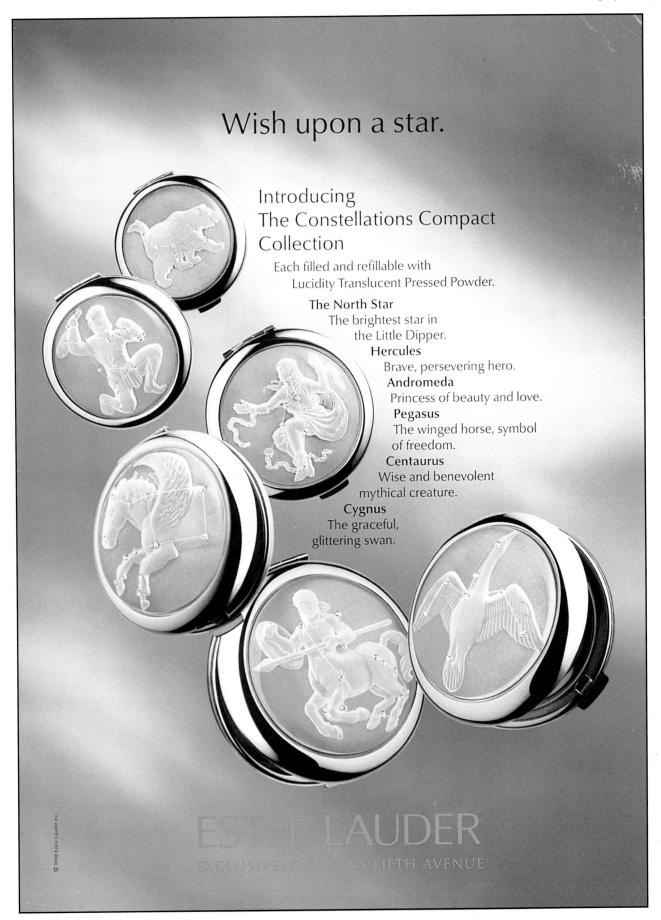

The Constellations Compact Collection. Courtesy Estee Lauder.

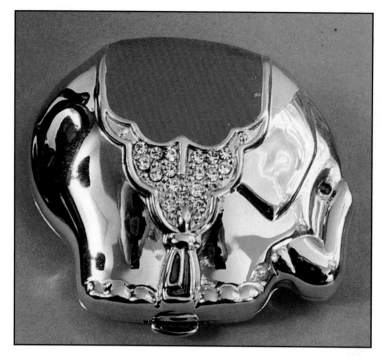

Estee Lauder 1994 "Little Prince" goldtone compact in the shape of a miniature elephant, red enamel blanket decorated with crystals, 2" x 2¼". $60.00 – 70.00.

Estee Lauder 1995 polished goldtone "Catnap" compact enhanced with red enamel collar (cat with black enamel collar, 1996), 2" x 2". $55.00 – 75.00.

Estee Lauder 1998 polished goldtone "Precious Bunny" compact, pink crystal eye, 2" x 2½". $45.00 – 65.00.

Estee Lauder 1998/1999 brushed goldtone "Precious Pillow" compact, decorative rhinestone bands divide pillow into four sections, 2¼" sq. $50.00 – 60.00.

Estee Lauder 1998 brushed goldtone "Magic Pillow" compact with gold tassel and lid enhanced with clear crystals, pillow w/red crystals, 2½" dia. $55.00 – 65.00.

Estee Lauder 1998 brushed goldtone "White Twinkling Rose" compact, lid enhanced with crystal design in the form of a rose, 2¼" dia. $150.00.

Estee Lauder 1997 round polished goldtone "New Cameo" compact, lid centered with cameo, 3" dia. $75.00 – 125.00.

Estee Lauder round brushed goldtone "Victory" compact, decorated with three stars, and red, white, and blue ribbon. Made for the 1996 Olympics in Atlanta, Georgia, "ATLANTA '96" engraved on reverse side, 2¼" dia. $75.00 – 100.00.

The next two paragraphs show six round goldtone Estee Lauder 1998 "Lucky Charm" compacts, lids enhanced with crystal, 1¾" dia., $55.00 each. Legend: Magical. Mystical. More than meets the eye. For years, people have passed along cherished charms to those they love — to keep them safe, to bring them good luck.

Left: "Lucky Clover" compact. Legend: One leaf for fame, one leaf for wealth, one leaf for romance, one leaf for health. This little rhyme kindles the magic of your Lucky Clover. Go ahead — make a wish.

Right: "Lucky Horseshoe" compact. Legend: Your Lucky Horseshoe helps wishes come true. When the ends are pointed up, you'll gather luck in ... turn the ends down to share it with a friend.

Bottom: "Lucky Penny" compact. Legend: Lucky you ... your Lucky Penny always lands heads up. Close your eyes and make a wish — but don't ever spend your penny, or you'll give away the magic as well as the money.

Left: "Lucky Butterfly" compact. Legend: It's a magical moment when Lucky Butterfly rests on your hand. All that you wish for is sure to come true — as long as you whisper your secret before she flutters away.

Right: "Lucky Elephant" compact. Legend: Treasure your Lucky Elephant — she always bring you good fortune. Rely on her for help when you need ancient wisdom (and a little modern-day patience) to see you through.

Bottom: "Lucky Ladybug" compact. Legend: Ladybug, ladybug, Fly away home ... When Lucky Ladybug lands on your hand, tell her your secret wish, then blow a kiss to make it come true.

Two goldtone Estee Lauder 1999 crystal studded fruits. Left: Yellow crystal "Lemon Drop;" right: green crystal "Lime," 2" x 2½". $125.00 – 135.00 each.

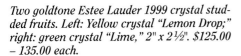

Round black enamel Masque compact, lid beautifully enhanced with a crystal and pearl jeweled decoration, interior reveals mirror, puff, and powder well, pink satin protector carrying case, presentation box is an unusual black hatbox, 3¼". Insert reads: "Masque presents the first limited edition powder compact to commemorate the Manor House Museum Exhibition of the Masque Collection Compacts of Character, July, 1944. Only ten pieces of this style have been made for the occasion. July '94 No 2/10. Proceeds from your purchase of this powder compact will be used to sponsor master apprenticeships to encourage young craftsmen and women to pick up the tools of their forebears and once again create beauty. This special commemorative powder compact has been made for you by the following firms of craftsmen: Jewelry by Kiashek, Compact by Stratton, Powder Puff and pouchette by Lambournes, Milliners Box by M. Petrushkin Ltd. for MASQUE." $150.00 – 175.00.

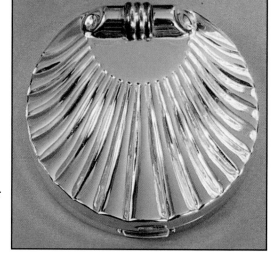

Estee Lauder 1988 goldtone "Shell" compact, 2¼" x 2¼". $60.00 – 75.00.

Two Estee Lauder goldtone compacts in the shape of a button. Left: 1993 "Golden Button" compact, cross stitch on lid enhanced with crystals, 2¼" dia. $100.00 – 125.00; right: 1994 "Button Button" compact, $80.00 – 100.00.

Two round goldtone Estee Lauder compacts, lids decorated with raised interlocking circular pattern. "Golden Braid" compact, 1997 lid enhanced with crystals, bottom, "Golden Twist" compact, 1998. 2¼" dia. Top, $55.00 – 75.00; bottom, $50.00 – 70.00.

Estee Lauder goldtone 1998 "Attitude" compact and "Attitude" pendant, lid centered with a dark stone that when pressed, reflects the color of your mood. Pendant complete with silk cord, worn by the Estee Lauder sales staff, 1⅝" dia. $15.00 – 20.00. Compact, 1¾" dia. $35.00 – 50.00. Insert reads: "What's your attitude? It's time for an attitude assessment. Are you in the mood for love? Is it a good time to ask for a raise? Or, are you a bit stressed out and just want to be left alone? How about your friends? Have you checked out their moods? Do you know if they have a good attitude or if simply have an attitude. Now, you have the power to instantly reveal any mood, any attitude. The answer is at your fingertips. To use: Hold the Attitude Compact in the palm of your hand. Press thumb firmly against top of compact and hold for approximately ten seconds. Instantly — all moods revealed. The color Black reveals a Stressed, Tense, Edgy attitude. The color Brown reveals a Cautious, Reserved, Hesitant attitude. The color Green reveals a Relaxed, Calm, Mellow attitude. The color Royal Blue reveals a Cheerful, Optimistic, Confident attitude."

Two beautiful round Venetian Murano glass compacts, millefiori decorated lids, similar to Murano glass paperweights, 2½" dia. $150.00 – 200.00 each.

229

Estee Lauder blue enamel "Color Play" blush compact designed to resemble spinning top, screws open to reveal blush and brush, 3½" x 2½" dia., 1990s. $25.00 – 35.00.

"Color Play" blush compact open.

Two round Estee Lauder compacts. Top: Polished silvertone "Evening Wear Rhinestone Pave" compact, 1996, lid decorated with clear rhinestones; bottom: brushed silvertone "Pink Pave" compact, 1996, lid decorated with pink rhinestones, each 2½" dia. $50.00 – 75.00 each.

"Clear Sailing," 1998 Estee Lauder round goldtone compact, lid decorated with blue and white horizontal enamel stripes centered with a small goldtone anchor, 2¼" dia. $50.00.

Round polished goldtone Estee Lauder "Equestrian" compact, 1998, quilted lid decorated with a silvertone horse bit and belt motif trim, 2¼" dia. $50.00.

Estee Lauder 1997 round mini "Red Rhinestone" compact, 1¾". $70.00 – 80.00.

Estee Lauder 1997 square "Golden Birthstone" compact, lid centered with a large faceted aquamarine, March birthstone, Legend: March – The Aquamarine Birthstone expresses the quiet harmony of nature. Sensitive souls have an affinity for aquamarines because they symbolize emotion, creativity, and perception. $50.00 – 60.00 each. "Golden Birthstone" compacts also available enhanced with appropriate colored faceted birthstones and legends for each of the 12 months, 1⅞" sq. $75.00 – 100.00.

Estee Lauder, "Glittering Heart" compact, front and back lids of the heart-shaped compact completely covered with clear crystals, complete with puff, powder, and mirror, $125.00 – 150.00.

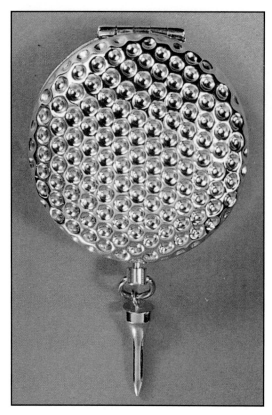

Estee Lauder 1998 round dimpled goldtone "Golf Ball" compact, complete with a tee charm suspended from thumbpiece, interior reveals puff, powder, and mirror, 1⅞" dia. $50.00.

Round brushed goldtone Estee Lauder "Tennis Ball" compact, 1998, lid decorated with rhinestone seams and tennis racket charm, interior reveals mirror, powder, and puff, 2¼" dia. $50.00 – 75.00.

Estee Lauder 1994 round "America the Beautiful" goldtone red, white, and blue enamel stars and stripes design, enhanced with rhinestones, interior reveals mirror, powder, and puff, 2¼" dia. $150.00 – 175.00.

Estee Lauder 1996 round goldtone "Lone Star" compact, lid decorated with red, white, and blue enamel and rhinestone cowboy boot and the Lone Star flag, interior reveals mirror, puff, and powder, either standard or magnifying mirror available, 2¼" dia. $150.00 – 175.00.

Estee Lauder 1994 round goldtone "American Dream" (American Painted) compact, lid decorated with red, white, and blue enamel swirls, enhanced with rhinestone stars, complete with mirror, puff, and powder, 2¼" dia. $125.00 – 150.00.

Estee Lauder 1997 round goldtone "French Flag" compact, lid decorated with red and blue enamel stripes centered with rhinestones, interior reveals mirror, puff, and powder, 2¼" dia., France exclusive. $125.00 – 150.00.

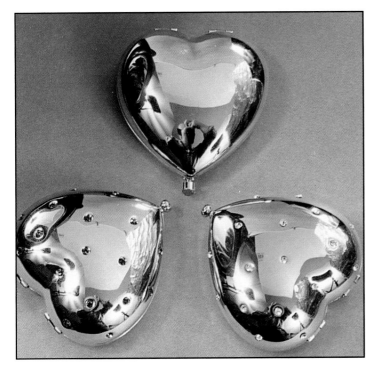

Three heart-shaped Estee Lauder goldtone compacts. Left: "True Blue," 1995 compact, lid decorated with blue rhinestones; right: "Starstruck" compact, lid decorated with clear rhinestones, 1994; top: "Plain Heart" compact, 1999, each 2¼" x 2". $55.00 – 65.00 each.

Estee Lauder goldtone seashell compacts. Left: Brushed goldtone "Golden Seashell," 1994; right: polished "Golden Seashell," 1995, complete with mirror, powder, and puff, 2½" x 2¾". $45.00 – 65.00 each.

Two Estee Lauder brushed goldtone compacts. Top: "Golden Leaf" compact, 1997, 2½" x 2½", $35.00 – 55.00; bottom: "Heart to Heart" compact, 1994, 2½" x 2½". $45.00 – 65.00.

Top: Estee Lauder "Golden Bough" round polished gold-tone compact, lid decorated with red rhinestones, 1994, reissued in 1995 with pearl decorated lid, 2¼" dia. $50.00 – 60.00. Bottom: Oblong brushed goldtone "Little Acorns" compact, 1995, contains powder, puff, and mirror, 2½" x 3". $45.00 – 65.00.

Two round Estee Lauder goldtone mini compacts. Top: "Brushed Golden Basket," 1995; bottom: polished "Golden Love Knot," 1997/1999 both complete with mirror, puff, and powder, each 1¾" dia. $27.50 – 30.00 each.

Two Estee Lauder round goldtone compacts. Top: "Sparkle Swirl," lid decorated with red crystal swirls, 1999, designed for and given (by Estee Lauder) to each of the 1999 Cape May Compact Collectors Convention-eers; bottom: "Sparkle Swirl," lid decorated with clear crystal swirls, 1998, interiors reveal puff, powder, and mirror, 2¼". $50.00 – 65.00 each.

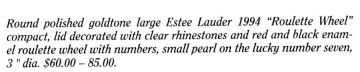

Round polished goldtone large Estee Lauder 1994 "Roulette Wheel" compact, lid decorated with clear rhinestones and red and black enam-el roulette wheel with numbers, small pearl on the lucky number seven, 3 " dia. $60.00 – 85.00.

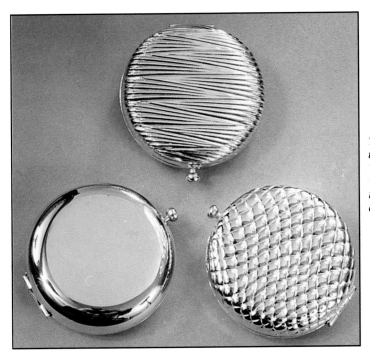

Three round goldtone mini Estee Lauder compacts, each complete with powder, puff, and mirror, each 1¾" dia. Left: Polished goldtone "After Hours" compact, 1996/1999, $30.00 – 40.00; top: goldtone "Golden Silk" compact, decorated with delicate criss-crossing threads, 1995, $35.00 – 45.00; right: "Golden Lizard" compact, lid decorated with lizard pattern, 1994, $40.00 – 50.00.

Estee Lauder 1992 round antique goldtone "Columbus Day Discovery" compact, lid decorated with detailed navigator's compass in high relief, interior contains powder, puff, and mirror, 2½" dia. $50.00 – 75.00.

Four round Estee Lauder goldtone compacts. Bottom: "Midnight Sun," 1994, outer rim of lid decorated with patterned edges, center engraved with the letters RG, $35.00 – 45.00; left: "Golden Weave" compact, 1968, woven goldtone and silvertone design on lid, $25.00 – 35.00; top: "Mobe" compact, 1994, centered with a raised, round faux mobe pearl framed by rings of gold circles, $45.00 – 55.00; right: "Golden Alligator" compact (original), 1967, re-issued in 1987, 1991, and 1999, lid engraved to resemble alligator skin, each contains mirror, powder, and puff, 2¼" dia. $30.00 – 40.00.

Round Estee Lauder 1994 beautiful hammered goldtone "Golden Jewel" compact, hammered lid decorated with seven cabochon and faceted colorful stones, complete with mirror, powder, and puff, 2¼" dia. $75.00 – 125.00.

Two goldtone heart-shaped Estee Lauder compacts. Bottom: "Gold Heart" 1998 compact, lid decorated with textured small balls. $50.00 60.00; top: "Heartfelt" compact, 1998, lid decorated with brushed and po ished goldtone wave design, interiors contain puff, powder, and mirr each 2¼" x 2¼". $35.00 – 45.00.

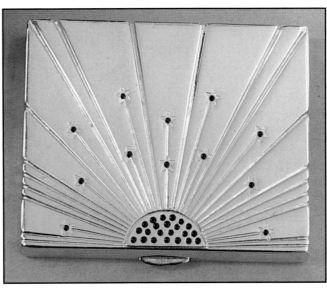

Estee Lauder 1996 round brushed goldtone "Go Fish" compact, lid decorated with goldfish in high relief enhanced with clear rhinestones; Canada release, 1995, lid decorated with goldfish in high relief enhanced with multi-colored rhinestones, both versions 2¼" dia. $55.00 – 75.00.

Rectangular polished goldtone Estee Lauder "Evening Star" compact, etched setting sun design, rays decorated with stars set with blue stones, 1991, reissued in 1994, 2¼" x 2¾". $100.00 – 125.00.

Red pave crystal Estee Lauder 1998 "Lady Apple" compact, in the form of an apple complete with goldtone leaf charm, 2" x 2". $150.00 – 175.00.

Estee Lauder 1998 "Sugar Plum" compact, in the shape of a plum, enhanced with pave amethyst crystals complete with goldtone leaf charm, 2" x 1¾". $150.00 – 175.00.

Yves Saint Laurent "In Love Again" pewter tone compact in the shape of a heart, barely discernible Yves Saint Laurent's signature underneath red plastic lid, reverse side reads "In Love Again," comes complete with red pouch and red box, 2" x 2⅜", 1998. $160.00.

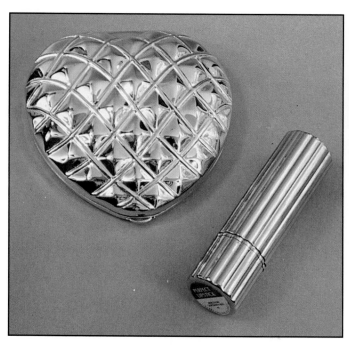

Estee Lauder polished goldtone "Heart and Soul" compact and lipstick set, 1990s, lid decorated with diamond-shaped raised puffs, 3" x 3", ribbed lipstick case, 2¾". $75.00 – 85.00 set.

Estee Lauder 1996, "Canada My Canada," round large polished goldtone compact, lid decorated with lovely red enamel maple leaf centered on a clear crystal background, Canada, 3" dia. $100.00 – 125.00.

Mini round Estee Lauder 1999 "Evening" compact, half of both lids decorated with clear pave crystals, other halves decorated with black pave crystals, red stone thumbpiece, 1¾" dia. $100.00 – 125.00.

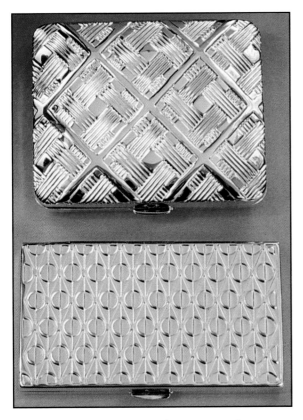

Two polished goldtone rectangular Estee Lauder compacts. Top: 1999 "Intricate Weave" compact, lid decorated with a raised woven pattern, interior reveals mirror, powder well with powder, and puff well with puff, 2½" x 3", $75.00 – 100.00; bottom: 1999 "Golden Optics" compact, lid decorated with raised triangles and circles, interior reveals mirror, powder well with powder, and puff well with puff, 1½" x 3½", $50.00 – 75.00.

Two square Estee Lauder goldtone compacts. Top: 1997 "Chocolate Box" compact, polished goldtone frames brown tortoise shell lid, $45.00 – 55.00; bottom: 1999 polished goldtone "Urban Block" compact, lid decorated with embossed mini squares, each 1⅞" square. $50.00 – 60.00.

Two square Estee Lauder goldtone "Bamboo Garden" compacts, each 2" square. Top: 1999 compact, lid decorated with bamboo design in high relief, $45.00 – 55.00; bottom: 1998 compact, lid decorated with bamboo design in high relief enhanced with clear crystals, $55.00 – 65.00.

Princess Marcella Borghese square goldtone compact, lid decorated with red and blue enamel hearts, framed interior mirror, puff, 2" sq. $45.00 – 55.00.

Three round Estee Lauder mini compacts, each 1¾" dia., lids completely covered with crystals. Top: 1995 "Black Jet," black crystal studded compact, $100.00 – 125.00; right: 1996 Pink Rhinestone, pink crystal studded compact, $100.00 – 125.00; left: 1995 "Nightlights," clear crystal studded compact. $100.00 – 125.00.

Estee Lauder goldtone oblong High Society, 1999 compact, lid decorated with swirling pattern, interior reveals mirror and two wells, one for puff and one for powder, 2" x 3¼". $50.00.

Polished and brushed stunning square goldtone Estee Lauder 1998 New York City compact. The New York City compact was made exclusively for the attendees of an Estee Lauder in-house sales meeting and was not available for general distribution. Lid enhanced with New York City's most famous skyscrapers in high relief: Chrysler Building, Empire State Building, and the World Trade Center Building; an Estee Lauder Lipstick is the third tower. Also comes with a silver sky, interior contains mirror, powder, and puff, 1⅞" sq. NPA.

Versace round silvertone compact and matching lipstick, 1990s, compact centered with head of Medusa surrounded by an engraved Grecian key design, interior reveals metal mirror, signed puff and powder impressed with head of Medusa, 3" dia. $36.00 – 50.00. Bullet-shaped silvertone lipstick tube decorated with a mini goldtone head of Medusa, 2½". $20.00 – 25.00.

Brushed goldtone Elizabeth Arden stylized round powder compact with matching lipstick, designed by renowned sculptor Robert Lee Morris for Elizabeth Arden, raised center peak in back and front lids of compact; compact, 2¾" dia. x 1½" high, lipstick 2¾". Instructions for inserting lipstick: "Hold bottom of lipstick case and pull out used lipstick cartridge. Insert refill into empty lipstick case pushing down gently until refill touches the bottom." $175.00 – 200.00 complete set.

Estee Lauder 1999 round goldtone "Personal Charm" compact, complete with loop to suspend the Personal Charms: New Year's Ball, Gift Box, Star Bright, Precious Poodle, Cuddly Kitten, Baby Shoes, Glittering Heart, and With this ring....; interior of compact reveals mirror, puff, and powder, compact 2", $35.00; charms $15.00 each.

Estee Lauder polished silvertone mini heart "Wedding Wishes" compact, 2000, pearl thumbpiece, complete with framed mirror, puff, and powder, 2" x 2". Legend on outside of enclosed card reads: "To have and to hold." Inside of card reads: "Especially for_____. With warmest wishes." $50. 00.

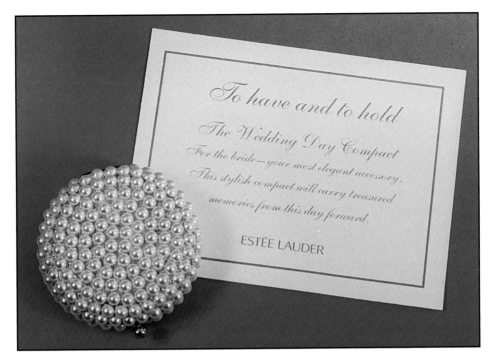

Estee Lauder mini round "Wedding Day" compact, 2000, lids completely covered with pearls, complete with framed mirror, puff, and powder, 2" dia. Legend on enclosed card reads: "To have and to hold. The Wedding Day Compact. For the bride — your most elegant accessory. This stylish compact will carry treasured memories from this day forward." $50.00.

Estee Lauder square goldtone "Purse Strings" compact, 2000, white enamel lid decorated with blue purse, 2" sq. $55.00.

Estee Lauder round goldtone "On Your Toes" compact, 2000, white enamel lid decorated with red shoes, 2¼" dia., $55.00.

Estee Lauder goldtone "Hats Off" oblong compact, 2000, white enamel lid decorated with straw hat, 2¾" x 2¼". $55.00.

Estee Lauder Precious Pet Collection, goldtone "Twinkling Toad" compact, 2000, goldtone lid designed to resemble toad, decorated with green crystals, 2¼" x 2¾". $75.00.

Estee Lauder Precious Pet Collection, goldtone "Brilliant Kitty" compact, 2000, goldtone lid designed to resemble kitty, decorated with black and clear crystals, 2½" x 2". $75.00.

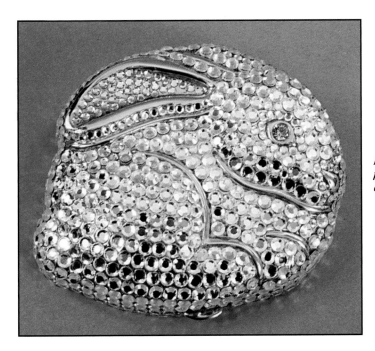

Estee Lauder Precious Pet Collection, goldtone "Brilliant Bunny" compact, 2000, goldtone clear crystal lid designed to resemble bunny, eye and ear decorated with pink crystals, 2½" x 2". $75.00.

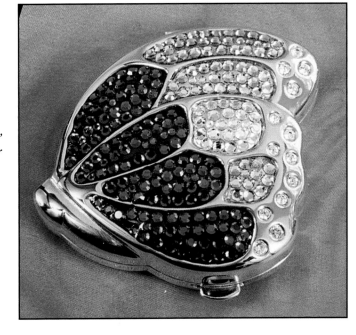

Estee Lauder Glitter Bug Collection, goldtone "Brilliant Butterfly" compact, 2000, goldtone lid decorated with blue, green, and clear crystals designed to resemble a butterfly, 2" x 2". $75.00.

Estee Lauder Glitter Bug Collection, goldtone "Sparkling Snail" compact, 2000, goldtone lid designed to resemble snail, completely covered with crystals, 2" x 2". $75.00.

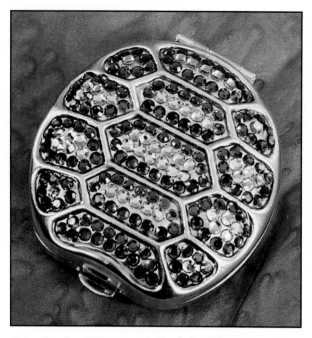

Estee Lauder Glitter Bug Collection, goldtone "Twinkling Tortoise" compact, 2000, goldtone lid designed to resemble a turtle, decorated with green and clear crystals, 2" x 2". $75.00.

Estee Lauder Glitter Bug Collection, goldtone "Glittery Ladybug" compact, 2000, goldtone lid decorated with red and black crystals, 2" x 1¾". $75.00.

Estee Lauder Glitter Bug Collection, round goldtone "Glamour Bee" compact, 2000, goldtone honeycomb lid decorated with yellow crystals and clear and black crystal bee, 1¾" dia., $75.00.

Estee Lauder Glitter Bug Collection, octagon-shaped goldtone "Shimmering Spider" compact, 2000, goldtone spider web lid decorated with clear crystals and black spider, 2". $75.00.

Estee Lauder Precious Pet Collection, goldtone "Tropical Fish" compact, 2000, goldtone lid designed to resemble fish, decorated with lavendar, green, and clear crystals, 2½" x 2". $75.00.

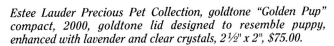

Estee Lauder Precious Pet Collection, goldtone "Golden Pup" compact, 2000, goldtone lid designed to resemble puppy, enhanced with lavender and clear crystals, 2½" x 2", $75.00.

Estee Lauder square black crystal "Sophisticated Lady" compact, 2000, lid decorated with a goldtone and pink crystal slide shoe, metal tassel attached at each corner, 1¾" sq. $125.00.

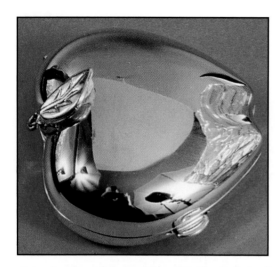

Estee Lauder polished goldtone "Golden Delicious" compact, 2000, designed to resemble an apple complete with goldtone leaf, 2" x 2". $30.00.

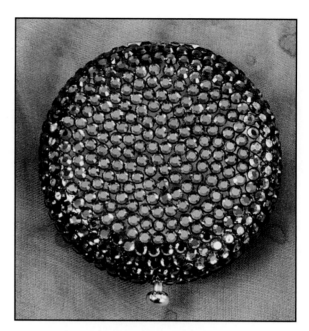

Estee Lauder Glitterball Compact Collection 2000, round mini "Heliotrope" compact, lids decorated with purple Austrian crystals, 2" dia. $125.00.

Following are twelve Estee Lauder round goldtone Zodiac compacts, 2000, lids decorated with appropriate zodiac signs enhanced with clear Austrian crystals, 2" dia., $50.00 each.

Left – "Golden Leo" compact. Legend reads: LEO, July 24 – August 23. You are the essence of exuberance. Enthusiastic, extravagant, expansive. You're flamboyant. Lavish with your affections. Generous with gifts. You love to be the center of attention. Your colors are gold and orange ... magnetic as the sun.

Center – "Golden Virgo" compact. Legend reads: VIRGO, August 24 – September 23. Yours is an intelligent mind. Truthful. Conscientious. Inquisitive. You thrive on challenges. A perfectionist bringing order out of chaos, you're known for your crystal-clear thinking. Your colors are navy blue and gray ... the colors of style and refinement.

Right – "Golden Libra" compact. Legend reads: LIBRA, September 24 – October 23. You have an effortless charm. Warm-hearted. Sentimental. Optimistic. You appreciate beauty in every form. And people are irresistibly drawn to you. You're a peacemaker striving for balance. Your colors are lavender and blue, the colors of harmony.

Left – "Golden Taurus" compact. Legend reads: TAURUS, April 21 – May 21. Yours is a devoted heart. Stong. Steadfast. And true. You enjoy all the finer things. The luxuries of life. And the warmth of love and home. Your colors are pale blue and mauve, the colors of tenderness.

Center – "Golden Gemini" compact. Legend reads: GEMINI, May 22 – June 21. You are curious about everything. Outgoing. Imaginative. And bright. You love the excitement of change. encountering new ideas. Making new friends. Traveling to new places. Your color is yellow, the color of novelty.

Right – "Golden Cancer" compact. Legend reads: CANCER, June 22 – July 23. Yours is a sympathetic soul. Perceptive. Sensitive. Loyal. You know exactly who you are. And you're intuitive about others. When you love, you love completely. Your home is a place of peace. Your colors are sea green and silver moon.

Left – "Golden Pisces" compact. Legend reads: PISCES, February 20 – March 20. You are a dreamer. Mysterious, intuitive, emotional. You're creative and imaginative. Always a good listener with a sensitive soul, you have an understanding nature. Your colors are turquoise and green like the sea.

Center – "Golden Aquarius" compact. Legend reads: AQUARIUS, January 21 – February 19. Yours is a friendly spirit. Open-minded. Original. Altruistic. You believe in the power of ideas. You want to change lives. And change the world. You see the big picture. Your color is blue like the limitless sky.

Right – "Golden Aries" compact. Legend reads: ARIES, March 21 – April 20. Yours is a courageous spirit. Energetic. Exciting. Spontaneous. You're a positive thinker. Gifted with the capacity to dream and to fall in love at first sight. You make things happen. Yours is the color of passion, red.

Left – "Golden Scorpio" compact. Legend reads: SCORPIO, October 21 – November 22. You're a passionate idealist. Intense. Emotional. Magnetic. You seek to live life fully. And you understand the depths of the heart. You are tempestuous in love. Disarmingly unpredictable. Your colors are crimson and burgundy, the colors of excitement.

Center– "Golden Sagittarius" compact. Legend reads: SAGITTARIUS, November 23 – December 21. Yours is an optimistic spirit. Independent. Adventurous. Free. You are direct, open and impetuous. Thriving on changes and challenges. you have a sense of honor and your spirit is absolutely irrepressible. Your color is purple the color of royalty.

Right – "Golden Capricorn" compact. Legend reads: CAPRICORN, December 22 – January 20. Yours is a confident spirit. Ambitious. Patient. Loyal. You have a strong sense of purpose. And a belief in our own abilities. You can be elusive yet your feelings run deep. Your colors are dark green, brown, and gray, the colors of nature.

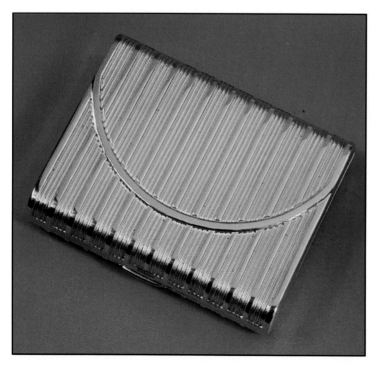

Estee Lauder ribbed oblong "Golden Envelope" compact, 1993, interior contains framed mirror, powder well, and puff, 3" x 2¼". $55.00 – 75.00.

Katherine Baumann round black, white, and red crystal Minnie Mouse compact. Minnie wears red crystal hat and holds a mirror in her hand, interior reveals powder compartment, framed mirror, and puff marked Stratton, 3" dia., case made by Stratton, England, for Katherine Baumann. Suggested retail price $290.00 – 362.50.

Katherine Baumann round black, white, and red crystal smiling Mickey Mouse compact, interior reveals powder compartment, framed mirror and puff marked Stratton, 3" dia., case made by Stratton, England, for Katherine Baumann. Suggested retail price $290.00 – 362.50.

Katherine Baumann round black, white, and red crystal Betty Boop compact, interior reveals framed mirror, powder compartment, and puff marked Stratton, 3" dia., case made by Stratton, England, for Katherine Baumann. Suggested retail price $290.00 – 362.50.

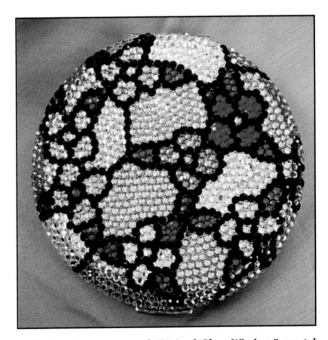

Katherine Baumann round "Stained Glass Window," crystal studded compact, lid beautifully decorated with red, pink, white, blue, green, and light blue crystal design, interior reveals framed mirror, powder compartment, and puff marked Stratton, 3" dia., case made by Stratton, England, for Katherine Baumann. Suggested retail price $250.00 – 312.50.

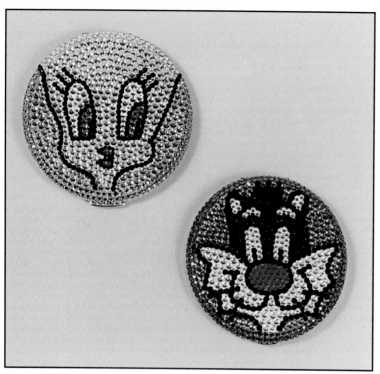

Two Madelin Beth round crystal compacts. Left: Yellow, pink, blue, white, red, and black crystal Tweety Bird compact; right: blue, black, red, and white Sylvester compact, interiors have puffs, mirrors, and powder wells, each 2¾" dia. $225.00 – 275.00.

Lancome square limited edition "Le Cherubim" goldtone compact, black enamel lid decorated with goldtone angel, 2¼" sq. $40.00 – 50.00.

Clinique 1998 mini silvertone "Compact Kisses," lid decorated with tic-tac-toe board, two red hearts, and two silvertone X's, complete with gray moiré, red-lined drawstring pouch, 1¾" sq. $25.00 – 35.00.

Clinique 1999 mini square silvertone compact, lid has four rows of four small indentations, indentations on bottom row have the millennium year "2000" in high relief, interior reveals framed mirror, puff, and powder well, complete with silvertone fabric carrying case, 1¾" sq. $25.00 – 35.00.

Debbie J. Palmer round goldtone "Quilted Compact," hatchmarks enhanced with crystals, black tassel, interior reveals powder well, puff, and framed mirror, 2¼" dia. $45.00 – 55.00.

Top: Debbie J. Palmer goldtone "Perfect Presents" pill case, lid decorated with repousse bow, 1990s, 1¾" dia., $40.00 – 50.00; bottom: square goldtone "Perfect Presents" compact, lid decorated with repoussé bow, 1990s, 2¼" x 2¼". $45.00 – 60.00.

Debbie J. Palmer round brushed silvertone "Odyssey compact," lid beautifully decorated with pastel-colored crystals, interior reveals mirror, puff, and pressed powder well, Nieman Marcus exclusive, 2¼" dia. $50.00 – 65.00.

Debbie J. Palmer round goldtone Cameo compact, lid decorated with cameo of two female profiles, black tassel on side of thumbpiece, interior reveals mirror, powder well, sifter, and puff, Nieman Marcus exclusive, 2¼" dia. $50.00 – 65.00.

Debbie J. Palmer brushed goldtone "Only Hearts" compact, heart-shaped compact's lid centered with repoussé keyhole, golden key on side of thumbpiece, interior reveals pressed powder well, mirror, and puff, 2¾" x 2¾". $30.00 – 45.00.

Debbie J. Palmer round brushed goldtone "Star" compact, golden stars attached near thumbpiece, interior reveals mirror, puff, and powder well, 1990s, 2¼" dia. $45.00 – 55.00.

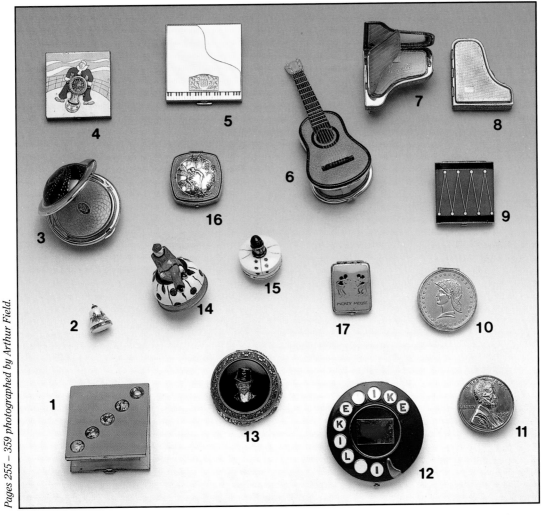

Pages 255 – 359 photographed by Arthur Field.

1 Lampl light blue enamel compact with five colorful three-dimensional scenes from "Alice in Wonderland" encased in plastic domes on lid. $250.00 – 350.00.

2 Sterling silver white cloisonné mini bell-shaped compact decorated with painted holly; diminishing mirror and loop for chain. $500.00 – 700.00.

3 Kigu "Flying Saucer" metal compact with blue celestial scene on both sides (shown open). $400.00 – 600.00.

4 Square goldtone compact with sailor steering ship and copper steering wheel mounted on lid. $80.00 – 120.00.

5 Volupté "Collector's Item" metal compact with grand piano on lid and raised keys on keyboard. $150.00 – 200.00.

6 Samaral brown leather and brass compact designed to resemble guitar with strings; Spain. $800.00 – 1,200.00.

7, 8 Pygmalion textured-brass compact designed to resemble grand piano; collapsible legs; England (7 shown open, 8 shown closed). $350.00 – 450.00.

9 Charbert red, white, and blue enamel "Drumstick" compact, c. 1930s. $150.00 – 200.00.

10 Elgin American silvered-metal compact designed to resemble coin. $150.00 – 200.00.

11 Avon copper-colored lip gloss container designed to resemble Lincoln penny. $40.00 – 60.00.

12 Red, white, and blue compact designed to resemble telephone dial with slogan "I Like Ike" imprinted on lid; red map of the United States on lid. $200.00 – 250.00.

13 Evans "Charlie McCarthy" mesh vanity pouch with raised Charlie McCarthy head on black enamel lid. $250.00 – 350.00.

14 Orange, blue, and white lusterware compact with colorful Asian figure mounted upright on screw-top lid. NPA.

15 French ivory mini compact with raised Bobby's head mounted upright on screw-top lid. NPA.

16 Djer-Kiss silvered-metal vanity case with raised nymphs on lid; powder and rouge compartments c. 1920s. $100.00 – 150.00.

17 Orange enamel mini compact with painted intaglio figures of Mickey and Minnie Mouse; powder sifter. $300.00 – 350.00.

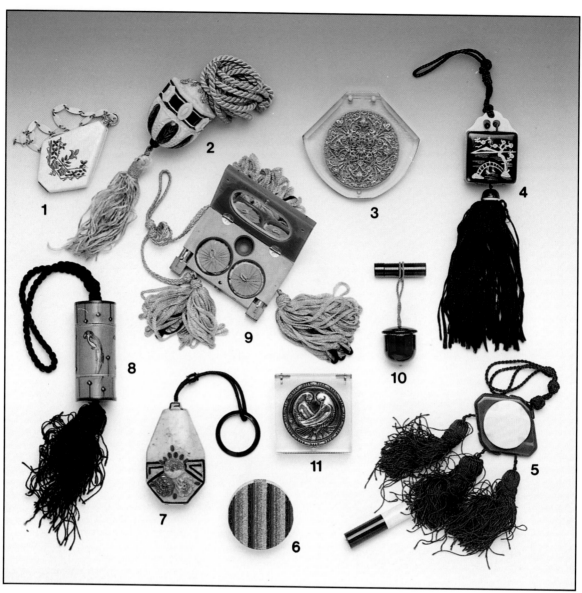

1 French ivory compact with painted red and green flowers; carrying chain made of plastic links; c. 1920s. $175.00 – 225.00.

2 French ivory and green molded plastic dual-opening vanity case with carrying chain and tassel; powder and rouge compartments; c. 1920s. $300.00 – 350.00.

3 Yellow Lucite compact with filigree metal lid, c. 1920s. $150.00 – 200.00.

4 Ebony and French ivory dual-opening vanity case with Asian scene on lid; powder and rouge compartments; carrying cord with lipstick concealed in tassel; c. 1920s. $250.00 – 300.00.

5 Blue and ivory plastic screw-top compact; carrying cord with lipstick concealed in tassel; c. 1920s. $350.00 – 550.00.

6 Multi-color striped glitter plastic compact, c. 1920s. $50.00 – 75.00.

7 Marbleized yellow plastic vanity case with raised multicolored flower on lid; ring carrying cord with ojime button; c. 1920s. $250.00 – 350.00.

8 Pink bolster-shaped vanity case decorated with painted parrot; carrying cord with lipstick concealed in tassel; c. 1920s. $350.00 – 450.00.

9 Oblong green plastic vanity case striped with ebony; compartments for powder, rouge, and slide-out lipsticks; tassel and tasseled carrying cord; c. 1920s (shown open). $350.00 – 450.00.

10 Brown plastic tango chain screw-top compact designed as an acorn; lipstick attached by gold cord. $125.00 – 200.00.

11 Blue Lucite compact with sterling repoussé medallion of two doves on lid. $150.00 – 175.00.

1 Gilded-metal embossed vanity case with multicolored intaglio decoration; prong set with red stones and pearls; compartments for powder and lipsticks; France, turn of the century (shown open). $200.00 – 275.00.

2 Oblong gilded-metal embossed vanity case with multicolored intaglio decoration; prong set with red stones and painted cloisonné inserts; powder and rouge compartments and sliding lipstick; France, turn of the century. $200.00 – 275.00.

3 Goldtone embossed compact with multicolored intaglio decoration; prong set with green stones; loop for chain; France, turn of the century. $100.00 – 150.00.

4 Gilded-metal embossed mini compact with multicolored intaglio decoration and lid set with blue stones and pearls; France, turn of the century. $100.00 – 150.00.

5 Gilded-metal embossed compact with multicolored intaglio decoration and enameled painted lid set with blue cabochon stones; France, turn of the century. $150.00 – 250.00.

6 Horseshoe-shaped gilded-metal embossed vanity case with multicolored intaglio decoration; prong set with purple stones; carrying chain and compartments for powder and lipsticks; France, turn of the century. $200.00 – 300.00.

7, 8 Oblong gilded-metal embossed vanity case with multicolored intaglio decoration; prong set with blue stones and painted disk; powder and rouge compartments; France, turn of the century. (7 shown closed, 8 shown open). $225.00 – 275.00.

9 Goldtone mini compact with multicolored intaglio decoration; prong set with purple stones; France, turn of the century. $125.00 – 175.00.

10 Gilded-metal embossed vanity case with multicolored intaglio decoration with cameo-like disk on lid; prong set with pink stones; France, turn of the century. $200.00 – 250.00.

11 Gilded-metal embossed compact with multicolored intaglio decoration; prong set with blue stones and pearls; loop for chain; France, turn of the century. $150.00 – 200.00.

12 Goldtone embossed vanity case with multicolored intaglio decoration; prong set with red and turquoise stones; tassel and carrying chain; France, turn of the century. $400.00 – 600.00.

13 Goldtone filigree miniature compact; prong set with turquoise stones; Continental, 19th century. $150.00 – 225.00.

14 Goldtone enameled compact with red, green, and goldtone enamel back and painted enamel scene on lid; Continental, turn of the century. $150.00 – 200.00.

15 Horseshoe-shaped gilded-metal embossed vanity case with multicolored intaglio decoration; openings for powder and rouge; prong set with blue stones, pearls, and painted disk; France, turn of the century. $200.00 – 275.00.

1 *Ebony wooden compact shaped as castanets with metal Paris ensignia on lid and orange tasseled carrying cord; France. $250.00 – 350.00.*

2 *Yellow bolster-shaped vanity case with silhouette and black polka dots; carrying cord with lipstick concealed in tassel; c. 1920s. $400.00 – 500.00.*

3 *Platé "Trio-ette" rose cameo molded-plastic vanity case shaped as hand mirror; powder on one side, rouge on the other; lipstick concealed in handle; c. 1940s. $125.00 – 250.00.*

4 *Crystal Lucite compact with polished metal cut-out of man taking siesta next to cactus plant, c. 1940s. $60.00 – 80.00.*

5 *Ebony plastic rhinestone-studded compact with screw top, c. 1920s. $60.00 – 80.00.*

6 *Red beetle-shaped novelty plastic compact. $80.00 – 125.00.*

7 *Oval red plastic compact set with rhinestones; carrying cord and tassel; c. 1920s. $250.00 – 350.00.*

8 *Pink Lucite-rimmed sterling silver compact with sterling hinge and catch. $150.00 – 200.00.*

9 *Venine blue plastic vanity case with goldtone filigree lid; compartments for powder and rouge. $60.00 – 80.00.*

10 *A. Bourjois & Co. "Novita" ebony plastic compact with canal scene painted on lid; fancy braided carrying cord with two lipsticks and perfume containers concealed in tassels; France. $700.00 – 900.00.*

1 Green and goldtone embossed oblong compact with painting of two girls in disk on lid; Italy, turn of the century. $125.00 – 175.00.

2 Vermeil etched silver and blue enamel compact, Italy, turn of the century. $300.00 – 400.00.

3 Silver etched compact with colorful enamel design on lid and French ivory cut-out; Continental, turn of the century. $250.00 – 350.00.

4 Octagonal champlevé, gilded and embossed compact with two shades of blue; Italy, turn of the century. $125.00 – 150.00.

5 Red and goldtone champlevé compact shaped as hand mirror; lipstick concealed in handle; red cabochon lipstick thumbpiece; Italy, turn of the century. $400.00 – 500.00.

6 Shaded red and green enamel goldtone compact designed to resemble purse; Italy, turn of the century. $150.00 – 250.00.

7 Gilded embossed compact with colorful enameled coats-of-arms on lid; Italy, turn of the century. $150.00 – 250.00.

8 Shaded red enamel goldtone compact with painted flowers on lid; Italy, turn of the century. $100.00 – 125.00.

9 Antiqued goldtone envelope compact with blue stone thumbpiece; Italy. $125.00 – 175.00.

10 Scalloped antique goldtone compact with blue enamel encircling French ivory miniature on lid; Italy, turn of the century. $150.00 – 225.00.

11, 12, 13 Vermeil engraved silver compact, lipstick, and comb set decorated with blue enamel and multicolored painted scenes; red cabochon lipstick thumbpiece; Italy, turn of the century. $600.00 – 700.00.

14 Goldtone embossed compact designed to resemble pocket watch; lid with Roman numerals and painted country scene; Italy, turn of the century. $200.00 – 250.00.

1 Evans blue enamel tango chain vanity with painted cloisonné lid; powder and rouge compartments (shown open). $150.00 – 200.00.

2 La Mode gilded metal cloisonné compact with painted flowers on lid; sliding lipstick. $100.00 – 150.00.

3 Gilded-metal engraved compact with blue enamel lid and rhinestones on outer edge; metal "Saint Genesius, Guide My Destiny" medallion on lid; Continental. $200.00 – 250.00.

4 Sterling silver hallmarked light blue cloisonné ball-shaped compact; loop for chain, Germany. $200.00 – 300.00.

5 Square, embossed silver, lavender cloisonné vanity case with painted basket of flowers on lid; goldtone interior with compartments for powder, rouge, and lipsticks; carrying chain. $250.00 – 350.00.

6 Shagreen tango chain compact with initial set with marcasites, c. 1930s. $250.00 – 300.00.

7 Richard Hudnut "Deauville" blue cloisonné tango chain vanity; metal mirror and powder and rouge compartments; lipstick attached to finger ring chain; c. 1920s. $200.00 – 250.00.

8 Green cloisonné goldtone vanity case with openings for powder and rouge; Austria, 19th century (shown open). $175.00 – 275.00.

9 Sterling silver hallmarked blue enamel vanity case with painted roses; adjacent openings for powder and rouge. $250.00 – 350.00.

10 Round nickel-silver red and black enamel compact; metal mirror and compartments for powder sifter and rouge; finger ring carrying chain; c. 1920s. $125.00 – 150.00.

11 Sterling silver hallmarked green cloisonné compact; lipstick in upper section; Germany. $250.00 – 300.00.

12 Sterling silver hallmarked yellow cloisonné compact with cutout silver medallion on lid; finger ring chain; Austria. $250.00 – 300.00.

13 Engine-turned nickel-silver compact/cigarette case/lighter combination with green enamel lid. $200.00 – 300.00.

14 Red and black champlevé and gilded vanity case with powder and rouge compartments and through handle. $150.00 – 200.00.

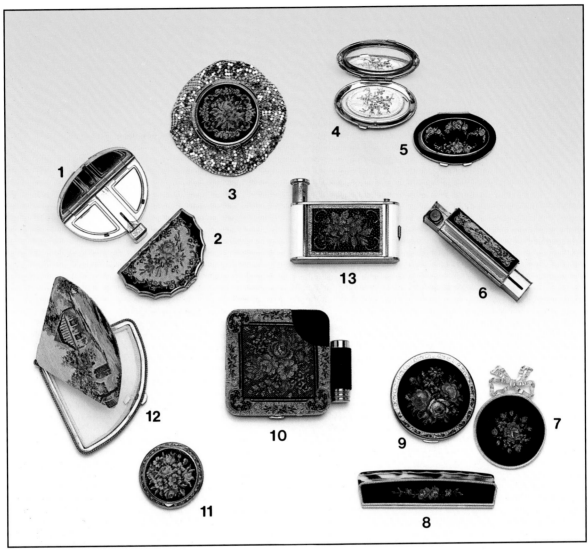

1 Petit point half-moon-shaped goldtone vanity case with powder and rouge compartments and sliding lipstick, c. 1930s (shown open). $100.00 – 150.00.

2 Petit point scalloped half-moon-shaped goldtone vanity case, c. 1930s. $80.00 – 125.00.

3 Evans petit point goldtone mesh vanity bag with metal mirror and powder and rouge compartments in lid, c. 1940 – 1950s. $150.00 –175.00.

4, 5 Rowenta oval enameled petit point compacts (4, brown enamel, shown opened; 5, black enamel, shown closed). $30.00 – 50.00.

6 Quinto petit point compact with sliding lipstick and perfume container (shown open). $125.00 – 175.00.

7, 8, 9 Petit point gilt mirror, comb, and compact set, Austria. $75.00 – 100.00.

10 Petit point goldtone compact backed in black faille with tandem lipstick. $150.00 – 225.00.

11 Petit point lid, rim, and back of round compact with powder sifter. $80.00 – 120.00.

12 Triangular petit point compact with swivel mirror. $150.00 – 175.00.

13 White enamel metal petit point compact with petit point lid designed to resemble camera; lipstick at top, cigarette case in back; West Germany. $150.00 – 200.00.

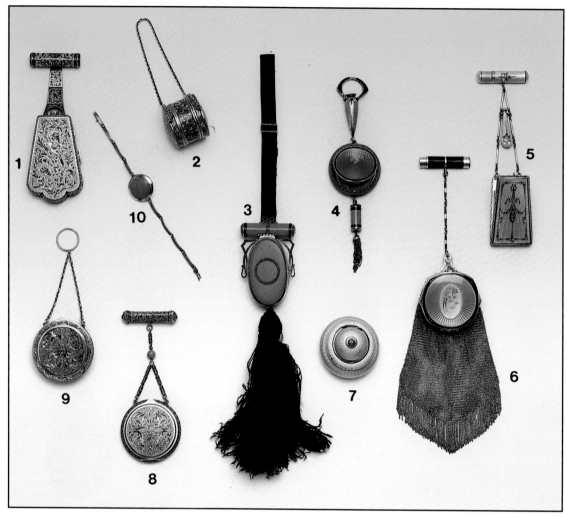

1 Sterling silver hallmarked green enamel vanity case with gold-tone interior; lipstick attached to vanity by enameled links; embossed perfume knob at base of links; partitions for powder, rouge, and cigarettes; Austria, turn of the century. $700.00 – 900.00.

2 Blue flowered enamel two-sided vanity case with powder on one side and rouge on the other; wrist chain; Continental, turn of the century. $250.00 – 350.00.

3 Sterling silver hallmarked salmon-colored plastic vanity case with marcasite trim; tandem lipstick and powder and rouge compartments; tassel and marcasite-decorated carrying cord; Continental. $1,500.00 – 2,000.00.

4 Foster & Bailey blue cloisonné vanity case suspended from enameled perfume container; powder and rouge compartments; lipstick attached at base; tassel and black enameled finger ring chain. $2,500.00 – 3,000.00.

5 Green cloisonné silver tango chain vanity with pink roses; pow-der and rouge compartments; lipstick attached by two enameled link chains with perfume suspended between the two chains. $700.00 – 900.00.

6 Foster & Bailey sterling silver mesh tango chain vanity bag with light blue cloisonné lid with painted flowers; powder and rouge compartments; lipstick attached by enamel chain; turn of the century. $900.00 – 1,200.00.

7 Peach copper and cloisonné vanity case with two-tier openings for powder and rouge; Germany, 19th century. $350.00 – 450.00.

8 Sterling silver hallmarked green champlevé tango chain with bar-brooch lipstick; Austria, turn of the century. $600.00 – 800.00.

9 Sterling silver hallmarked green champlevé compact with fin-ger ring chain; Austria, turn of the century. $300.00 – 500.00.

10 Sterling silver hallmarked blue cloisonné compact/bracelet with enameled links; Germany, 19th century. $750.00 – 1,000.00.

262

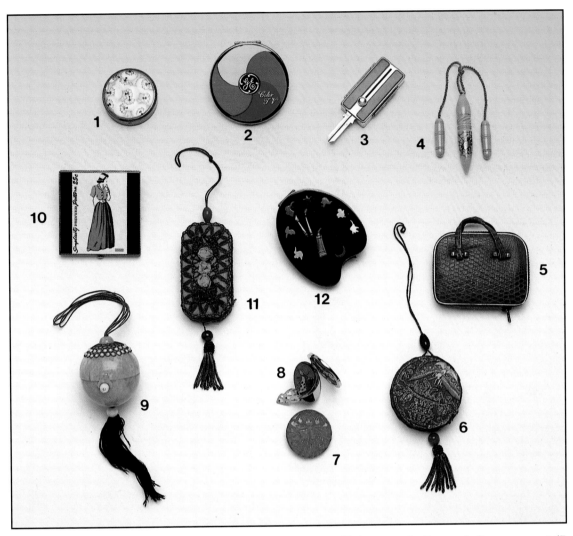

1 Coty goldtone compact with Coty trademark (stylized white puffs on an orange background) on lid. $60.00 – 80.00.

2 Elgin American goldtone compact with colorful enamel swirls and "G.E. Color T.V." logo on lid. $175.00 – 225.00.

3 Segal red enamel nickel-silver compact with sliding key blank in lid, c. 1930s. $225.00 – 300.00.

4 Turquoise plastic screw-top perfume container with lipstick and eye make-up containers suspended from gold cord. $100.00. – 150.00.

5 Brown lizard zippered compact designed to resemble suitcase with carrying handles. $125.00 – 175.00.

6 Vantine's blue silk compact decorated with embroidery and gold thread; beaded tassel and carrying cord with ojime bead; c. 1920s. $100.00 – 175.00.

7, 8 Molded orange plastic round clip-on compact (7 shown closed, 8 shown open). $100.00 – 150.00.

9 Yellow marbleized plastic ball compact decorated with faux pearls; tassel and carrying cord. $350.00 – 450.00.

10 Wadsworth compact with "Simplicity Printed Pattern 25 cents" on lid. $225.00 – 400.00.

11 Pink satin vanity case with gold braid; powder and rouge compartments; carrying cord with ojime bead and beaded tassel; c. 1920s. $100.00 – 175.00.

12 Volupté black enamel goldtone compact designed to resemble artist's palette with raised paint tube, brushes, and colors on lid. $350.00 – 450.00.

1 White enamel tango chain vanity case with country scene on lid; lipstick attached by two link chains; powder sifter and rouge compartments; original fitted presentation box. $300.00 – 400.00.

2, 3 Embossed vermeil compact and lipstick set with enameled country scene on lid; Italy, turn of the century. $125.00 – 150.00; $350.00 – 450.00.

4 Octagonal silvered-metal blue cloisonné vanity case with roses; powder sifter and rouge compartment and through handle; c. 1920s. $200.00 – 225.00.

5, 6 Antiqued goldtone oval embossed vanity case with cloisonné lid, carrying chain, and compartments for powder sifter, rouge, lipstick, and coins (5 shown open, 6 shown closed). $500.00 – 600.00.

7 Lavender cloisonné silvered-metal vanity case with blue flowers; powder sifter and rouge compartment; swivel handle. $100.00 – 150.00.

8 Green enamel tango chain vanity case with flowers on lid and lipstick; powder sifter and rouge compartment; double-link chain; c. 1920s. $200.00 – 250.00.

9 La Mode blue cloisonné goldtone vanity case with metal mirror; compartments for powder and rouge, and two sliding lipsticks, one on either side. $100.00 – 150.00.

10 La Mode green cloisonné goldtone vanity case with picture locket in lid; and metal mirror, compartment for powder, and two sliding lipsticks, one on either side (shown open). $100.00 – 150.00.

11 Silvered-metal and enameled vanity case with painted raised tree and house on lid; engine-turned link chain; compartments for powder, rouge, and lipsticks; c. 1930s. $150.00 – 250.00.

12 Sterling silver blue cloisonné vanity case with pink flowers; openings on either side for powder and rouge; two loops for chain. $175.00 – 275.00.

13 Black enamel goldtone vanity case with pink rose; two sides open (one for powder, the other for rouge); carrying cord with lipstick concealed in tassel. $125.00 – 150.00.

1, 2 Richard Hudnut "Deauville" vanity case with red and black enamel profiles on lid; powder and rouge compartments; lipstick holder attached to compact and finger ring; c. 1920s (1 shown open, 2 shown closed). $250.00 – 300.00.

3 Richard Hudnut "Deauville" vanity case with white and green enamel profiles on lid; powder and rouge compartments; original fitted presentation box; c. 1920s. $200.00 – 300.00.

4 Evans "Tap Sift" white cloisonné vanity case with black stylized "skyscraper" motif and key pattern around rim; powder sifter and rouge compartment; c. 1920s. $125.00 – 150.00.

5 Evans "Tap Sift" green cloisonné tango chain vanity case with black stylized "skyscraper" motif; powder sifter and rouge compartment; lipstick attached by double chain; c. 1920s. $150.00 – 250.00.

6 Richard Hudnut "le Debut" silvered-metal vanity case with powder and rouge compartments; lipstick attached to compact and finger ring; c. 1920s. $150.00 – 250.00.

7 Art Deco abstract cloisonné vanity case with link carrying chain; compartments for powder, rouge, and lipstick. $200.00 – 300.00.

8 Silvaray Art Nouveau red enamel metal compact. $80.00 – 100.00.

9 Bree green enamel vanity case with metal profile on lid; powder slide and compartments for rouge and lipstick; c. 1930s. $100.00 – 125.00.

10 Art Nouveau silvered half-moon-shaped enameled vanity case with multicolored swirls; goldtone interior, link carrying chain, and compartments for powder, rouge, and lipstick. $150.00 – 250.00.

1 Cylindrical etched-glass compact/perfume container with goldtone compact on top; probably France (shown open). $500.00 – 600.00.
2 Tiffany & Co. gold octagonal two-sided tango-chain mini compact with floral design around rim; turn of the century. $1,000.00 – 1,500.00.
3 Octagonal gold compact/bracelet with engraved lid and band. $500.00 – 600.00.
4 Gold engraved mini compact shaped as hand mirror; loop for chain. $300.00 – 400.00.
5 Gold mesh vanity bag with sapphire cabochon thumbpieces and fringes set with pearls; carrying chain; c. 1920s. $2,500.00 – 3,500.00.
6 Etched-glass compact/perfume container with goldtone lids, glass striped with blue enamel; carrying ring (shown open). $500.00 – 600.00.

Compact with three enameled shields on screw-top lid, suspended from dance-program book; "Bal Kolejowy, Stanislawowie, 8 lutego, 1908" in goldtone on cover; white velvet fringed belt hook; Poland. NPA.

Embossed brass vanity/hatpin; 1½" round, with raised fleur-de-lis on lid; 11½" steel pin. $500.00 – 800.00.

1, 2, 3 Enameled compact shaped as hand mirror; interior and exterior mirrors and matching comb (1 shown closed, 2 shown open, 3 matching comb). $200.00 – 250.00 set; $150.00 – 200.00 compact.
4 Sterling-silver hallmarked white cloisonné miniature oval compact shaped as hand mirror with painted roses on lid; loop for chain; Continental. $300.00 – 350.00.
5 Sterling-silver hallmarked pink cloisonné enameled miniature compact shaped as hand mirror with painted flowers on lid; loop for chain; Continental. $300.00 – 350.00.
6 Brass miniature compact shaped as hand mirror with painted flowers on lid; loop for chain; Continental. $200.00 – 250.00.
7 Sterling-silver blue cloisonné miniature oval compact shaped as hand mirror; interior and exterior mirrors and loop for chain; Continental. $300.00 – 350.00.
8 Sterling-silver hallmarked yellow cloisonné miniature compact shaped as hand mirror; loop for chain; Continental. $300.00 – 350.00.
(Continued on next page.)

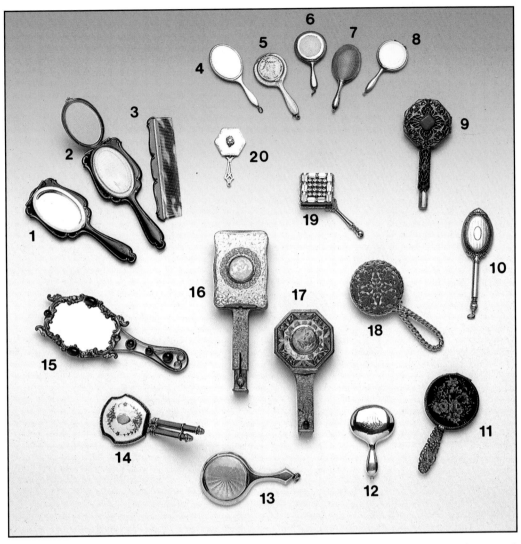

9 Octagonal silvered-filigree metal vanity case shaped as hand mirror; interior reveals powder sifter; two-sided mirror, and rouge compartment decorated with red stones; lipstick in handle. $175.00 – 225.00.

10 Sterling silver oval miniature compact shaped as hand mirror; handle unscrews to reveal lipstick and perfume containers; loop for chain; Continental. $300.00 – 350.00.

11 Petit point compact shaped as hand mirror; filigree handle and interior and exterior mirrors; Austria. $60.00 – 80.00.

12 Sterling silver miniature oval compact shaped as hand mirror; exterior diminishing mirror and loop for chain; Continental. $250.00 – 300.00.

13 Vermeil sterling silver hallmarked compact shaped as hand mirror with pink cloisonné lid and exterior mirror; interior lid incorporates writing slate; loop for chain. $350.00 – 400.00.

14 White cloisonné compact shaped as hand mirror with painted flowers on lid; fold-over handle contains compartments for lipstick and eye makeup; interior and exterior mirrors. $350.00 – 450.00.

15 Goldtone compact shaped as hand mirror decorated with colored cabochon stones; interior and exterior mirrors; France. $300.00 – 500.00.

16 Blue and white champlevé goldtone compact shaped as hand mirror with painting of man and woman on lid; lipstick in handle and blue cabochon thumbpiece; Italy. $400.00 – 500.00.

17 Red and white champlevé octagonal goldtone compact shaped as hand mirror with painting of girl on swing on lid; lipstick in handle and red cabochon thumbpiece; Italy. $400.00 – 500.00.

18 Goldtone compact shaped as hand mirror with green enamel-decorated lid; interior and exterior mirrors; France. $100.00 – 125.00.

19 Art Deco miniature compact shaped as hand mirror with rhinestones on lid; interior and exterior mirrors. $75.00 – 100.00.

20 Sterling silver, hexagonal mini compact shaped as hand mirror with coat-of-arms on lid; loop for chain; Continental. $150.00 – 175.00.

1 Antique goldtone vanity case with faux baroque pearls and blue stones on filigree lids; opening on either side for powder and rouge; pearl-decorated tassel and braided finger ring chain. $300.00 – 400.00.

2 Antique goldtone chatelette; compact with lipstick case, coin holder, and belt hanger decorated on both sides with filigree overlay set with aquamarine-colored stones; Continental. $350.00 – 450.00.

3 Pierced silvered-metal bolster-shaped necessaire with onyx filigree disk set with blue stones and marcasites on lid; tassel and carrying chain (shown open). $400.00 – 600.00.

4 Pattie Duette "Vivaudou" antique goldtone-filigree vanity bag set with blue stones; vanity case on inside hinge; lined interior; carrying chain with lipstick concealed in tassel; Continental, turn of the century (shown open). NPA.

5 Antique goldtone-filigree vanity case with multicolored stones on lid; opening on either side for powder and rouge, sliding lipsticks at sides, and perfume vial at top; tassel and carrying cord; Continental, turn of the century. $350.00 – 450.00.

6 Antique goldtone filigree oval vanity case with stones and center cabochon stone; braid carrying chain with lipstick concealed in tassel; Austria, turn of the century. $275.00 – 350.00.

7 Antique goldtone vanity bag with blue stones and pearls; cover incorporates compact with onyx disk set with blue stones; tassel and carrying chain; silk back; Continental, turn of the century. $450.00 – 650.00.

8 Antique goldtone tango-chain vanity bag compact with green stones; tassel and filigree lipstick holder; silk back; Continental, turn of the century. $350.00 – 450.00.

9 Gilded filigree compact with turquoise stones; butterflies suspended from neck chain. $350.00 – 450.00.

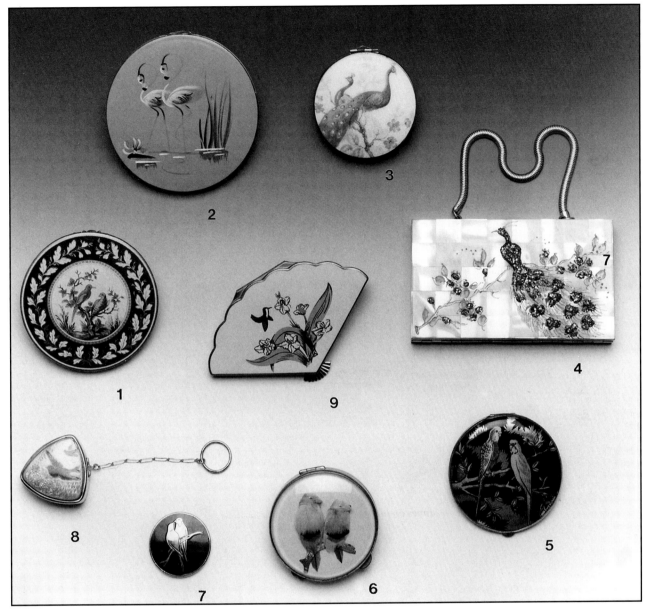

1 Stratton goldtone compact with scenic transfer on lid, c. 1950s. $40.00 – 60.00.

2 Rex Fifth Avenue painted, enameled compact with two pink flamingoes on a turquoise background. $75.00 – 100.00.

3 Schildkraut goldtone cloisonné compact with two blue peacocks on a white background. $30.00 – 50.00.

4 Marhill mother-of-pearl carryall with painted peacock and glitter on lid. $200.00 – 250.00.

5 Gwenda goldtone enameled painted foil compact, England. $80.00 – 100.00.

6 Goldtone compact with two pink and gray simulated feathered birds enclosed in a plastic dome. $150.00 – 200.00.

7 Blue enameled silvertone mini-flapjack compact, c. 1930s. $50.00 – 70.00.

8 Goldtone triangular enameled compact with two green birds in flight on a light blue background and finger ring chain. $80.00 – 120.00.

9 Wadsworth goldtone hand-painted yellow enamel fan-shaped compact, c. 1940s. $80.00 – 100.00.

1 Volupté goldtone hand-shaped compact, c. 1940s. $100.00 – 125.00.

2 Volupté goldtone "faux diamond engagement ring" hand-shaped compact, c. 1940s. $200.00 – 250.00.

3 Volupté goldtone "manicured" hand-shaped compact, c. 1940s. $150.00 – 175.00.

4 Volupté goldtone "lace gloved" hand-shaped compact, c. 1940s. $300.00 – 450.00.

5 Volupté goldtone hand-shaped compact, c. 1940s, shown open.

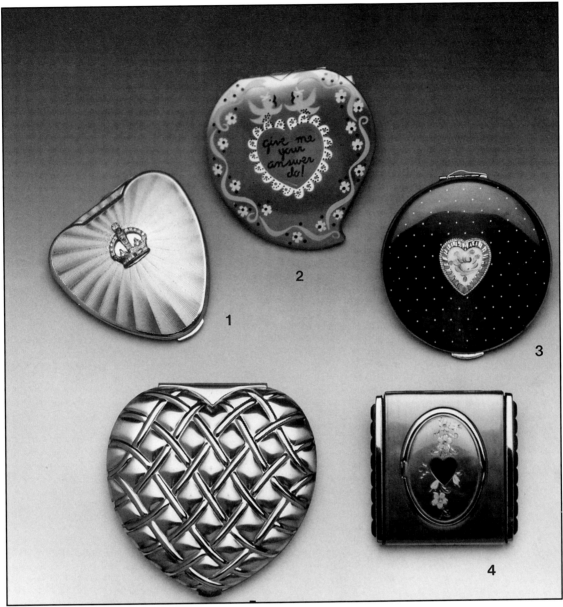

1 Kigu "Cherie" goldtone heart-shaped compact with jeweled crown on lid; England, c. 1940 – 1950s. $50.00 – 80.00.

2 Elgin American stylized heart-shaped enameled compact with "Give me your answer do!" on lid, c. 1940 – 1950s. $80.00 – 120.00.

3 Kigu goldtone blue enamel compact with heart-shaped enameled flower on lid; England, c. 1940–50s. $50.00 – 75.00.

4 Marathon goldtone compact with heart on lid; lid opens to reveal a locket; compact opens by pressing the plastic side panels. $60.00 – 80.00.

5 Evans pink and yellow goldtone basket weave compact, c. 1946. $150.00 – 225.00.

1 Goldtone heart-shaped compact with brocade lid, c. 1930s. $40.00 – 60.00.

2 American Maid goldtone heart-shaped compact with engraved lid (shown open). $40.00 – 60.00.

3 La Mode silver-plated heart-shaped compact. $50.00 – 75.00.

4 Enameled goldtone heart-shaped lock-motif compact. $150.00 – 200.00.

5 Engraved silver-plated heart-shaped compact with carrying chain. $75.00 – 100.00.

6 Matte goldtone mini compact. $30.00 – 60.00.

7 Goldtone heart-shaped compact with purple orchid inlaid in black plastic on lid. $60.00 – 90.00.

8 Evans goldtone heart-shaped compact with lipstick concealed in black tassel and black carrying cord, c. 1940s. $250.00 – 350.00.

1 *Amita damascene compact inlaid with gold and silver view of Mt. Fuji capped in silver on black matte-finish lid; Japan, c. 1920s. $100.00 – 150.00.*

2 *Gilt inlaid vanity case with carrying chain, mirror, coin holder, and powder compartment; Japan, c. 1920s (shown open). $225.00 – 275.00.*

3 *Damascene compact inlaid with gold and silver view of Mt. Fuji capped in silver on black matte-finish lid; complete with hinged, fitted presentation box; K24. $150.00 – 200.00.*

4 *Damascene compact black matte-finish inlaid with gilt Egyptian scene. $75.00 – 100.00.*

5 *Damascene vanity case, with gold and silver view of Mt. Fuji capped in silver on black matte-finish lid; carrying chain and compartments for powder, lipstick, and rouge; K24. $150.00 – 200.00.*

6 *Damascene compact with elaborate gold inlaid pagoda scene on front lid; bamboo inlaid on back lid; loop for chain; c. 1920s. $250.00 – 300.00.*

7 *Amita damascene compact with gold and silver floral motif on black matte-finish lid; Japan, c. 1920s. $100.00 – 150.00.*

8 *Damascene-style gilt compact with scene of man and horse on lid, c. 1930s. $40.00 – 60.00.*

1 *Silver-plated vanity case with white pearlized miniature of woman walking a dog on black background mounted on the front lid; carrying chain; compartments for powder, lipstick, rouge, and compartment that "May be used for either Cigarettes, Money, Calling Card or Rosary;" c. 1920s. $150.00 – 225.00.*

2 *Black enamel silvered-metal tango-chain vanity case with silvered Scottie dogs; compartment for powder, metal mirror opens to reveal rouge; lipstick attached with a chain; c. 1920 – 1930s. $150.00 – 225.00.*

3 *Sabor gilt and plastic compact with Lucite dome enclosing two kissing poodles made of thread; France, c. 1930s. $60.00 – 80.00.*

4 *Small blue enamel vanity case with Scottie dog transfer; powder compartment and metal mirror opens to reveal rouge compartment; c. 1920 – 1930s. $30.00 – 50.00.*

5 *Zell Fifth Avenue goldtone compact with poodle motif set with red cabochon stones; lipstick in a fitted black grosgrain case, c. 1940 – 1950s. $125.00 – 175.00.*

6 *Sterling ¾" square compact with chain attached to a ring mounted with a hunting dog, c. 1920s. $200.00 – 250.00.*

7 *Sterling black enamel compact with small plastic dome enclosing a three-dimensional head of a Scottie; Germany, c. 1920 – 1930s. $150.00 – 200.00.*

8 *Black enamel compact with painted poodle on a white enamel disk on lid, c. 1930s. $40.00 – 60.00.*

9 *Black enamel gilt vanity case with gilt Scottie on lid; powder compartment; metal mirror lifts to reveal rouge compartment; c. 1920–30s. $50.00 – 75.00.*

10 *Plastic cigarette/compact combination with metal cut-out Scottie on lid, c. 1940s. $80.00 – 110.00.*

11 *Tooled leather bulldog-motif compact with beaded eyes and bell at base. NPA.*

1 Girey "Kamra-Pak" sparkling confetti plastic vanity case resembling camera; mirror, powder and rouge compartments, and slide-out lipstick; c. 1930 – 1940s. $50.00 – 80.00.

2 Wadsworth "Compakit" black plastic vanity case resembling camera with carrying case; powder compartment in front of case, lipstick, and cigarette lighter on top, opening for cigarettes at bottom of case; c. 1940s (shown open). $300.00 – 350.00.

3 Same as 2, shown in carrying case. $300.00 – 350.00.

4 Kamra-Pak-style blue checkerboard enamel vanity case with compartments for powder and lipstick; reverse side opens to reveal manicure kit; c. 1940. $150.00 – 200.00.

5 Kamra-Pak-style lizard vanity case for powder and lipstick; reverse side opens to sewing kit; c. 1940s (shown open). $150.00 – 200.00.

6 Snakeskin Kamra-Pak-style vanity purse with carrying handle; compartments for lipstick, powder, rouge, comb, and coins; other side reveals manicure kit; c. 1940 – 1950s (shown open). $250.00 – 300.00.

7 Black suede Kamra-Pak-style vanity purse with carrying handle; compartments for lipstick, powder, rouge, comb, and coins; other side has cigarette compartment and lighter; c. 1940 – 1950s. $225.00 – 275.00.

8 Kamra-Pak-style black enamel vanity case with powder compartment, lipstick, and perfume bottle. $100.00 – 175.00.

9 Girey "Kamra-Pak" vanity case in blue leather with pink plastic top resembling camera; mirror, powder and rouge compartments, and slide-out lipstick; c. 1930 – 1940s. $50.00 – 75.00.

10 Multicolored tooled leather-covered Persian-design compact. $125.00 – 175.00.

11 Kamra-Pak-style blue painted enamel vanity case with girl leaning against lamp post mounted on front lid; compartments for powder, lipstick, and cigarettes; c. 1940s. $125.00 – 175.00.

12 Mireve black enamel vanity case with powder compartment, sliding lipstick, and perfume bottle; France. $125.00 – 175.00.

13 Kamra-Pak-style green painted enamel vanity case with Asian scene on front lid; compartments for powder, lipstick, and cigarettes; c. 1940s. $100.00 – 150.00.

1 Black and white mother-of-pearl vanity case with attached lipstick, c. 1930s. $50.00 – 75.00.

2 Mother-of-pearl fan-shaped miniature compact with rhinestones, Japan. $40.00 – 60.00.

3 Miniature 1"-round mother-of-pearl compact with faux ruby surrounded by rhinestones. $30.00 – 40.00.

4 Volupté mother-of-pearl "Swinglok" carryall, c. 1940 – 1950s. $150.00 – 200.00.

5, 6, 7 Marhill mother-of-pearl set with compact, comb, and lipstick/mirror. $75.00 – 100.00.

8 Stylized mother-of-pearl checkerboard compact designed as a book. $50.00 – 75.00.

9 Petit point bordered mother-of-pearl compact. $90.00 – 100.00.

10 Max Factor mother-of-pearl lipstick case. $35.00 – 50.00.

11 K & K gray mother-of-pearl compact with faux sapphires and rhinestones, c. 1930 – 1940s. $50.00 – 75.00.

12 Pierced mother-of-pearl light blue and white compact with a dove mounted in center. $75.00 – 100.00.

13 Round mother-of-pearl checkerboard compact, c. 1930s. $60.00 – 75.00.

14 Volupté "Pocket watch" mother-of-pearl compact, c. 1940 – 1950s. $60.00 – 75.00.

15 Mother-of-pearl 5"-round checkerboard compact, c. 1940s. $150.00 – 200.00.

16 Maxley mother-of-pearl compact with inlaid black diagonal stripes and mother-of-pearl cameo, c. 1930s. $175.00 – 200.00.

1 *Evans petit point goldtone mesh vanity bag with metal mirror and powder and rouge compartments, c. 1940 – 1950s. $150.00 – 225.00.*

2 *Evans rhinestone and white velvet vanity bag with carrying chain, metal mirror, and powder and rouge compartments, c. 1940 – 1950s. $150.00 – 225.00.*

3 *Gilt mesh vanity bag with multicolored synthetic stones; metal mirror and powder compartment; c. 1930 – 1940s. $100.00 – 150.00.*

4 *Tapestry vanity pouch with floral pattern on lid, c. 1920 – 1930s. $40.00 – 60.00.*

5 *Rex gilt mesh vanity pouch with mini white plastic beads, c. 1930s. $40.00 – 60.00.*

6 *Pink satin vanity pochette with pink and green trim; mirror on outside base; c. 1920s. $75.00 – 100.00.*

7 *Gilt mesh vanity bag with blue synthetic stone; finger-ring chain, metal mirror, and powder compartment; c. 1930 – 1940s. $60.00 – 100.00.*

8 *Evans rhinestone and black velvet vanity bag with mirror and powder and rouge compartments, c. 1940 – 1950s. $150.00 – 225.00.*

1 Rex Fifth Avenue multicolor-striped taffeta vanity pochette with mirror on outside base, c. 1940s. $75.00 – 100.00.

2 Pale blue satin vanity pochette with a border of lace and colored beads, possibly handmade; mirror on outside base; c. 1920s. $75.00 – 100.00.

3 Silvered mesh vanity pouch with silvered repoussé disk on black enamel lid, c. 1930s. $50.00 – 75.00.

4 Beaded vanity pouch with silvered lid, c. 1930s. $50.00 – 75.00.

5 Evans oval gilt mesh, red enamel vanity pouch. $50.00 – 60.00.

6 Square leather vanity pouch with gilded lid. $60.00 – 80.00.

7 Rex Fifth Avenue navy blue taffeta vanity pochette with green polka dots; mirror on outside base; c. 1940s. $75.00 – 100.00.

8 Pink satin vanity pochette with lace and pink and green trim; mirror on outside base; c. 1920s. $60.00 – 80.00.

9 Brown fur vanity pouch with collapsible bottom. $50.00 – 75.00.

1 Evans black velvet vanity bag with transfer picture of apple; metal mirror and powder and rouge compartments; c. 1940–50s. $200.00 – 250.00.

2 Evans gilt mesh, white enamel vanity bag with metal mirror and powder and rouge compartments, c. 1940 – 1950s. $150.00 – 225.00.

3, 4 Evans gilt mesh vanity pouch with painted flowers on white enamel lid, c. 1930s (front and back view). $80.00 – 100.00.

5 Rex Fifth Avenue pink fabric vanity pochette; mirror at base of compact; c. 1940s. $75.00 – 100.00.

6 Volupté light blue collapsible leather vanity pouch, c. 1930s. $75.00 – 95.00.

7 Evans silvered-metal mesh vanity pouch with black enamel lid, c. 1930s. $65.00 – 80.00.

8 Gilt-mesh vanity pouch with picture of butterfly on lid, c. 1930s. $60.00 – 80.00.

9 Brown suede vanity pochette, c. 1930s. $70.00 – 90.00.

10 Blue cloisonné enameled silvered mesh vanity pouch with painted roses on lid, c. 1930s. $80.00 – 100.00.

11 Evans gilt-mesh white cloisonné vanity pouch, c. 1930s. $80.00 – 100.00.

12 Evans miniature gilt-mesh white cloisonné vanity pouch, c. 1930s. $75.00 – 95.00.

13 Evans black rhinestone vanity pouch made of bead-like material, c. 1930s (shown open). $60.00 – 80.00.

1 Blue leather one-piece horseshoe-shaped compact. $40.00 – 60.00.

2 Zell Fifth Avenue blue leather compact; sides open to reveal billfold and coin purse; c. 1940s. $70.00 – 90.00.

3 Maroon gold-tooled leather-covered horseshoe-shaped compact, possibly Spain. $60.00 – 80.00.

4 Mondaine white leather-covered book-motif compact, c. 1930s. $75.00 – 125.00.

5 Mondaine blue gold-tooled leather compact, c. 1930s. $40.00 – 80.00.

6 Alligator compact with pull-out mirror, possibly Spain. $80.00 – 100.00.

7 Square gold-tooled leather compact, possibly Italy. $30.00 – 50.00.

8 Mondaine maroon gold-tooled leather compact, c. 1930s (shown open). $60.00 – 80.00.

9 Square leather-buckle compact, c. 1950s. $60.00 – 80.00.

10 Lesco Bond Street small green alligator compact. $70.00 – 90.00.

1 Lin-Bren green leather compact with envelope-motif coin holder on lid, c. 1940s. $70.00 – 100.00.

2 Gold-tooled leather compact with Venice canal scene on lid, possibly Italy. $40.00 – 60.00.

3 Lin-Bren green leather compact/cigarette holder combination (shown with open cigarette case); U.S. Patent No. 2,471,963; c. 1940s. $150.00 – 200.00.

4 Same as 3 in black leather (shown closed). $150.00 – 200.00.

5 Same as 3 in red leather (shown open). $150.00 – 200.00.

6 Maroon leather compact with sleeve for lipstick, c. 1930s. $60.00 – 90.00.

7 Dorette small snakeskin vanity purse with zippered compartments for powder and purse; lipstick concealed in front lid. $200.00 – 250.00.

8 Lady Vanity oval blue leather compact with snap closing. $40.00 – 60.00.

9 Square alligator compact with goldtone lipstick attached to side. $80.00 – 100.00.

1 Green lizard compact with lipstick hinged on top of lid, probably Argentina. $150.00 – 200.00.

2 Gold-tooled brown leather horseshoe-shaped compact, Argentina. $50.00 – 70.00.

3 Persian gold and black compact with padded lid. $30.00 – 50.00.

4 Larue green-gold tooled leather compact designed as a book; lid contains sliding mirror (shown open). $100.00 – 125.00.

5 Brown gold-tooled leather compact, Italy. $150.00 – 200.00.

6 Mondaine green leather vanity case with carrying cord and miniature portrait of a woman within a gold-tooled border; mirror, powder, rouge, and lipstick compartments; c. 1930 – 1940s. $125.00 – 150.00.

7 Light brown lizard horseshoe-shaped purse-motif compact, Argentina. $60.00 – 80.00.

8 Round brown leather compact. $50.00 – 70.00.

9 Marcee handmade horseshoe-shaped gold-tooled leather compact. $80.00 – 100.00.

10 Persian gold and navy blue compact with padded lid and back. $50.00 – 70.00.

1 Croco square white leather zippered compact with decorative multicolored cord inset on lid, Israel. $50.00 – 75.00.

2 Navy blue horseshoe-shaped leather compact with gold-tooled fleur-de-lis on lid. $60.00 – 80.00.

3 Horseshoe-shaped gilt-metal compact with decoratively tooled leather inserts on lid and back, probably Argentina. $100.00 – 125.00.

4, 5 Mondaine tooled leather-covered case designed as a book, c. 1930 – 1940s (shown open and closed). $60.00 – 100.00.

6 Horseshoe-shaped red leather zippered compact with attached sleeve for lipstick. $80.00 – 100.00.

7 Croco round light blue zippered compact with decorative multicolored cord inset on lid, Israel. $40.00 – 60.00.

8 Fur compact with coin-purse snap closure, Argentina. $75.00 – 85.00.

9 Square gold-tooled leather compact with Venice canal scene, possibly Italy. $40.00 – 60.00.

10 Nan Co-ed zippered horseshoe-shaped compact with scene of cowboy on a horse with branding-iron marks. $100.00 – 125.00.

11 Leather compact with colorful Persian scene. $40.00 – 60.00.

12 Wadsworth cobra envelope-shaped compact. $120.00 – 150.00.

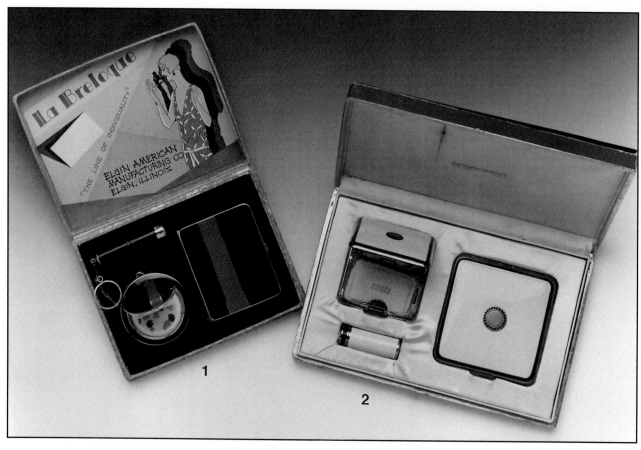

1 Elgin American "La Breloque" tango-chain red and black enameled compact; lipstick with matching cigarette case in original presentation box. $200.00 – 250.00.

2 Richard Hudnut compact in white with black enamel border; lipstick and matching cigarette case in original presentation box, c. 1920 – 1930s. $200.00 – 250.00.

1 Ronson "Fourteencase" white Art Deco enamel combination compact/lighter/cigarette case with flannel pouch and original presentation box. $200.00 – 250.00.

2 Ronson white and brown marbleized Art Deco enamel combination compact/lighter/cigarette case, c. 1930 – 1940s. $125.00 – 150.00.

3 Black enamel gilt-decorated combination compact/cigarette case; black enamel compact with white flower cloisonné disk on lid; c. 1930s. $125.00 – 150.00.

4 Ronson brown marbleized Art Deco enamel combination compact/lighter/cigarette case, c. 1930 – 1940s. $125.00 – 175.00.

5 Evans light blue enamel combination compact/lighter/cigarette case with marcasite decoration on lid of compact, c. 1930s. $150.00 – 175.00.

6 Marathon black-enamel silvered-metal combination compact/lighter/cigarette case with initialed medallion on compact lid, c. 1930 – 1940s. $150.00 – 175.00.

1 Evans bronzed-metal combination compact/cigarette case with engine-turned design and white cloisonné disk on front lid, c. 1930s. $60.00 – 80.00.

2 Richard Hudnut green and black enamel metal compact and cigarette case, 1930s. $125.00 – 175.00.

3 Ronson silvered-metal compact/cigarette case combination, c. 1930 – 1940s. $125.00 – 150.00.

4 Enameled white cloisonné side-by-side compact/cigarette case/calling card combination, c. 1930 – 1940s (shown open). $125.00 – 150.00.

5 Enameled blue cloisonné side-by-side compact/cigarette case/calling card combination, c. 1930 – 1940s. $125.00 – 150.00.

6 Marathon white enamel and silvered combination compact/lighter/cigarette case with enameled scene on lid of compact, c. 1930 – 1940s. $125.00 – 150.00.

7 Lampl black enamel goldtone compact/cigarette case combination with rhinestone and green faux gemstones on lid; compact in center flanked by compartments for cigarettes; c. 1930s. $125.00 – 150.00.

8 La Mode light and dark blue enamel compact/cigarette case with pearl-beaded removable compact centered on lid of cigarette case. $100.00 – 150.00.

1 Dunhill Vanity silvered vanity case designed to resemble cigarette lighter; powder and rouge compartments; top reveals sliding lipstick; c. 1920s. $100.00 – 150.00.

2 Dunhill Vanity goldtone vanity case designed to resemble cigarette lighter; powder and rouge compartments; top reveals sliding lipstick; U.S. Patent No. 1,639,628; c. 1920s (shown open). $100.00 – 150.00.

3 Green and black enamel metal compact/cigarette case combination (shown open). $100.00 – 125.00.

4 Maroon marbleized plastic-covered goldtone two-sided compact/cigarette case combination. $100.00 – 125.00.

5 Mascot brick-design engine-turned goldtone two-sided compact/cigarette-case combination, England. $80.00 – 100.00.

6 Tan and brown enamel metal compact/cigarette case combination with white cloisonné flowered disk on lid. $80.00 – 100.00.

7 Evans silvered green enamel Art Deco miniature compact designed to resemble cigarette lighter; top releases powder, bottom slides out to reveal lipstick. $150.00 – 200.00.

8 Ronson brown enamel goldtone compact/cigarette case combination, c. 1930 – 1940s. $125.00 – 150.00.

9 Lampl goldtone compact/cigarette case combination with rhinestones and green faux gemstones on lid of compact; compact in center flanked by compartments for cigarettes; c. 1930s. $125.00 – 150.00.

10 Black enamel combination compact/lighter/cigarette case with yellow cloisonné and painted rose on lid of compact. $200.00 – 250.00.

1 *Illinois Watch Case Co. square goldtone compact/watch combination with three initials monogrammed on lid, c. 1930s. $100.00 – 150.00.*

2 *Evans oblong silvered-metal compact/watch combination, c. 1950s. $100.00 – 150.00.*

3 *Illinois Watch Case Co. round goldtone compact/watch combination with engraved design on lid, c. 1930 – 1940s. $150.00 – 225.00.*

4 *Evans square goldtone compact/watch; lid designed to resemble trunk with straps, c. 1940s. $125.00 – 175.00.*

5 *Goldtone oblong compact/watch/coin holder combination with carrying chain, Germany. $125.00 – 150.00.*

6 *Black enamel silvered-metal vanity case/watch combination with powder and rouge compartments (shown open). $100.00 – 125.00.*

7 *Evans square goldtone engine-turned checkerboard compact/watch combination, c. 1940s. $125.00 – 150.00.*

8 *Elgin American round goldtone compact/watch combination with black grosgrain carrying case; lid engraved to resemble pocket watch; c. 1950s. $150.00 – 175.00.*

9 *Illinois Watch Case Co. yellow enameled bronze clamshell vanity case/watch combination with gold-plated interior and compartments for powder and rouge; c. 1930s. $150.00 – 175.00.*

1 Elgin American silvered compact/music box combination with three gilded deer on lid; melody is "Anniversary Waltz;" black carrying case; c. 1950s. $100.00 – 150.00.

2 Pale yellow enamel goldtone vanity case/compass combination with powder and rouge compartments; lid contains compass and pictures of ships and their destinations; France. $100.00 – 150.00.

3 Elgin American gilt and satin-finish compact/compass combination with engraved scene on lid depicting the continents, c. 1950s. $150.00 – 225.00.

4 Marbleized brown enamel and goldtone decorated compact/thermometer combination, France. $125.00 – 175.00.

5 Goldtone compact with silvered music score or "Stardust" mounted on lid, c. 1920s. $100.00 – 125.00.

6 Black matte enamel goldtone compact/music box combination with slide-out lipstick; lid designed as piano keyboard; French melody; c. 1930s. $125.00 – 150.00.

1 Black enamel goldtone vanity case with U.S.N. insignia in gilt heart on lid; powder and rouge compartments; c. World War II. $80.00 – 100.00.

2 Navy blue and white small vanity case with nautical motif on lid; powder and rouge compartments; c. World War II. $40.00 – 60.00.

3 Sterling-silver compact with Marine Corps insignia on lid; gilded interior with diminishing mirror in lid and finger-ring chain; c. World War I. $200.00 – 250.00.

4 Wood compact with painted serviceman and girl; "Until We Meet Again" painted on lid; c. 1940s. $80.00 – 100.00.

5 Zell yellow marbleized plastic Kamra-Pak-style vanity case with Navy insignia on lid; powder and rouge compartments and slide-out lipstick; c. 1940s. $75.00 – 100.00.

6 Sterling-silver shield-shaped compact with carrying chain; Red Cross enameled insignia disk on lid; monogrammed; c. World War I. NPA.

7 Yellow enameled suitcase-motif vanity case with stickers depicting New York's points of interest; metal Marine Corps insignia on lid; powder and rouge compartments; c. 1940s. $125.00 – 150.00.

8 Brown marbleized enamel Kamra-Pak-style compact with U.S. Navy insignia on lid and sliding lipstick; Germany c. 1940s. $100.00 – 150.00.

9 Black enamel round clip-on compact with U.S. Navy insignia on lid, c. World War II. $100.00 – 150.00.

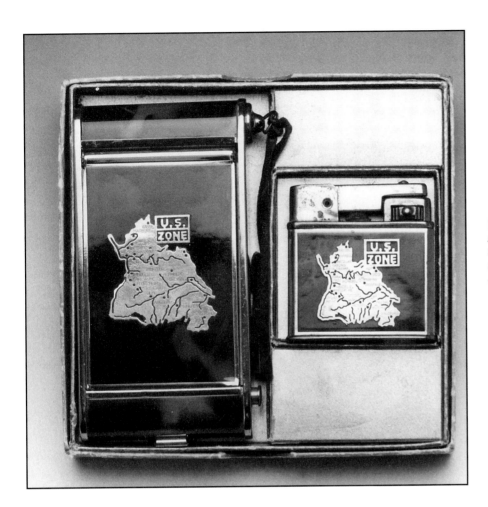

Weltzunter blue marbleized enamel Kamra-Pak-style vanity case and matching cigarette lighter with silvered metal cut-out map of U.S. Zone on lid; original presentation box; Germany, c. 1940s. $175.00 – 225.00.

Coty "Flying Colors" gilt-metal triple vanity case designed to resemble spread eagle wings; red, white, and blue lipstick tube in center; original presentation box and packet of Coty Airspun face powder; c. 1940s. $175.00 – 250.00.

1 *Bronzed-metal compact designed as Air Force officer's cap with jeweled Armed Forces disk on top, c. 1940s. $60.00 – 100.00.*

2 *Khaki plastic compact designed as Army officer's cap, c. 1940s. $50.00 – 80.00.*

3 *Red, white, and blue plastic compact designed as Navy officer's cap, c. 1940s. $60.00 – 100.00.*

4 *Goldtone compact with copper Armed Forces cap mounted on lid, c. 1940s. $60.00 – 100.00.*

5 *Navy blue and white plastic compact designed as Navy officer's cap, c. 1940s. $50.00 – 90.00.*

6 *Red, white, and blue plastic compact designed as Navy officer's cap, c. 1940s (shown open). $50.00 – 90.00.*

7 *Black enamel goldtone heart-shaped vanity case with Armed Forces emblem on lid; powder and rouge compartments; arrow slides out to reveal lipstick; c. 1940s. $100.00 – 150.00.*

8 *Rex Fifth Avenue red enamel oval compact; mother-of-pearl Army hat mounted on lid, inscribed "Mother Love Son," U.S. Army; c. 1940s. $80.00 – 100.00.*

9 *Satin goldtone compact with copper replica of Army officer's hat mounted on lid, c. 1930s. $80.00 – 125.00.*

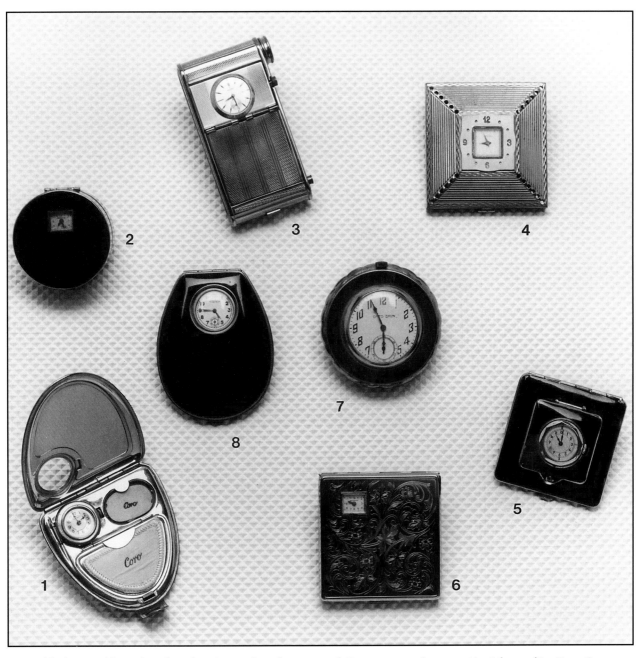

1 Coro black enamel horseshoe-shaped vanity case/watch combination with snap closing; powder and rouge compartments; c. 1920s. $150.00 – 200.00.
2 Illinois Watch Case Co. compact/watch combination, c. 1930s. $60.00 – 100.00.
3 Medana goldtone engine-turned Kamra-Pak-style compact/watch combination; back contains cigarette compartment; sliding lipstick case; West Germany, c. 1940 – 1950s. $175.00 – 250.00.
4 Ameré goldtone engine-turned compact, Switzerland. $125.00 – 150.00.

5 Brown enamel compact/watch combination, Germany. $125.00 – 150.00.
6 American Beauty goldtone engraved vanity case/watch combination with powder and rouge compartments, c. 1940 – 1950s. $125.00 – 150.00.
7 Goldtone compact/watch combination, Germany. $125.00 – 175.00.
8 Timepact black enamel elongated horseshoe-shaped vanity case/watch combination with powder and rouge compartments. $150.00 – 175.00.

1 Volupté goldtone compact with Cub Scout, Den Mother emblem. $60.00 – 80.00.
2 Satin goldtone Girl Scout compact. $60.00 – 80.00.
3 Sterling-silver octagonal miniature compact with Harvard University emblem on lid; loop for chain. $75.00. – 100.00.
4 Stork Club goldtone compact and lipstick. $200.00 – 225.00.
5 Arthur Murray presentation goldtone compact with picture of Arthur Murray Dancers on front lid. $100.00 – 150.00.
6 Satin-finish goldtone compact with silvered shovel mounted on lid; souvenir of ground breaking for office in Worcester, Massachusetts; presentation box. $40.00 – 60.00.
7 Enameled "Eastern Star" jeweled compact. $30.00 – 50.00.
8 Silvered "Veterans of Foreign War" vanity case with powder and rouge compartments. $40.00 – 60.00.

1 Goldtone compact designed as suitcase decorated with travel stickers. $160.00 – 180.00.

2 Silver octagonal compact with cutout map of India on lid. $150.00 – 200.00.

3 Goldtone compact with scenes of Paris mounted on lid. $80.00 – 120.00.

4 Painted brown enamel compact, Paris. $125.00 – 150.00.

5 Satin-finish goldtone vanity case designed as suitcase decorated with travel stickers, c. 1930s. $160.00 – 180.00.

6 Green enamel goldtone compact with scenes of Ireland on lid, England. $30.00 – 50.00.

7 Goldtone compact with scenes of Scotland on black plastic lid, England. $60.00 – 100.00.

8 Miref goldtone compact with "Paris, 1412" enclosed in plastic dome on lid. $80.00 – 120.00.

1 *Silvered-metal compact with gilt design of the State of Alaska on lid. $40.00 – 60.00.*

2 *Agme goldtone compact with scenes of North America on satin-finish lid, Switzerland. $60.00 – 80.00.*

3 *Green painted enamel compact depicting the Empire State Building, New York. $50.00 – 60.00.*

4 *Compact with scene of Pennsylvania Turnpike on lid. $40.00 – 60.00.*

5 *Elgin American compact with Georgia state flag and flower on lid, c. 1940 – 1950s. $50.00 – 75.00.*

6 *Oblong wood compact with map, state flower, and scenes of California on lid. $80.00 – 100.00.*

7 *Silvered-metal vanity case with "Souvenir of Washington, D.C." printed on lid. $30.00 – 60.00.*

1 White plastic-covered metal compact with "The Woman's Shop, Springfield, Mass." printed on slip-cover lid. $75.00 – 100.00.

2 Engine-turned goldtone compact with "Compliments of The Rainbow Inn" printed on yellow marbleized plastic disk decorated with simulated sapphires, c. 1920s. $60.00 – 80.00.

3 Silvered-metal repoussé floral-decorated compact with shield with scene of the White House mounted on lid; loop for chain. $60.00 – 80.00.

4 Silvered-metal horseshoe-shaped compact with shield of "Battle Bennington Vt." mounted on lid. $60.00 – 80.00.

5 Artcraft round blue enamel compact with "Indian and Mohawk Trail" painted on lid. $60.00 – 80.00.

6 Goldtone engine-turned compact with "Summit Pikes Peak" on white plastic disk set with red stones mounted on lid. $60.00 – 80.00.

7 Silvered-metal compact with photograph of "Old Orchard Beach, Maine" on lid, c. 1930s. $75.00 – 100.00.

8 Engine-turned silvered-metal vanity case with shield of "The Pier, Old Orchard Beach, Maine" mounted on lid; powder and rouge compartments. $60.00 – 80.00.

9 Black enamel compact with photograph of "Bellingrath Gardens, Mobile, Ala." printed on lid, c. 1920s. $60.00 – 80.00.

1 Engine-turned goldtone compact with "Sesquicentennial 1776 – 1926, Philadelphia, Pa." printed on plastic disk on lid. $60.00 – 80.00.

2 Wooden compact with tapestry design of 1939 New York World's Fair on lid. $80.00 – 100.00.

3 White enamel miniature flapjack compact with "A Century of Progress, 1833 – 1933" on silver disk mounted on lid. $70.00 – 90.00.

4 Columbia Fifth Avenue mesh vanity pouch with orange and blue scene of 1939 New York World's Fair on lid. $80.00 – 125.00.

5 Octagonal silvered-metal vanity case with copper coin inset in lid, inscribed "Sesquicentennial International Exposition, Philadelphia, 1926." $100.00 – 125.00.

6 Columbia Fifth Avenue navy blue moiré vanity pouch with orange and blue scene of 1939 New York World's Fair on lid. $80.00 – 125.00.

7 Light blue enamel metal compact with "Trylon & Perisphere 1939" disk mounted on lid. $70.00 – 100.00.

1 Elizabeth Arden light blue harlequin-shaped compact, c. 1940s. $125.00 – 175.00.

2 Dorothy Gray oval goldtone compact with black enamel harlequin mask on lid, c. 1940s. $80.00 – 100.00.

3 Silver Drill Instructor's hat compact with finger-ring and metal mirror. $150.00 – 250.00.

4 Pilcher silvered compact with horse's head mounted on lid, "Thoroughbred" printed below, Kentucky Derby, 1953. $80.00 – 100.00.

5 Pilcher "Slimpact" wood compact with chess knight set on inlaid checkerboard lid, c. 1940 – 1950s. $60.00 – 80.00.

6 Pilcher wood compact with horse's head mounted on lid, c. 1940 – 1950s. $60.00 – 80.00.

7 Lady's silvered and black metal pistol/compact, c. 1950s. NPA.

Antiqued gilt parure designed with a Fede type decoration applied to the mesh vanity pouch; locket, pillbox, screw-back earrings, necklace, and two bracelets, one with secret opening; c. 1930s. NPA.

1 Goldtone compact designed as hand mirror with decorated, engraved lid. $80.00 – 100.00.

2 Engine-turned decorated goldtone compact designed as hand mirror; ring for chain; Germany, c. 1920s. $100.00 – 125.00.

3 Engine-turned decorated goldtone compact designed as hand mirror; Germany, c. 1920s (shown open). $125.00 – 150.00.

4 Silver engraved scalloped-edged compact formed as hand mirror with lipstick in handle. $200.00 – 275.00.

5 Sterling silver compact formed as hand mirror with bloodstone cabochon thumbpiece; lipstick in bolster-shaped handle; Italy, c. 1920s. $200.00 – 275.00.

6 Sterling silver compact formed as hand mirror with coral cabochon thumbpiece; lipstick in cylindrical handle; Italy, c. 1920s. $250.00 – 350.00.

7 Blue enamel compact formed as hand mirror with painted scene on lid. $60.00 – 80.00.

8 Silvered miniature Limoges compact formed as hand mirror with painted scene on lid, France. $40.00 – 75.00.

9 Goldtone Limoges compact formed as hand mirror with painted scene on lid, France. $100.00 – 125.00.

10 Miref gilt compact formed as hand mirror with lipstick in handle; beveled mirror on both sides of compact, France. $125.00 – 150.00.

11 Antique silver-plated triangular compact designed as hand mirror with turquoise cabochon thumbpiece; lipstick in handle. $125.00 – 175.00.

12 Hoechst silver-plated compact designed as hand mirror with lipstick in handle; flannel case; probably Germany. $125.00 – 175.00.

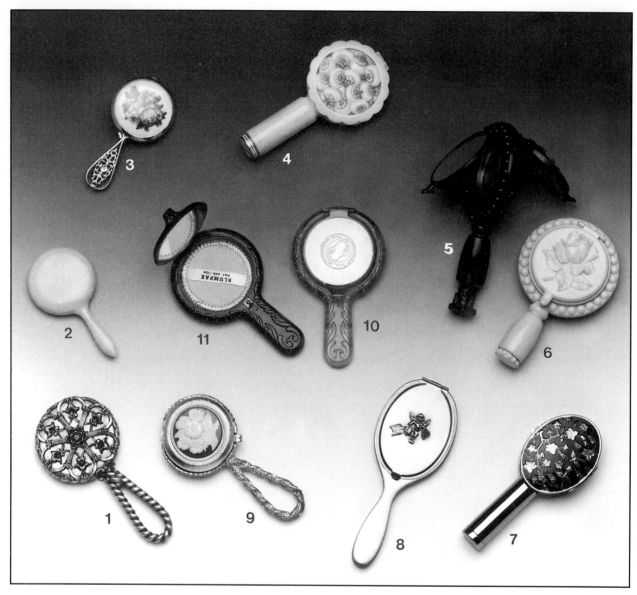

1 Pewter-colored metal compact shaped like a hand mirror; lid decorated with stylized cutout flowers; France. $100.00 – 150.00.

2 Ivory-colored plastic miniature compact shaped like hand mirror; Germany, c. 1920s. $60.00 – 75.00.

3 Silvered miniature compact shaped like hand mirror, lid decorated with petit point; France. $40.00 – 75.00.

4 Coty plastic compact designed as hand mirror; lid decorated with Coty trademark powder puffs; lipstick in handle. $50.00 – 75.00.

5, 6 Platé "Trio-ette" plastic vanity case designed as hand mirror; powder and puff on one side, rouge on other side; lipstick in handle; c. 1940s (black case shown open, white case shown closed). $125.00 – 250.00.

7 Black and gilt enameled compact formed as hand mirror with lipstick in handle. $75.00 – 125.00.

8 Satin-finish goldtone compact shaped like hand mirror with cupid centered on lid. $40.00 – 60.00.

9 Goldtone compact shaped like hand mirror with plastic floral decoration on lid. $40.00 – 60.00.

10, 11 Blumpak plastic compact shaped like hand mirror (amber compact shown open, yellow compact shown closed). $30.00 – 50.00.

1 Oval rose-colored velvet vanity case with cameo medallion on lid; compartments for powder, rouge, and lipstick; carrying cord with ring and ojime bead; c. 1920s. $80.00 – 100.00.

2 Black velvet vanity case with embroidered butterfly and edged with gold trim; compartments for powder, rouge, and lipstick; carrying cord with ring and ojime bead; c. 1920s. $80.00 – 100.00.

3 Fuller plastic compact with sleeve for comb mounted on lid. $40.00 – 60.00.

4 Elgin American red, white, and blue enamel "Drumstick Set;" compact and lipstick in drum-and-drumstick motif; original presentation box. $100.00 – 150.00.

5 Ivory-colored marbleized plastic compact with red trim around edge and sailing ship picture on lid; snap closure; c. 1920s. $60.00 – 80.00.

6 Evening in Paris wood compact with decorated lid, c. 1940s. $40.00 – 60.00.

7 Plastic compact with copper-etched lid depicting scene of lady and lamb; signed Biscay; France. $100.00 – 125.00.

8 La Faveur de Paris "Sifta-Pak" blue tooled-leather powder bag with mirrored lid and drawstring powder puff; France, c. 1920s. $60.00 – 80.00.

9 Elmo navy blue moiré vanity powder bag with mirror and drawstring powder puff; snap closure, c. 1920s. $60.00 – 80.00.

10 Pink silk double compact box with lace and gold braid trim and compartments for powder and rouge; snap closure; c. 1920s (shown open). $80.00 – 100.00.

11 Blue silk compact with netting and ribbon with slip-cover lid, c. 1920s. $80.00 – 100.00.

12 Rose silk compact with lace and braid trim and slip-cover lid, c. 1920s. $40.00 – 60.00.

13 Delettrez "Wildflower" pale blue paper compact with colorful floral spray on lid, c. 1940s. $50.00 – 60.00.

14 Harmony of Boston tan box-shaped compact with snap closure, c. 1920s (shown open). $50.00 – 60.00.

1 Zell Fifth Avenue black suede vanity clutch with compact, two lipstick tubes, and comb; metal trim on outer lid and snap closing; c. 1940s. $60.00 – 80.00.

2 Silver lamé vanity clutch with silver lamé compact and lipstick, c. 1940s. $40.00 – 60.00.

3 Navy blue moiré and gilt vanity clutch with gilt compact, lipstick, and comb; c. 1940s. $40.00 – 60.00.

4 Richard Hudnut white and gold fabric vanity clutch with compact and lipstick; decorated with "Tree of Life" motif set with green stones; c. 1940s. $75.00 – 100.00.

5 Ciner black satin vanity clutch with rhinestone-decorated compact and lipstick, c. 1940s. $175.00 – 200.00.

6 Lin-Bren red lizard vanity clutch with compact and lipstick, c. 1940s. $75.00 – 100.00.

7 Renard black and gold fabric vanity clutch with pull-up compact and lipstick in sleeve at bottom of clutch, c. 1940. $40.00 – 60.00.

8 Majestic floral vanity clutch with compact, two lipstick tubes, and comb; c. 1940s. $60.00 – 80.00.

Vanity clutches on page 304, with several shown open.

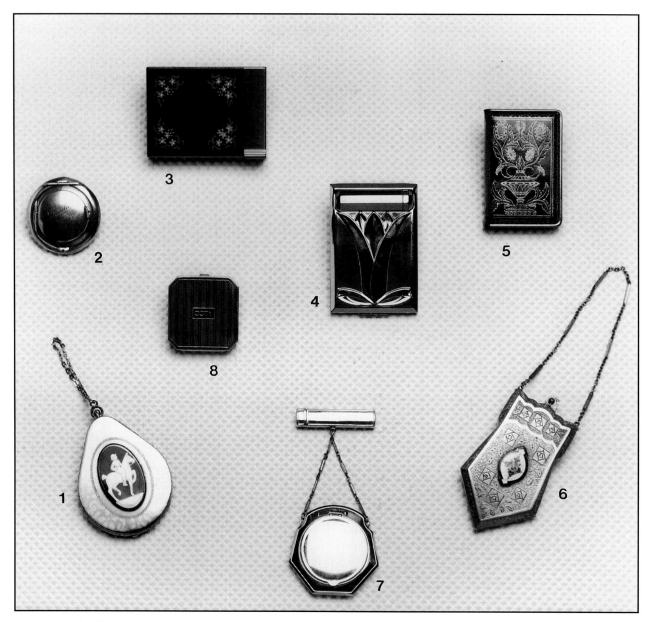

1 Tear-shaped gilt and silvered vanity case with silvered man and horse encased in plastic dome; gilt interior, carrying chain, and compartments for powder, rouge, and lipstick. $150.00 – 200.00.

2 Sterling-silver hallmarked double-tier compact; upper lid reveals locket; compartment for powder in lower lid; c. 1915. $200.00 – 225.00.

3 Volupté black enamel gilt compact with sliding lipstick; black enamel inner and outer lids decorated with flowers. $80.00 – 125.00.

4 Richard Hudnut gilt compact with raised tulip design; lipstick encased in lid cover. $40.00 – 60.00.

5 Mondaine multicolored tooled leather vanity case designed to resemble book; compartments for powder, rouge, and cigarettes. $80.00 – 125.00.

6 Marathon gilt and silvered engraved vanity case with enameled disk on lid; gilt interior, carrying chain, and compartments for powder, rouge, and lipstick. $150.00 – 200.00.

7 E.A.M. nickel-finish tango-chain vanity; lid holds metal mirror and rouge compartment; lower half contains powder compartment. $150.00 – 200.00.

8 Coty octagonal polished nickel-finish vanity case; upper lid for rouge, lower opening for powder. $60.00 – 80.00.

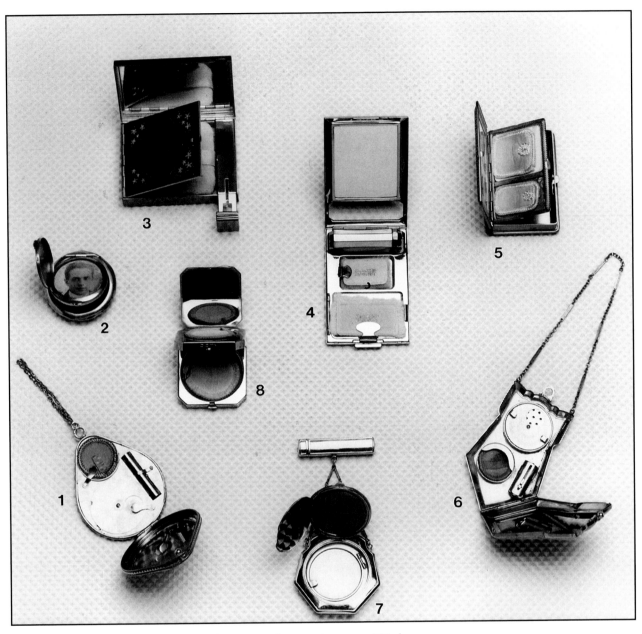

Vanity cases and compacts on page 306 shown open.

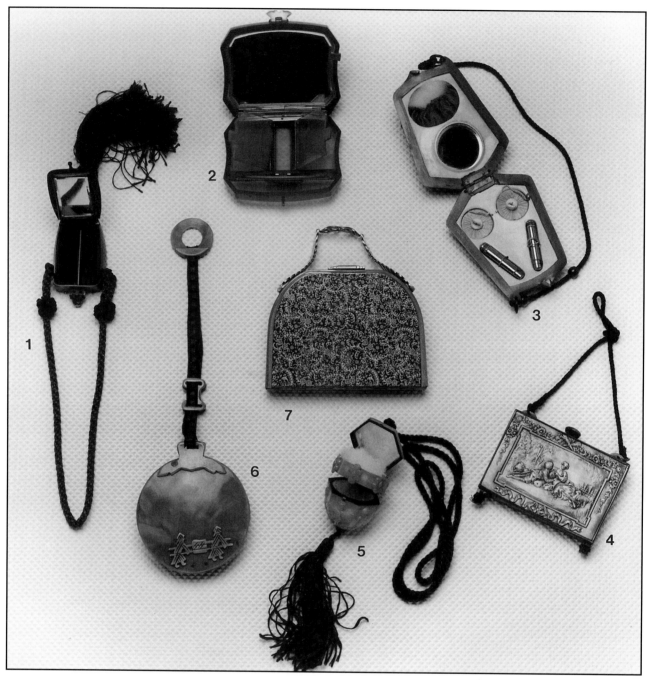

1 Brown plastic vanity case with carrying cord and tassel; powder and rouge compartments; c. 1920s (shown open). $125.00 – 175.00.

2 Butterscotch-colored plastic vanity case; writing slate on back of mirror and compartments for powder, rouge, lipstick, and comb; c. 1920s (shown open). $150.00 – 175.00.

3 Tan plastic vanity case with maroon flowers; carrying cord and compartments for powder, rouge, two lipsticks, mirror, and pocket for puff; c. 1920s (shown open). $200.00 – 250.00.

4 Tan and brown vanity case with country scene on lid; carrying cord and compartments for powder, lipstick, and perfume; c. 1920s. $200.00 – 225.00.

5 Egg-shaped yellow plastic vanity purse with cherubs; black tassel and carrying cord; powder and rouge compartments; c. 1920s. $300.00 – 350.00.

6 Gold-colored plastic vanity reticule with Asian motif; black and gold carrying cord with ring and buckle ojime; compartment for powder and puff; c. 1920s. $100.00 – 125.00.

7 Stratton black and gold floral-decorated metal vanity reticule with fancy metal carrying chain; compartments for compact, coin purse, and comb; c. 1950s. $250.00 – 300.00.

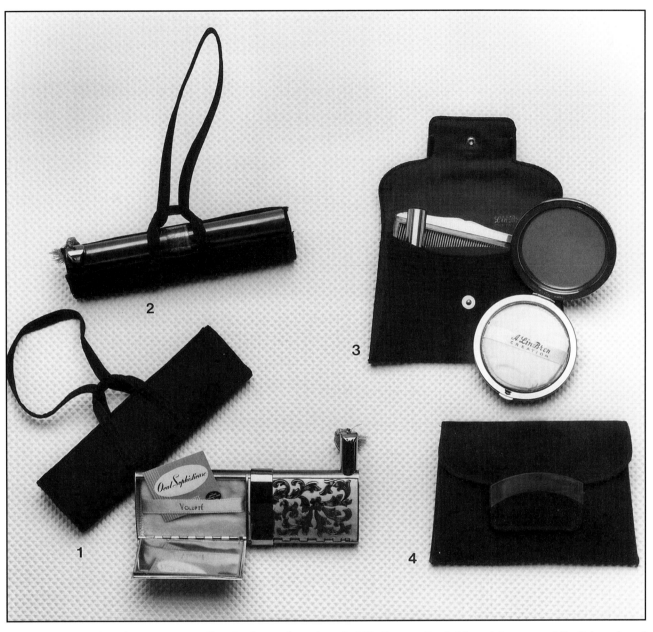

1, 2 Volupté "Oval Sophisticase" carryall with silver-embossed gilt lid; center band slides to open compartments for powder and utilities, tassel pulls out to reveal lipstick; black faille carrying case; c. 1950s; (1 shown open, 2 shown closed). $125.00 – 150.00.

3, 4 Lin-Bren vanity clutch contains compact, lipstick, and comb (3, navy blue faille, shown open; 4, maroon suede, shown closed). $60.00 – 80.00.

1 *Majestic gold and black lace vanity clutch with black and gold carrying chain and compartments for compact, lipstick, and comb (shown open). $60.00 – 80.00.*
2, 3 *Graceline small vanity reticule with wrist chain; compartments for puff, compact, and lipstick, (2, maroon velvet, shown open; 3, multicolor woven fabric, shown closed). $50.00 – 70.00.*
4 *Zell gilt-padded vanity clutch with compartments for compact, lipstick, and comb (shown open). $40.00 – 60.00.*

*1, 2 Coty "Envelope" goldtone compact, c. 1940s. $60.00 – 80.00.
3, 4 Vanity case with compartments for powder, rouge, and cigarettes; tassel pulls out to reveal lipstick; probably England (3, blue plastic resembling cloisonné top, leather-lined interior, shown closed; 4, black silk, leather-lined interior, shown open). $150.00 – 200.00.*

5, 6 Le Rage goldtone vanity case with chain-attached lipstick; center lid with enamel painted flowers reveals compartment for rouge, photo, tablets; interior reveals snap-on comb/whisk broom combination; second opening reveals powder compartment and perfume container; moiré carrying case contains perfume funnel; England, c. 1950s. $450.00 – 550.00.

1 Silvered-metal purse-motif vanity case with enamel bluebird and engine turned back; contains loose powder sifter, two puffs, rouge, mirror, and carrying chain; c. 1920s. $60.00 – 80.00.

2, 3 Wadsworth two-sided mini vanity case with powder and rouge compartments and finger loop (2, green suede, shown open; 3, black leather, shown closed). 2, $50.00 – 75.00; 3, $40.00 – 60.00.

4 Coty "Buckle" goldtone vanity case with white enamel buckle, c. 1940s. $80.00 – 125.00.

5 Fillkwik Co. "Van-Mist" silver vanity case designed to resemble camera; compartments for powder, rouge, lipstick, and perfume; c. 1930s. $125.00 – 175.00.

6 Sterling silver hallmarked two-sided miniature vanity case with floral-engraved powder and rouge compartments and finger ring chain; England, c. 1900s. $125.00 – 150.00.

7 Jonteel repoussé silver-plated compact with finger ring chain, c. 1920s. $60.00 – 80.00.

8, 9 Houbigant six-sided vanity case with basket of flowers on lid; compartments for powder and rouge (8, goldtone small version; 9, silvered-metal larger version). $40.00 – 60.00 each.

10 Coty "Jingle Bells" goldtone compact, c. 1940s. $125.00 – 175.00.

11 Coty silvered-metal compact with cutout design of boy and girl, c. 1920 – 1930s. $40.00 – 60.00.

1 *Gun-metal clover-shaped purse-motif compact.* $60.00 – 80.00.
2 *Sterling silver hallmarked compact designed to resemble hand mirror; lid decorated with blue faux cloisonné; loop for chain.* $75.00 – 100.00.
3 *White enamel compact with "Yes" in green and "No" in red.* $100.00 – 150.00.
4 *Six-inch-round pink and goldtone compact with sixteen stars with faux diamonds on lid.* $150.00 – 200.00.
5 *Volupté green and yellow triangular checkerboard compact.* $65.00 – 80.00.
6 *Gold-filled compact decorated with blackbird; finger ring chain and tassel; c. 1920s.* $125.00 – 175.00.

7 *K & K small oval black enamel compact with rhinestone lipstick tube mounted on lid.* $100.00 – 125.00.
8 *Flato goldtone compact with brass key mounted on lid; red leather-like protective case.* $100.00 – 125.00.
9 *Majestic goldtone compact with comb and black faille case.* $40.00 – 60.00.
10 *Silver compact with blue and white Delft enamel windmill scene.* $50.00 – 60.00.
11 *Light and dark blue guilloche enamel 1" compact; loop for chain.* $80.00 – 125.00.

1 La Mode gilt and black-striped enamel vanity case with black silhouette on cover; powder, rouge, and lipstick compartments; loop for chain. $100.00 – 125.00.

2, 3 Slim oval compact designed as a locket with chain; black silhouette on cover (2, yellow enamel, shown in presentation box; 3, red enamel with loop for chain). $100.00 – 150.00 each.

4 Divine lavender-striped enamel miniature compact with white silhouette on cover. $30.00 – 50.00.

5 Ivory-colored enamel vanity case; silver silhouette within black disk; powder and rouge compartments. $40.00 – 50.00.

6 La Mode ivory and black enamel vanity case with black silhouette on ivory; powder and rouge compartments and through handle. $100.00 – 150.00.

7 Plastic and goldtone compact with molded silhouette on plastic slip-cover lid. $40.00 – 50.00.

8 Black enamel and goldtone vanity case with black transfer silhouette; powder and rouge compartments. $60.00 – 80.00.

9 Rex Fifth Avenue blue plastic and gilt compact with white plastic silhouette on blue lid, c. 1940s. $40.00 – 60.00.

10 Silver and black-enamel vanity case with white silhouette; finger-ring chain; powder sifter and rouge compartment; c. 1920s. $80.00 – 125.00.

11 Armand red enamel compact with silhouette on lid, "Pat'd Aug. 14, 1917." $40.00 – 60.00.

12 Blue and clear plastic compact with white silhouette on screw-top lid. $20.00 – 30.00.

13 Rigaud "Mary Garden" gilt miniature compact with embossed silhouette on slip-cover lid, c. 1919. $40.00 – 60.00.

14 Armand silver-plated compact with engraved silhouette on lid and engine-turned back, "Pat. 7–1–24." $60.00 – 80.00.

15 Rigaud "Mary Garden" brass compact with embossed silhouette on cover, c. 1919. $60.00 – 80.00.

1 Black enamel vanity case with lipstick compartment centered on lid; powder and rouge compartments. $60.00 – 100.00.

2 Kigu blue enamel compact with Limoges-type locket centered on lid, c. 1940 – 1950s. $60.00 – 100.00.

3 Goldtone vanity case with locket centered on lid; powder, rouge, and lipstick compartments; c. 1930s. $60.00 – 100.00.

4 Maroon enamel vanity case with lipstick compartment centered on lid; powder and rouge compartments. $60.00 – 100.00.

5 Lazell goldtone vanity case with powder compartment; rouge compartment centered on lid "Pat'd. July 18, 1922." $70.00 – 125.00.

6 Mondaine red enamel vanity case with lipstick compartment centered on lid; compartments for powder and rouge; c. 1920 – 1930s. $70.00 – 125.00.

7 Silvered-metal compact with goldtone locket centered on lid, c. 1930s. $75.00 – 150.00.

1 Woodworth "Karess" egg-shaped vanity case in engine-turned silvered metal; edge of lid enameled with blue Greek key design; powder and rouge compartments; c. 1920s. $30.00 – 60.00.

2 Yardley goldtone vanity case with red, white, and blue embossed design on lid; powder and rouge compartments; c. 1940s. $60.00 – 75.00.

3 Alwyn blue enamel suitcase-motif compact. $80.00 – 120.00.

4 Yardley black enamel and goldtone vanity case with powder and rouge compartments and swing-out lipstick, c. 1930s. $60.00 – 75.00.

5 La Mode goldstone and enameled vanity case with powder and rouge compartments and slide-out lipsticks (shown open). $100.00 – 150.00.

6 Rosenfeld zippered goldtone compact with multi-color confetti sparkles and thread, Israel. $30.00 – 50.00.

7 Volupté "Swinglok" stippled goldtone compact with multicolored synthetic gems on swinglok, c. 1940s. $60.00 – 100.00.

8 Lucite compact mirrored on inner and outer lid, c. 1940s. $80.00 – 100.00.

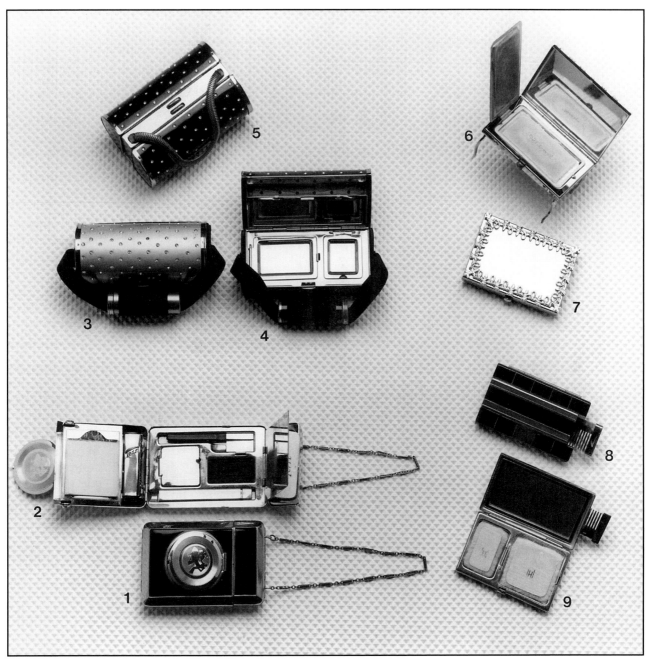

1, 2 Terri black enamel goldtone vanity case with carrying chain; compartments for powder, rouge, lipstick, and lip-tissues; complete eye makeup kit included; c. 1950s. $225.00 – 350.00.

3, 4 Rhinestone-studded vanity case; black faille carrying case incorporates sleeves for lipstick and comb; compartments for powder, rouge, and cigarettes (3, goldtone, shown closed; 4, black enamel, shown open). $125.00 – 175.00 each.

5 Rhinestone-studded black enamel double vanity case with car-rying chain and compartments for powder, rouge, comb, lip-stick, and cigarettes. $200.00 – 300.00.

6, 7 Wadsworth goldtone compact designed to resemble vanity table; collapsible cabriole legs. $150.00 – 275.00.

8, 9 Houbigant enameled vanity case with powder and rouge compartments and sliding comb on lid (8, black enamel, shown closed; 9, white enamel, shown open). $100.00 – 150.00.

1, 2 Silver-plated compact with swivel lipstick on lid, c. 1930s. $125.00 – 150.00.

3 Engine-turned silvered-metal compact with through handle, c. 1920s. $100.00 – 125.00.

4 Silvered compact with hammered surface and fleur-de-lis mounted on lid; carrying chain; c. 1920s. $100.00 – 150.00.

5 Silvered vanity case with carrying chain and compartments for powder, rouge, lipstick, and coins, "Pat. Aug. 9, 1921" (shown open). $125.00 – 150.00.

6 Silver-plated metal miniature vanity case with floral-engraved decoration on all sides; goldtone interior, through handle, and compartments for powder, rouge, and lipstick; c. 1920s. $100.00 – 125.00.

7 German silver engraved vanity case with carrying chain and compartments for powder, rouge, and coins; c. 1915. $100.00 – 175.00.

8 Silver-plated metal vanity case with engraved decoration on all sides; goldtone interior, through handle, and compartments for powder, rouge, and lipstick; c. 1920s. $125.00 – 150.00.

9 Silvered-metal oblong vanity case with through handle and compartments for powder, rouge, and lipstick; c. 1920s (shown open). $125.00 – 150.00.

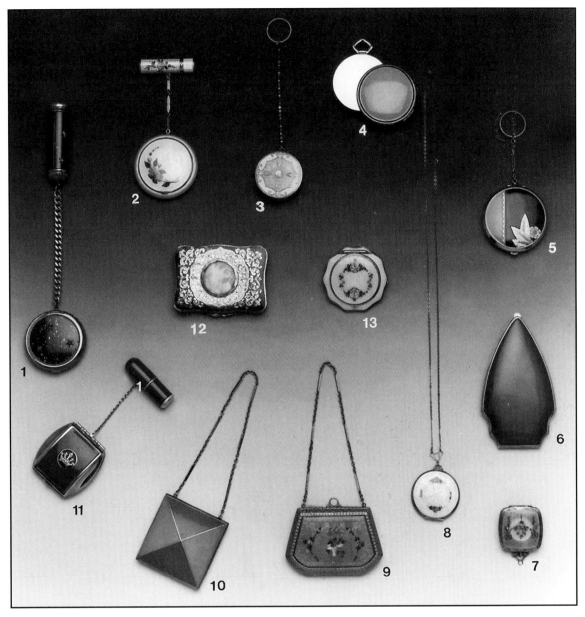

1 Navy blue enamel on goldtone tango-chain compact and lipstick case with star-shaped studs mounted on a blue celestial scene. $175.00 – 200.00.

2 B.B.Co. sterling silver enameled tango-chain with light blue and cream-colored cloisonné flowers on lid, c. 1920s. $250.00 – 300.00.

3 Blue and white guilloche enamel compact with finger-ring chain, c. 1917. $100.00 – 125.00.

4 Green enamel round compact with slide-out mirror, Germany. $60.00 – 80.00.

5 Green and black enamel metal compact with finger-ring chain, c. 1920s. $100.00 – 125.00.

6 Shaded blue enamel on metal shield-shaped vanity case, c. 1920 – 1930s. $40.00 – 60.00.

7 R & G Co. green cloisonné and silver miniature compact with painted flowers on lid; loop for chain; c. 1910. $125.00 – 175.00.

8 Yellow cloisonné locket compact with painted roses on lid; complete with chain; c. 1920s. $100.00 – 125.00.

9 Blue cloisonné purse-motif vanity case with painted flowers on lid; carrying chain and compartments for powder, rouge, and lipstick; c. 1920 – 1930s. $150.00 – 200.00.

10 Square blue and ivory-colored enamel vanity case with carrying chain, c. 1920s. $100.00 – 125.00.

11 Green enamel tango-chain vanity with silvered-metal crown mounted on lid, c. 1920s. $100.00 – 125.00.

12 Green champlevé vermeil compact with painted ivory disk on lid; Italy, late 19th century. $125.00 – 150.00.

13 R & G Co. yellow cloisonné vanity case with painted flowers on lid, c. 1920s. $135.00 – 150.00.

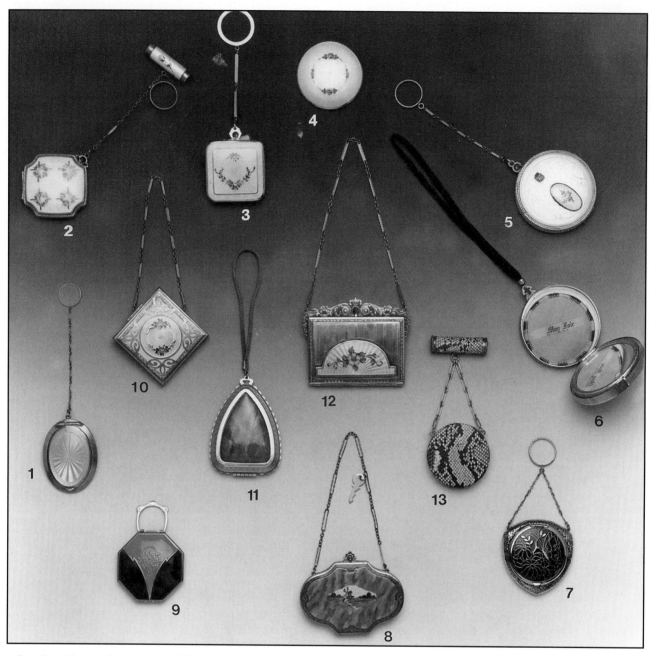

1 Vermeil sterling silver oval compact with blue cloisonné decorated lid and finger-ring chain, c. 1920s. $125.00 – 150.00.

2 R & G Co. sterling silver yellow cloisonné tango-chain vanity with painted flowers on lid; lipstick and perfume tube suspended from enameled and silver finger-ring chain; c. 1920s. $250.00 – 300.00.

3 G.L.B. Co. sterling silver yellow and blue cloisonné vanity case with painted flowers; powder sifter and rouge compartment; enameled finger ring chain; c. 1920s. $225.00 – 250.00.

4 Flapjack green cloisonné compact with painted flowers on lid, c. 1930s. $60.00 – 80.00.

5 Engine-turned silvered-metal compact with enameled disk on lid and finger ring chain, c. 1920s. $100.00 – 125.00.

6 May Fair engine-turned goldtone vanity case with enameled disk on lid; powder and rouge compartments; carrying cord and tassel; c. 1920s (shown open). $100.00 – 125.00.

7 Evans "Tap Sift" black enameled white-nickel triangular vanity case with finger ring chain, c. 1920s. $80.00 – 100.00.

8 D.F.B. Co. blue enamel vanity case with painted windmill scene; chain with key; powder sifter and rouge compartment, "Pat'd Feb 9, 1926." $150.00 – 250.00.

9 La Mode octagonal green enamel vanity case with etched basket on lid; compartments for powder and rouge and through handle; c. 1920 – 1930s. $70.00 – 90.00.

10 Lavender and green champlevé vanity case with powder sifter, rouge and coin compartments; carrying chain; c. 1920s. $175.00 – 200.00.

11 Triangular vanity case with engine-turned decoration and lustrous simulated cloisonné disk on lid; compartments for powder and rouge; carrying chain; c. 1920 – 1930s. $80.00 – 100.00.

12 Goldtone and silvered-metal vanity case with lavender cloisonné inset on lid; compartments for powder, rouge, and lipstick; carrying chain; c. 1920s. $150.00 – 200.00.

13 Snakeskin tango chain compact and lipstick. $125.00 – 175.00.

1 *Rigid mesh multicolored bolster-shaped vanity bag with faux pearls and blue stones; tassel and carrying chain (shown open). $250.00 – 300.00.*

2 *Maroon enamel vanity case with compartments for powder, rouge, lipstick, comb, and eye makeup (shown open). $80.00 – 125.00.*

3 *Sterling silver hallmarked lavender cloisonné compact / perfume combination with painted flowers; finger ring chain suspended from perfume ring. $300.00 – 350.00.*

4 *Highly finished white-nickel compact designed as hand mirror. $60.00 – 80.00.*

5 *R & G Co. "Nuwite" octagonal green enamel compact with scalework design on lid, c. 1920s. $100.00 – 125.00.*

6 *Rigid multicolored mesh purse-motif vanity case; compartments for powder, rouge, and coins; carrying chain (shown open). $150.00 – 225.00.*

7 *Daniel black leather compact with plastic dome enclosing portrait of lady, Paris. $80.00 – 100.00.*

8 *Black plastic compact with Lucite top enclosing painted picture of lady on sparkling confetti, c. 1920s. $150.00 – 175.00.*

9 *Black plastic compact with Lucite top enclosing painted "Pierrot" on sparkling confetti, c. 1920s. $125.00 – 150.00.*

10 *Evans goldtone mesh vanity bag decorated with multicolored stones; scene of man and woman on lid; satin lines; wrist chain; metal mirror and powder and rouge compartments; c. 1940 – 1950s. $300.00 – 400.00.*

11 *Red damask bolster-shaped vanity bag with tassel and carrying chain with carved plastic ojime bead. $100.00 – 125.00.*

12 *Leather-textured blue silvered vanity case with enamel painting on lid; wrist chain; c. 1930s. $80.00 – 100.00.*

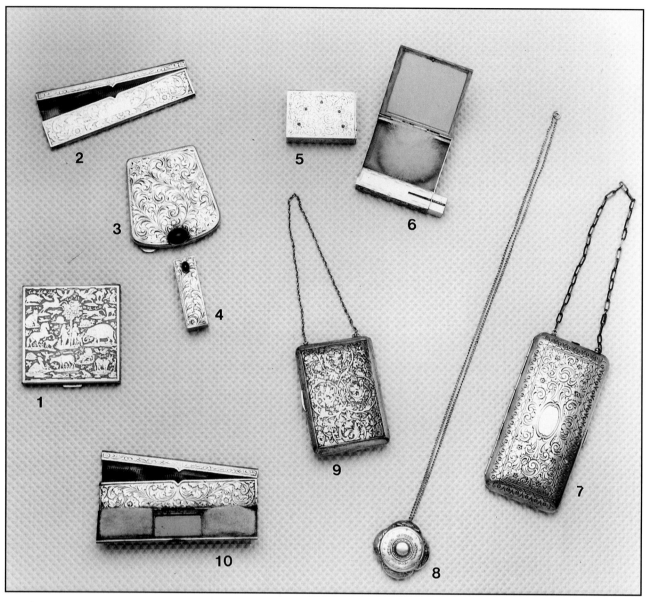

1 Volupté silvered-metal compact embossed on all sides with "Adam and Eve" as central motif. $60.00 – 80.00.

2, 3, 4 Sterling silver engraved compact, lipstick, and comb set with green cabochon on compact and lipstick, Italy. $250.00 – 300.00.

5 Sterling silver miniature engraved vanity case with small rubies; sliding lipstick. $150.00 – 225.00.

6 Sterling silver engraved vanity case; sliding lipstick (shown open). $175.00 – 250.00.

7 German silver engraved oblong carryall with carrying chain

and compartments for powder, rouge, coins, and bill-clip. $175.00 – 250.00.

8 Clover-shaped silvered repoussé compact/locket with chain. $80.00 – 125.00.

9 German silver engraved carryall with carrying chain and compartments for powder, rouge, coins, and bill-clip. $125.00 – 200.00.

10 Silver engraved compact/comb combination with compartments for powder and rouge in comb case. $75.00 – 125.00.

1 Silver filigree compact with two lids mounted with damascene scenes of India; interior lid opens to reveal powder compartment; India. $200.00 – 250.00.

2 Antique goldtone compact with Asian scene on lid, Austria. $60.00 – 80.00.

3 Asian brass engraved double-tier swivel vanity case (shown open). $250.00 – 300.00.

4 Octagonal silver compact with repoussé Siamese dancer on lid. $100.00 – 150.00.

5 Chinese hallmarked handmade silver filigree compact; lid lifts to reveal mirror, drawer pulls out for powder; loop for chain (shown with drawer open). $200.00 – 300.00.

6 Chinese handmade silver filigree compact; multicolored lid lifts to reveal mirror, drawer pulls out for powder (shown open). $250.00 – 350.00.

7 Suzuyo sterling silver compact inlaid with copper bamboo branches, Japan. $175.00 – 200.00.

8 Silver and black damascene compact with Siamese dancer on lid. $100.00 – 175.00.

9 Sunc sterling silver compact with jade cut-out mounted on lid, China. $175.00 – 250.00.

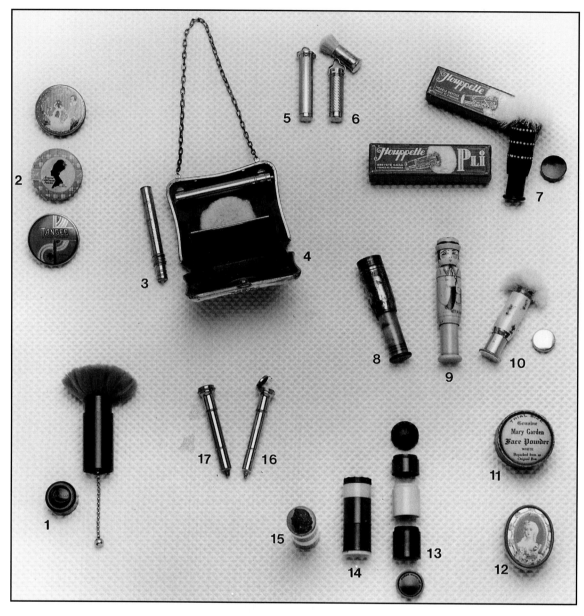

1 Lamkin pink and black plastic powder-puff container and carrying chain, England. $50.00 – 75.00.

2 Three miniature powder boxes; Tangee, Armand, and Richard Hudnut; c. 1920s. $50.00 each.

3 Paris Fashion Co. silvered powderette, c. 1900s. $50.00 – 100.00.

4 Silvered repoussé vanity purse with mirror, powder puff, and powderette, "Pat'd Oct. 17, 1914." $150.00 – 225.00.

5, 6 Gold-filled Puf-Kase, c. 1920s (5 shown closed; 6, smaller version, shown open). $125.00 – 150.00; $100.00 – 125.00.

7, 8 Houppette plastic pli, France, c. 1920s (7, turquoise-beaded black, shown open; 8, goldtone decorated, shown closed). $60.00 – 100.00; $80.00 – 125.00.

9 Pink plastic pli painted to resemble doll; hat contains lipstick; France, c. 1920s. $150.00 – 225.00.

10 Sterling-silver hallmarked pli with vermeil overlay and painted cloisonné, France (shown open). $200.00 – 250.00.

11 Mary Garden face powder in a puff in original box, c. 1917. $25.00 – 75.00.

12 Richard Hudnut "Du Barry" face-powder sampler in original box; France, c. 1920s. $40.00 – 60.00.

13, 14, 15 Colt Purse Make-Up Kit with plastic tubular colored makeup containers, c. 1930s (13 shown open, 14 shown closed, 15 top view). $40.00 – 60.00; $40.00 – 60.00; $60.00 – 90.00.

16, 17 Princess Pat powderette-lipstick, c. 1920s (16, goldtone, shown open; 17, silvered, shown closed). $50.00 – 75.00 each.

1 Antique embossed goldtone-finish vanity case with multicolored stones; carrying chain and compartments for powder, rouge, and lipstick; turn of the century. $100.00 – 150.00.

2 Antique goldtone compact with filigree lid set with pearls and turquoise; jeweled tassel and carrying chain; turn of the century. $200.00 – 250.00.

3 Antique goldtone vanity bag lined with pink satin; multicolored silk back; filigree compact set with pearls and blue stones; jeweled tassel and carrying chain; turn of the century. $350.00 – 450.00.

4 Antique silvered-metal vanity bag; filigree compact set with multicolored stones; black velvet back, carrying chain, and tassel; turn of the century. $350.00 – 450.00.

5 Two-sided antique goldtone vanity case; filigree lids set with red stones; powder and rouge compartments; tassel conceals lipstick; carrying chain; turn of the century. $250.00 – 300.00.

6 Antique silvered-filigree metal vanity bag set with marcasites and blue stones; gray moire lining, jeweled tassel, and carrying chain; turn of the century. $350.00 – 450.00.

7 Antique goldtone filigree compact set with green stones; lipstick case bonded to top; tassel and carrying chain; turn of the century. $250.00 – 300.00.

1 Goldtone vanity case with filigree lid set with colored stones and green cabochon stone; red faille lining; multicolored silk back set with stones; jeweled tassel and carrying chain; compartments for powder, rouge, and lipstick; turn of the century. $300.00 – 325.00.

2 White cloisonné goldtone vanity reticule with lid mounted with multicolored gemstones and filigree back; silk-lined interior; tassel conceals lipstick; carrying chain; Austria, turn of the century. $400.00 – 500.00.

3 Embossed brass collapsible compact with edge set with multicolored cabochons; France, turn of the century (shown open). $250.00 – 300.00.

4 Antique goldtone tango-chain; compact and rouge have filigree lids set with green stones and micro-mosaic disks; c. 1920s. $125.00 – 175.00.

5 Antique goldtone compact with red stones on embossed lid; tassel and carrying chain; c. 1920s. $200.00 – 250.00.

6 Goldtone filigree vanity case set with pearls and yellow stones; openings on both sides for powder and rouge, lipstick attached on bottom; tassel and carrying chain. $350.00 – 400.00.

7 Goldtone compact with honeycomb lid set with multicolored stones; fabric back; turn of the century. $200.00 – 250.00.

8 E.A. Bliss Co. brass filigree purse-motif vanity case with multicolored stones and carrying chain, turn of the century. $150.00 – 200.00.

9 Embossed goldtone compact with multicolored stones on lid; Czechoslovakia, late 19th century. $125.00 – 200.00.

10 Antique goldtone compact; filigree lid incorporates lipstick holder set with blue stones; turn of the century. $250.00 – 300.00.

1 Evans 5"-round sterling gold-wash compact with pink, yellow, and white basket weave. $200.00 – 250.00.
2 Evans 5"-round sterling compact with pink, yellow, and white basket weave (shown open). $200.00 – 250.00.
3 Evans 4"-round sterling gold-wash compact with pink, yellow, and white basket weave. $175.00 – 200.00.
4 Evans oval sterling gold-wash compact with pink, yellow, and white basket weave. $125.00 – 150.00.
5 Evans pink, yellow, and white basket weave metal carryall, c. 1940 – 1950s (shown open). $125.00 – 150.00.

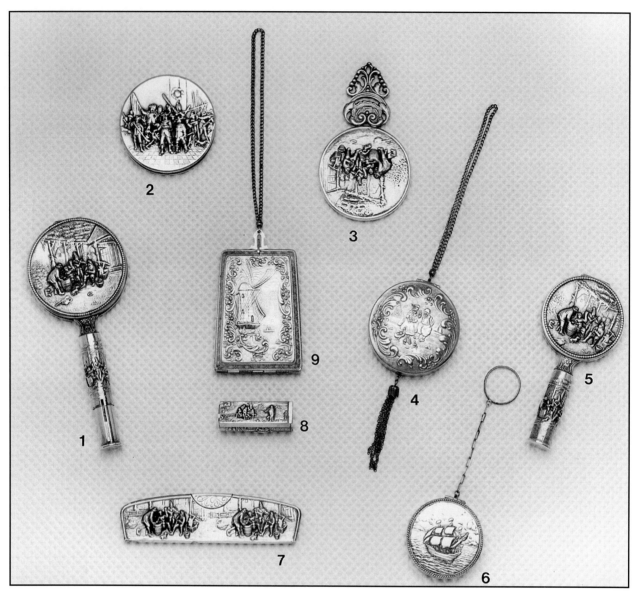

1 S & F silver-plated compact designed to resemble hand mirror; lipstick in handle; repoussé cracker-barrel scene on lid; Denmark. $125.00 – 150.00.

2 Silver-plated mirror with Danish scene on lid, Denmark. $60.00 – 80.00.

3 Silver-plated mirror with repoussé cracker-barrel scene, Denmark. $30.00 – 50.00.

4 Silver-plated compact with Dutch scene on lid; tassel and carrying chain; c. 1920s. $125.00 – 150.00.

5 S & F silver-plated compact designed to resemble hand mirror; lipstick in handle; repoussé cracker-barrel scene on lid, Denmark. $125.00 – 150.00.

6 Silver-plated vanity case with sailing ship on lid; powder and rouge compartments and finger ring chain; c. 1920s. $100.00 – 125.00.

7 Silver-plated comb with repoussé cracker-barrel scene, Denmark. $20.00 – 30.00.

8 Silver-plated lipstick with repoussé cracker-barrel scene, Denmark. $40.00 – 60.00.

9 Silver-plated vanity case with Dutch scene on lid; compartments for powder, rouge, and lipstick; carrying chain; c. 1920s. $150.00 – 175.00.

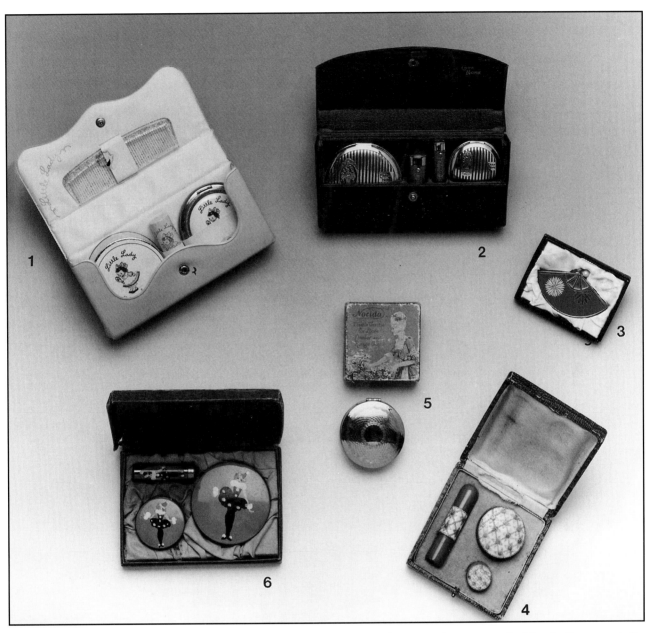

1 Little Lady child's vanity box containing compact, lipstick, powder, and comb in blue carrying case. $50.00 – 75.00.
2 Langlois "Cara Noma" blue vanity clutch containing silver-plated powder compact, rouge, lipstick, and eye make-up containers, "Pat. 7-1-24." $125.00 – 175.00.
3 Goldtone miniature red enamel fan-motif compact in original fitted presentation box, c. 1950s. $50.00 – 60.00.

4 Edouardo "Bag-Dabs" green and white plastic compact; lipstick and sachet container decorated with red flowers; original fitted presentation box; France. $125.00 – 200.00.
5 Norida nickel-silver vanity case with powder and rouge compartments in original box, "Pat. Aug. 5, 1924." $60.00 – 80.00.
6 Goldtone compact with painted clown, rouge, and lipstick set in original fitted presentation box. $80.00 – 150.00.

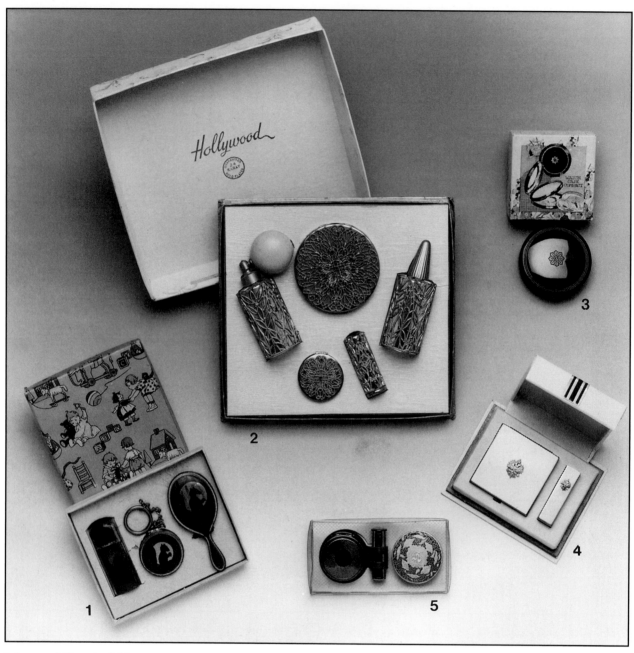

1 Annette "Chypre" child's green cosmetic set; compact with finger chain; hand mirror and perfume bottle; original fitted presentation box. $125.00 – 200.00.
2 Hollywood 24-karat gold-plated multicolored stone-studded filigree cosmetic set with compact, rouge case, lipstick, perfume bottle with atomizer, and lotion bottle in original fitted presentation box. $150.00 – 225.00.
3 Colgate & Co. "Watch Case" brown metal vanity case with

powder and rouge compartments in original presentation box. $40.00 – 60.00.
4 Anna Pavlova white and gold enamel goldtone compact and lipstick case set with goldtone coat-of-arms in original fitted presentation box, c. 1930s. $100.00 – 120.00.
5 Coty "Trio" goldtone metal rouge and lipstick case; tandem set in red plastic "invitation"-size face powder; c. 1930s. $60.00 – 80.00.

1 Goldtone compact with colorful South Seas scene encased in Lucite lid. $40.00 – 60.00.

2 Coty goldtone embossed book-motif compact, c. 1940s. $40.00 – 60.00.

3 Majestic copper-colored basket weave compact. $30.00 – 50.00.

4 Damascene goldtone and black metal compact, c. 1930s. $30.00 – 40.00.

5 Blue and white enamel plaid vanity case with powder and rouge compartments. $40.00 – 60.00.

6 Octagonal silvered and black enamel compact with powder sifter, c. 1920s. $75.00 – 90.00.

7 Black and white plastic compact. $20.00 – 30.00.

8 B C brass engine-turned vanity case with powder and rouge compartments, mirror and writing slate, and brass writing pencil enclosed on side lid; Germany, c. 1920s. $125.00 – 150.00.

9 Copper compact with black enamel bull's-eye center. $60.00 – 80.00.

10 Black plastic bolster-shaped vanity bag with painted blue and white flowers set with rhinestones; black carrying cord; lipstick concealed in tassel; c. 1920s. $250.00 – 300.00.

11 Volupté goldtone basket weave compact with red stones on lid; sliding lipstick; c. 1940s. $50.00 – 60.00.

12 Antique goldtone compact with goldtone leaves mounted on lid and red cabochon stone in center, c. 1930s. $40.00 – 60.00.

1 B.Co. green crackle plastic vanity case with enamel decoration on lid, carrying chain, and compartments for powder, rouge, and lipstick. $80.00 – 125.00.

2 Volupté blue enamel "Watchcase Compact," set with faux pearls with painted disk on lid and black tassel, c. 1940s. $60.00 – 80.00.

3 Red and black enamel tango-chain vanity with red and black enamel chain; powder sifter, rouge compartment, and metal mirror; c. 1920s. $125.00 – 150.00.

4 Silvered-metal compact with enameled medallion on lid and through handle, c. 1920s. $100.00 – 125.00.

5 Zell simulated lavender cloisonné vanity case (shown open). $40.00 – 60.00.

6 Marbleized brown Bakelite tango-chain vanity with red enamel disk on lid. $80.00 – 125.00.

7 Chrome cookie-shaped compact with loop for chain, c. 1910. $30.00 – 50.00.

8 Richard Hudnut black and goldtone enamel vanity case; metal mirror and powder and rouge compartments; c. 1920s. $40.00 – 60.00.

9 Schildkraut rhinestone compact with black faille and rhinestone carrying case. $80.00 – 100.00.

10 Square champlevé compact with blue, gold, and green enamel flowers and yellow cabochon stone on lid; engraved sides; Czechoslovakia. $100.00 – 125.00.

11 Goldtone compact with Lucite dome enclosing heather on a plaid background. $40.00 – 60.00.

12 Orange enamel metal vanity case with metal mirror and powder and rouge compartments; lipstick compartment centered on back lid; c. 1920s. $75.00 – 100.00.

1 Horseshoe-shaped zippered compact with painted dancing girl on lid, signed Annette Honeywell. $50.00 – 75.00.

2 Avon oval compact with blue and green checkerboard lid. $20.00 – 30.00.

3 Royal blue ribbed-silk compact; catch set with blue stones; England. $100.00 – 125.00.

4 Dorset Fifth Avenue bolster-shaped goldtone compact. $50.00 – 60.00.

5 Terri silvered-metal vanity case with black carrying cord, c. 1950s. $60.00 – 80.00.

6 Majestic brass compact with spinning roulette wheel set on lid. $90.00 – 150.00.

7 Volupté brass and black enamel oblong vanity case with compartments for powder, rouge, lipstick, and comb. $30.00 – 50.00.

8 Wooden painted compact, c. 1940s. $40.00 – 60.00.

9 E.A.M. sterling pentagonal vanity case with goldtone engraved interior; powder and rouge compartments and carrying chain; c. 1920s (shown open). $150.00 – 175.00.

Kigu brown marbleized enameled compact/camera combination; working camera incorporates compact, lipstick holder, and 16 mm film-cartridge holder; England, c. 1940 – 1950s. $1,500.00 – 2,000.00.

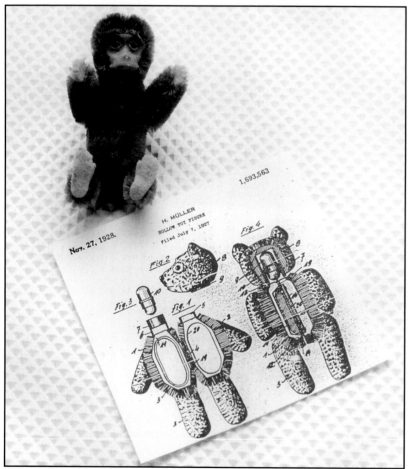

Schuco miniature monkey that opens to reveal compact and lipstick; patent shown is for hollow toy teddy bear compact/lipstick combination, c. 1920s. $500.00 – 700.00.

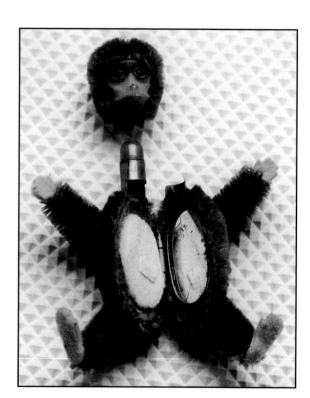

Schuco monkey at left shown open.

1 Nickel-silver engine-turned vanity case with painted enamel flowers on lid; carrying chain and compartments for powder, lipstick, and rouge; c. 1920s. $125.00 – 200.00.

2 Woodworth "Karess" embossed silver-metal miniature vanity with compartments for powder, rouge, and lipstick, c. 1920s. $60.00 – 80.00.

3, 4 Volupté "Watchcase Compact" with picture locket on flower-decorated lid, c. 1940s (3 shown closed, 4 shown open). $70.00 – 100.00.

5 Stratton goldtone compact with crown motif, c. 1940 – 1950s. $150.00 – 250.00.

6 Elizabeth Arden engraved goldtone powder-sifter compact, Switzerland. $60.00 – 100.00.

7 Richard Hudnut nickel-silver complimentary powder sifter, c. 1920s. $25.00 – 75.00.

8 White enamel goldtone compact with lock motif. $75.00 – 125.00.

9 Coty "Sub-Deb" red and white plastic compact, c. 1940s. $25.00 – 40.00.

10 Napier sterling-silver clamshell compact, c. 1940s. $200.00 – 250.00.

11 Givenchy goldtone clamshell compact with blue stone thumbpiece (shown open). $100.00 – 125.00.

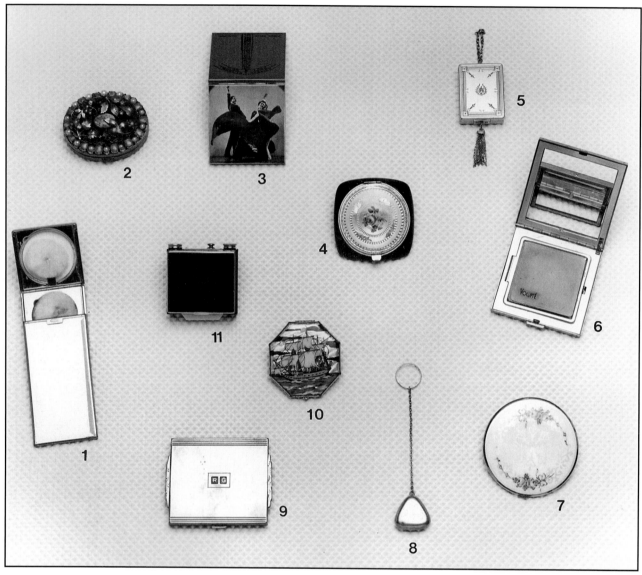

1 Yardley goldtone embossed vanity case; sliding mirror reveals powder and rouge compartments; England, c. 1930 – 1940s. $60.00 – 80.00.

2 Evans oval antique goldtone compact encrusted with faux cabochon jade and pearls. $40.00 – 60.00.

3 The Rainbow Room and Grill "First Prize for Dancing" compact with picture of dancers. $80.00 – 125.00.

4 Brown plastic and goldtone compact with painted flowers on lid. $40.00 – 60.00.

5 Melba goldtone engraved vanity case with powder and lipstick compartments, tassel, and finger ring chain. $40.00 – 60.00.

6 Volupté engraved goldtone compact with swivel mirror lid. $80.00 – 125.00.

7 La Mode cloisonné flapjack vanity case. $50.00 – 70.00.

8 Goldtone and silvered miniature triangular compact with finger ring chain $40.00 – 60.00.

9 Agme goldtone compact with adjustable initials on lid, Switzerland. $80.00 – 120.00.

10 Gwenda octagonal painted foil compact. $40.00 – 80.00.

11 Cambi illuminated, enameled goldtone and plastic vanity case with powder compartment, sliding lipstick, and eye make-up in lid; France. $60.00 – 100.00.

1 *Norida hammered goldtone-metal compact with powder sifter, c. 1920s. $40.00 – 60.00.*

2 *French ivory compact with mirror encircled with bluebirds on lid; "Compliments of Van Raalte" on inner lid. $30.00 – 50.00.*

3 *Rhinestone silvered-metal compact, c. 1930s. $80.00 – 100.00.*

4 *Volupté rigid goldtone mesh compact with buckle closure. $80.00 – 100.00.*

5 *Embossed goldtone cookie-shaped compact, c. 1910. $40.00 – 60.00.*

6 *Woodworth "Karess" blue enamel goldtone vanity case with carrying chain and compartments for powder, rouge, and lipstick; c. 1920s. $60.00 – 80.00.*

7 *Rex Fifth Avenue oval red enamel goldtone compact; lid inset with mirror. $80.00 – 100.00.*

8 *Volupté black enamel and goldtone buckle-motif compact. $60.00 – 80.00.*

9 *La Mode black enamel vanity case with painted enamel disk on lid; powder and rouge compartments and sliding lipstick on either side. $100.00 – 150.00.*

10 *Wadsworth crystal deep-cut cross-bar plastic compact with polished goldtone back, c. 1930s. $100.00 – 150.00.*

11 *Gucci black enamel goldtone compact. $80.00 – 100.00.*

12 *Oblong black enamel polished goldtone compact with colorful butterfly-wing scene under clear plastic on lid, c. 1930s. $75.00 – 100.00.*

13 *Compact set into square yellow plastic frame with transfer scene on lid. $50.00 – 75.00.*

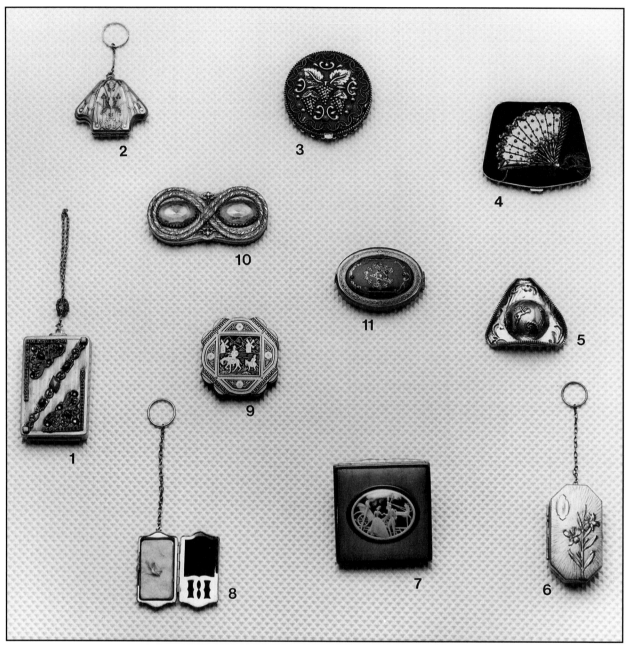

1 Engine-turned brass-tone metal vanity case with multicolored stones encrusted on lid; powder and rouge compartments and carrying chain. $80.00 – 100.00.

2 Enameled silvered-metal miniature vanity case with powder sifter and rouge compartment; finger ring chain; c. 1920s. $40.00 – 60.00.

3 Silvered-metal compact decorated with red stones. $40.00 – 60.00.

4 Black silk compact decorated with beaded pink fan, France. $60.00 – 80.00.

5 Silvered-metal compact designed in shape of a hat with repoussé cherub on lid. $100.00 – 125.00.

6 Imperial-plate goldtone-metal vanity case with flower design on lid; finger ring chain; c. 1920s. $80.00 – 100.00.

7 Daniel satin-finish goldtone compact with three-dimensional white plastic courting scene under plastic dome. $80.00 – 125.00.

8 Engraved silvered-metal powder-vial container with puff, metal mirror, and finger ring chain. NPA.

9 Damascene scalloped goldtone compact with windmill scene on lid. $30.00 – 40.00.

10 Engraved, embossed goldtone compact with harlequin mask-shaped lid decorated with two large yellow stones, France. $80.00 – 100.00.

11 Oval goldtone compact with blue plastic lid set with faux gems. $40.00 – 60.00.

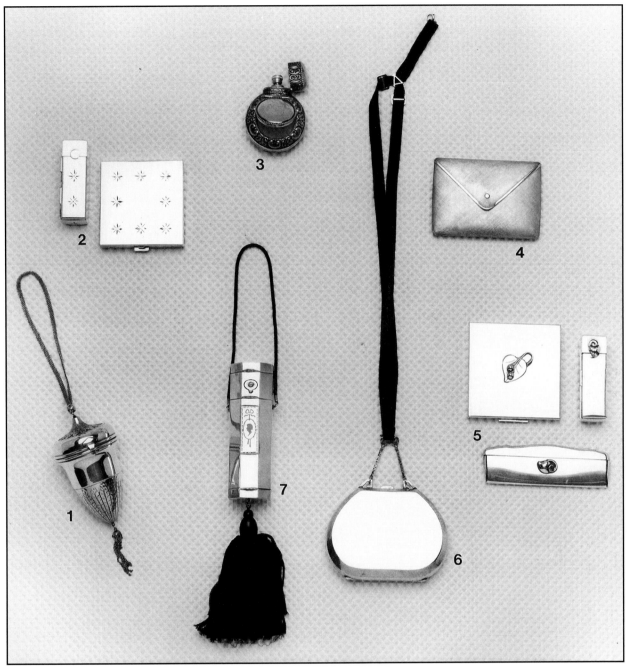

1 Silver embossed acorn-shaped vanity case with tassel and mesh chain; powder and rouge compartments; turn of the century. $475.00 – 575.00.

2 Tiffany & Co. sterling-silver compact and lipstick case set with etched snowflakes. $400.00 – 500.00.

3 Sterling-silver compact/perfume combination with repoussé leaf design around edges; Germany, turn of the century. $325.00 – 450.00.

4 Tiffany & Co. sterling-silver antique-finish compact designed to resemble envelope, Italy. $250.00 – 300.00.

5 Sterling-silver compact, lipstick, and comb set with grape leaf; possibly Georg Jensen. $500.00 – 600.00.

6 Sterling hallmarked purse-motif vanity case with carrying cord; powder and rouge compartments, lipstick tube, and mirror; England, turn of the century. $450.00 – 550.00.

7 Sterling-silver hallmarked necessaire, silhouettes on lid and front; cord and tassel; sliding lipstick and compartments for powder, rouge, and cigarettes. $700.00 – 1,000.00.

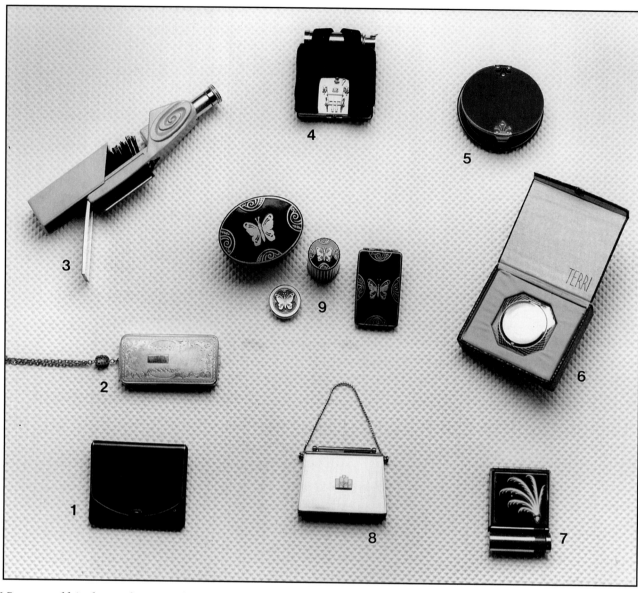

*1 Brown marbleized enamel compact designed to resemble enve-
lope, with cabochon blue stone on lid, Germany. $60.00 – 80.00.
2 Richard Hudnut "Du Barry Beauty Box" engraved goldtone
vanity box with carrying chain; compartments for powder,
rouge, and lipstick. $60.00 – 80.00.
3 Light blue plastic novelty carryall with concealed compact, lipstick, hairbrush, and comb. $125.00 – 200.00.
4 Flato goldtone compact with jeweled horse and carriage
mounted on lid in blue velvet protective case with lipstick sleeve.
$250.00 – 300.00.
5 Kreisler red and black enamel goldtone compact with ornate
hinge and closure. $40.00 – 60.00.*

*6 Terri octagonal goldtone compact with scale-work engraved
edges and dancers on lid; original fitted presentation box. $80.00
– 100.00.
7 Yardley goldtone vanity case with white enamel feather on lid;
powder and rouge compartments and tandem lipstick; c. 1940s.
$60.00 – 80.00.
8 Satin goldtone compact designed to resemble purse, with blue
enamel disk on lid; carrying chain. $150.00 – 200.00.
9 Lucretia Vanderbilt blue enamel silvered-metal set decorated
with silver butterflies; miniature round compact, oblong vanity
case, boudoir-size face powder container, and sample-size
extract container. NPA.*

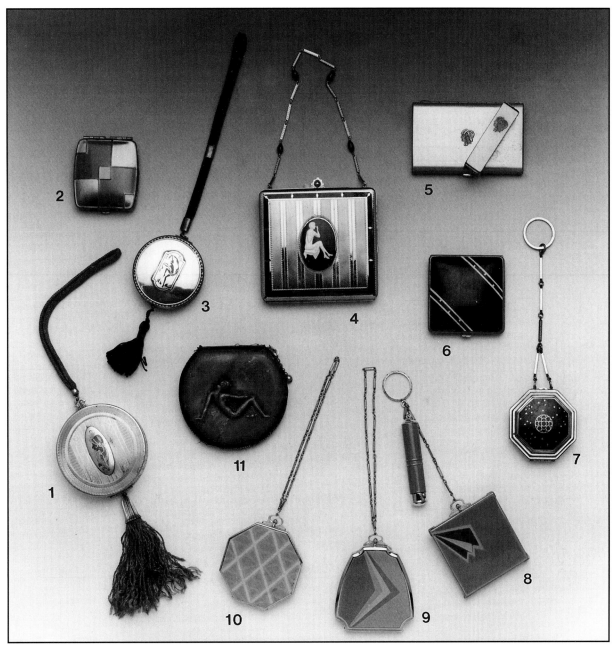

1 Silvered and goldtone vanity case with blue enamel profile of woman on lid; faded blue tassel and carrying cord; compartments for powder, rouge, and lipstick; turn of the century. $100.00 – 150.00.

2 Art Deco blue enamel and goldtone vanity case with compartments for powder and rouge. $60.00 – 80.00.

3 Sterling silver hallmarked Art Nouveau compact with silhouette of dancing woman; carrying cord and tassel. $150.00 – 175.00.

4 D.F. Briggs Co. engine-turned silvered carryall with oval disk of woman applying makeup centered and black enamel border; carrying chain and compartments for powder, rouge, lipstick, coins, and necessities. $200.00 – 250.00.

5 Chantrey bronze-colored metal vanity case and lipstick set with red and black silhouettes of man and woman. $100.00 – 125.00.

6 Black and white enamel vanity case with compartments for powder and lipstick. $60.00 – 80.00.

7 Richard Hudnut "Le Debut" octagonal vanity case with black enamel celestial scene; powder and rouge compartments and finger-ring chain. $150.00 – 225.00.

8 E.A.M. Art Deco blue enamel tango chain with red and yellow abstract design; powder sifter and attached lipstick; finger-ring chain; c. 1920s. $150.00 – 200.00.

9 E.A.M. Art Deco enameled compact blue, yellow, and gray abstract design; powder sifter and carrying chain; c. 1920. $150.00 – 200.00.

10 Octagonal Art Deco compact with pink, yellow, and blue abstract design; powder sifter and carrying chain; c. 1920. $150.00 – 200.00.

11 Horseshoe-shaped pewter and leather zippered compact with repoussé woman on lid. $150.00 – 200.00.

1, 2 Goldtone and black lip-blotter tissue case with mirrored lid (1 shown closed, 2 shown open). $20.00 – 40.00 each.

3 Dorothy Gray engine-turned goldtone compact designed to resemble a hat, c. 1940s. $125.00 – 175.00.

4 Lederer "Sacs" goldtone compact with red pompon black suede beret; original presentation box, France. NPA.

5 Miniature red enamel goldtone bolster-shaped compact (shown open). $25.00 – 30.00.

6 Multicolored micro-mosaic goldtone compact, Italy. $80.00 – 100.00.

7 Wadsworth polished and satin-finish engraved compact designed to resemble a fan. $60.00 – 80.00.

8 Octagonal wood-marquetry compact inlaid with light and dark wood veneers. $75.00 – 100.00.

9 Brass cookie-shaped basket weave compact, c. 1920s. $60.00 – 80.00.

10 Langlois "Shari" green enamel and goldtone vanity case with compartments for powder, rouge, and lipstick (shown open). $80.00 – 100.00.

11, 12 Two goldtone and red cloisonné compacts in original silk-lined leather fitted presentation box (11 shown open, 12 shown closed). $100.00 – 125.00.

13 Goldtone tango chain vanity case with black painted strap-work. $100.00 – 125.00.

1 Antiqued silver-filigree and engraved belt chatelette with compact, pencil, perfume holder, and writing slate; Continental, 19th century. NPA.

2 Engraved silver compact shaped as a hand mirror with lipstick in handle; Italy, turn of the century. $150.00 – 225.00.

3 Whiting & Davis silvered mesh vanity bag with etched and engraved lid and braided carrying chain, c. 1920s. $500.00 – 600.00.

4, 5 Powder-Tier triple-tier vanity case with swivel compartments for powder, rouge, and lipstick, c. 1920s (4, sterling silver, shown open; $350.00 – 450.00; silvered metal, shown closed). $225.00 – 275.00.

6 Silvered compact with spider and fly repoussé on both sides; neck chain. $175.00 – 225.00.

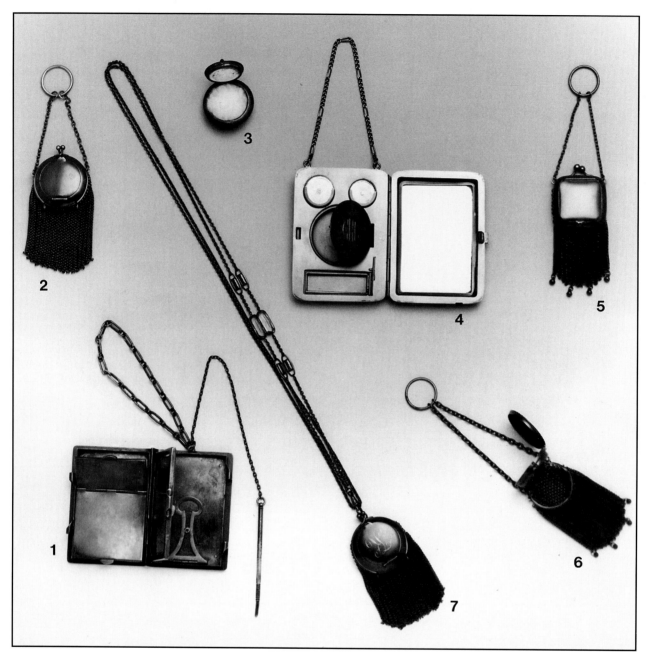

1 Gun-metal mini carryall designed to resemble book, with four faux amethysts on lid; carrying chain and compartments for powder, rouge, bills, writing slate, and slim metal pencil (shown open). $200.00 – 225.00.

2 Gun-metal mini mesh vanity bag with diminishing mirror and finger ring chain, France. $150.00 – 200.00.

3 Gun-metal mini compact with loop for chain, Germany. $50.00 – 75.00.

4 Gun-metal black beaded mini carryall monogrammed ERC; carrying chain and compartments for powder, lipstick, and coins (shown open). $200.00 – 250.00.

5 Gun-metal mini mesh vanity bag with finger ring chain. $150.00 – 200.00.

6 Gun-metal mini mesh vanity bag with finger ring chain, France. $150.00 – 200.00.

7 Gun-metal mini mesh vanity bag with monogrammed lid; diminishing mirror and neck chain; France. $200.00 – 250.00.

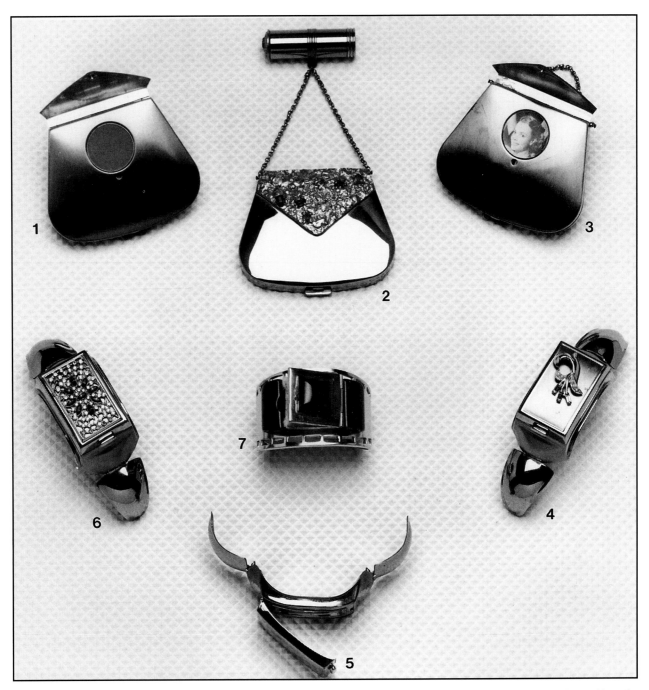

1 Volupté "Lucky Purse" satin-finish metal compact; outer lid reveals rouge; c. 1940s (shown open). $80.00 – 100.00.
2 Volupté "Lucky Purse" polished-metal tango-chain compact with multicolored stones; lipstick; c. 1940s. $150.00 – 200.00.
3 Volupté "Lucky Purse" satin-finish metal compact; outer lid reveals picture locket; c. 1940s (shown open). $80.00 – 100.00.
4 K & K polished satin-finish compact/bracelet set with pearls and blue stones; hinged bracelet. $250.00 – 300.00.

5 K & K polished satin-finish compact/bracelet; hinged bracelet (shown open). $200.00 – 250.00.
6 K & K polished satin-finish compact/bracelet set with rhinestones and red stones; hinged bracelet. $250.00 – 300.00.
7 Deva-Dassy polished goldtone compact/bracelet set with large green stones, France. $200.00 – 275.00.

1 Hexagonal engine-turned brass tango chain compact. $100.00 – 125.00.

2 Sterling-silver engraved miniature compact with locket mounted on top. $125.00 – 200.00.

3 Brass ball compact with pair of dice under plastic dome lid. $125.00 – 200.00.

4 Champlevé goldtone compact with painted ivory disk on lid, Italy. $40.00 – 60.00.

5 Goldtone miniature compact with Limoges painting set in pearl disk on filigree lid. $60.00 – 80.00.

6 Green champlevé and vermeil compact, Italy. $80.00 – 100.00.

7 Green cloisonné and silver four-leaf-clover vanity case with painted flowers on lid; goldtone interior; metal mirror, powder sifter, and rouge compartment; c. 1920s. $100.00 – 125.00.

8 Evans engine-turned nickel-silver triangular vanity case with yellow cloisonné lid with painted flowers; powder and rouge compartments and through handle. $100.00 – 125.00.

9 Terri blue plastic compact with silver dancers on metal lid. $30.00 – 40.00.

10 Goldtone compact with micro-mosaic flowers on lid and four stones set around base. $60.00 – 80.00.

11 Divine miniature orange enamel compact with white silhouette on lid. $40.00 – 60.00.

12 Divine miniature pink enamel compact with white picture on lid (shown open). $40.00 – 60.00.

13 Divine miniature yellow compact with painted picture of woman on lid. $40.00 – 60.00.

14 White enamel compact with molded pink and green plastic floral design on lid, c. 1930s. $60.00 – 80.00.

15 Flato goldtone compact with etched cat with green cabochon stone eyes on lid; lipstick sleeve in maroon velvet case; c. 1950s. $250.00 – 350.00.

16 Blue enamel goldtone compact with multicolored painted flowers on lid, France. $100.00 – 125.00.

17 Cheramy "Cappi" goldtone vanity case with powder and rouge compartments and sliding mirror, c. 1920s (shown open). $80.00 – 100.00.

1 *E.A. Bliss Co. vermeil nickel-silver compact/bracelet with etched floral decoration on lid; applied cut-out leaf-shape metal band; turn of the century. $150.00 – 250.00.*

2 *F.J. Co. antique goldtone compact/bracelet with filigree lid and flowers on band, c. 1930s. $225.00 – 300.00.*

3 *La Mode satin-finish flapjack vanity case and bracelet set with rhinestone trim. $150.00 – 200.00.*

4 *Sterling silver hallmarked vermeil cloisonné compact/bracelet with painted flowers on lid and grosgrain band, Continental. $250.00 – 400.00.*

5, 6 *Mello-Glo nickel-silver "Wrist Compact" with grosgrain band, c. 1920s. $75.00 – 125.00.*

7 *Octagonal goldtone compact/bracelet with rhinestone and filigree overlay on lid and grosgrain band. $80.00 – 125.00.*

8 *Sterling-silver hallmarked blue cloisonné compact/bracelet with black grosgrain band; Continental, turn of the century. $350.00 – 450.00.*

9 *Black plastic compact/bracelet set with rhinestones; grosgrain band; c. 1920s. $175.00 – 200.00.*

10 *Silvered compact/bracelet with filigree and engraved decoration; removable pin-hinge closure; Continental, 19th century. $175.00 – 275.00.*

11, 12 *Marlowe Co. "Parisienne" plastic cosmetic bracelet with decorative metal band that slides to reveal two mirrors and five cosmetic compartments (11, ivory, shown closed; 12, black, shown open). $225.00 – 325.00.*

1 *French ivory plastic bolster-shaped vanity case with rhine-stones and blue stones; faded blue carrying cord with lipstick concealed in tassel, c. 1920s. $250.00 – 300.00.*

2 *Crystal plastic compact with blue Wedgwood disk on lid. $80.00 – 100.00.*

3 *Vani-Pak black plastic compact/cigarette case combination with sliding mirror (shown open). $80.00 – 100.00.*

4 *Black plastic vanity case with rhinestone geometric design on lid; front opens to reveal mirror and powder and rouge com-partments; back contains coin pocket; black carrying cord with*

lipstick concealed in tassel; c. 1920s. $350.00 – 400.00.

5 *Richelieu yellow plastic egg-shaped vanity case with mono-grammed lid; powder and rouge compartments. $40.00 – 60.00.*

6 *Goldtone and orange plastic compact with filigree overlay on lid set with stones; neck chain. $100.00 – 150.00.*

7 *Oval simulated-tortoise shell plastic compact with raised grape and leaf design on lid; sterling-silver catches; c. 1940s. $60.00 – 80.00.*

1 K & K brass-colored, engine-tooled, basket-shaped compact with dice enclosed in plastic domed lid; embossed swinging handle. $125.00 – 200.00.

2 Kigu engraved brass-colored, basket-shaped compact with filigree flowers centered with faux pearl on lid; embossed swinging handle; England, c. 1940–50s. $125.00 – 200.00.

3 K & K brass-colored, engine-tooled, basket-shaped compact with embossed swinging handle (shown open). $80.00 – 100.00.

4 K & K brass-colored, engine-tooled, basket-shaped compact with satin-finish lid and embossed swinging handle. $80.00 – 125.00.

5 K & K brass-colored, engine-tooled, basket-shaped compact with multicolored silk flowers enclosed in plastic domed lid; embossed swinging handle. $125.00 – 200.00.

6, 7 Brass walnut-motif compact; inner partition incorporates writing slate and diminishing mirror; compartments for powder and combination hinged scent bottle and pin holder; loop for chain; 19th century (6 shown open, 7 shown closed). $200.00 – 250.00.

8 Silver walnut-motif compact; inner partition has picture locket and diminishing mirror; compartments for powder and hinged scent bottle; loop for chain (shown open). $250.00 – 350.00.

9 Zell goldtone engraved basket-motif compact with engraved pink and green flowers and embossed rigid handle. $100.00 – 150.00.

10 Polished goldtone basket compact with red, white, and green painted flowers on lid and engraved swinging handle. $125.00 – 175.00.

1 Blue plastic sphere-shaped compact with multicolored plastic flowers; carrying cord and tassel. $250.00 – 350.00.
2 Polished goldtone ball-shaped compact with roulette wheel enclosed in plastic domed lid. $125.00 – 200.00.
3 Green lizard oval compact with brass decoration and closure and lizard wrist strap. $400.00 – 450.00.
4 Ebony enamel "eight-ball" compact. $125.00 – 200.00.
5 Kigu brass musical globe compact, England, c. 1940–50s. $350.00 – 450.00.
6 Henriette brass compact, c. 1930s (shown open). $60.00 – 80.00.

7 Vogue Vanities "PomPom" ivory enamel ball compact decorated with painted flowers; powder sifter and multicolored tassel; England. $100.00 – 125.00.
8 Enameled red, white, and blue hot air balloon motif compact; balloon basket contains rouge. $650.00 – 750.00.
9 Asprey sterling silver hallmarked miniature ball compact with vermeil blue enamel; loop for chain. $150.00 – 250.00.
10 Henriette polished brass-ball compact with multicolored flowers enclosed in plastic domed lid, c. 1930s. $125.00 – 200.00.

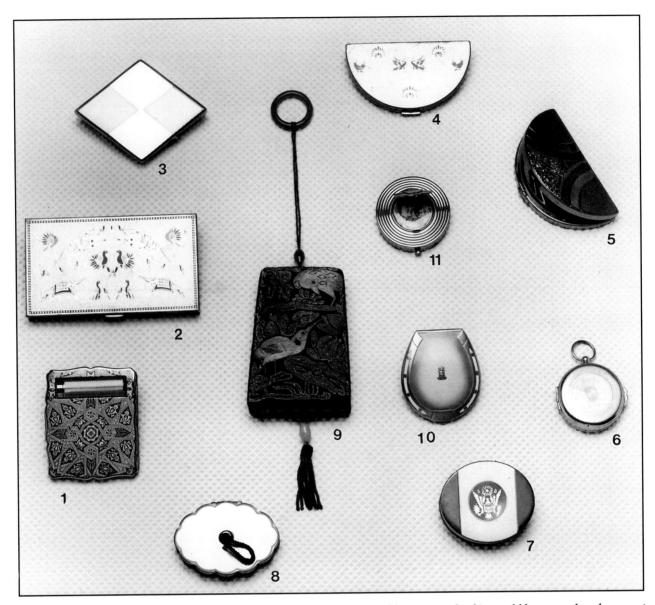

1 Stratton scalloped oblong multi-color enamel goldtone compact with lipstick in lid. $60.00 – 80.00.

2 Volupté goldtone carryall with multicolored enameled animals on lid; compartments for powder, rouge, cigarettes, and comb. $125.00 – 150.00.

3 K & K satin and polished goldtone diamond-shaped compact. $40.00 – 60.00.

4 Coro half-moon-shaped goldtone compact with enameled Persian design on lid. $40.00 – 60.00.

5 Coro half-moon-shaped satin and polished goldtone compact (shown open). $40.00 – 60.00.

6 Miref engine-turned goldtone compact designed to resemble pocket watch; carrying ring; France. $100.00 – 150.00.

7 Rex Fifth Avenue red, white, and blue enamel oval compact with military emblem on lid. $50.00 – 75.00.

8 Volupté scalloped goldtone compact with black enamel border and finger-ring cord. $40.00 – 60.00.

9 Black silk vanity case with embroidered birds on lid; blue beaded tassel with green ojime bead and carrying ring; compartments for powder, rouge, and lipstick; c. 1920s. $150.00 – 225.00.

10 Shaded yellow enamel horseshoe-shaped vanity case with coat-of-arms on lid; powder and rouge compartments. $40.00 – 60.00.

11 Zell Fifth Avenue goldtone compact with picture locket in lid. $40.00 – 60.00.

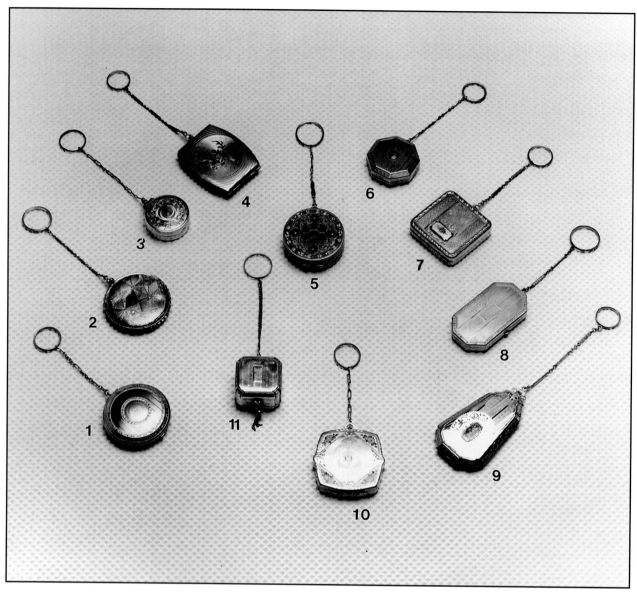

1 Engine turned silvered-metal vanity case with powder sifter, rouge compartment, and finger ring chain; c. 1920 – 1930s. $80.00 – 100.00.

2 Etched silvered-metal compact with rhinestone decoration around rim and finger-ring chain, c. 1920 – 30s. $80.00 – 100.00.

3 Silver-plated compact with finger ring chain, c. 1920 – 1930s. $40.00 – 60.00.

4 Rounded-oblong silvered and goldtone vanity case with powder sifter, rouge compartment, and finger ring chain, c. 1920 – 1930s. $80.00 – 100.00.

5 Engine-turned goldtone vanity case with blue and white enamel flowers set with cabochon blue stones; powder sifter, rouge compartments, and finger ring chain; c. 1920 – 1930s. $100.00 – 125.00.

6 Engine-turned nickel-finish octagonal compact with green enamel disk on lid and finger ring chain, c. 1920 – 1930s. $80.00 – 100.00.

7 May Fair goldtone vanity case with yellow cloisonné disk on lid; compartments for powder and rouge and finger ring chain; c. 1920 – 1930s. $80.00 – 100.00.

8 Silvered goldtone oblong octagonal vanity case with powder and rouge compartments and finger ring chain, c. 1920 – 1930s. $60.00 – 80.00.

9 Silver-plated engine-turned vanity case with green enamel disk on lid; powder sifter, rouge compartment, lipstick, and finger ring chain; c. 1920 – 1930s. $80.00 – 100.00.

10 Engine-turned silvered-metal vanity case with yellow cloisonné on lid; powder and rouge compartments and finger ring chain; c. 1920 – 1930s. $90.00 – 100.00.

11 Sterling silver hallmarked double-sided vanity case with powder and rouge compartments and finger ring chain; Continental. $200.00 – 250.00.

1 *Goldtone compact with painted peacock on plastic disk set with red stones. $40.00 – 60.00.*

2 *Melba miniature oblong compact with enameled scene on lid. $40.00 – 60.00.*

3 *Woodworth "Karess" polished goldtone vanity case with powder and rouge compartments, c. 1920s. $30.00 – 50.00.*

4 *Navy blue enamel silvered-metal vanity case with marcasite flower on lid; lid opens to reveal pop-up-mirror and compartments for powder, rouge, and lipstick. $60.00 – 80.00.*

5 *Pale yellow vanity case with raised mountain scenes; tassel and carrying cord; compartments for powder, rouge, and lipstick; c. 1920s. $175.00 – 225.00.*

6 *Evans goldtone tap-sift powder compact with red enamel goldtone lid. $40.00 – 60.00.*

7 *Multicolored damask compact with wallet-type closure and plastic ring on lid, France. $40.00 – 60.00.*

8 *Estée Lauder Lucite compact with monogrammed metal lid. $40.00 – 60.00.*

9 *Silvered-metal vanity case with abalone disk; "Chicago, Ill" printed on cover; c. 1920s. $60.00 – 80.00.*

10 *Oblong engine-turned silvered-metal vanity case with raised basket on lid; sliding mirror reveals powder and rouge compartments. $100.00 – 125.00.*

1 Mary Dunhill satin goldtone compact with hinges and thumbpiece set with rhinestones and green stones. $60.00 – 80.00.

2, 3 Jet set, compact and matching pillbox. $40.00 – 60.00 set.

4 Volupté brown oblong vanity case with compartments for powder, rouge, pills, and comb (shown open). $40.00 – 60.00 set.

5 Silvered compact with purple enamel lid set with rhinestones. $50.00 – 60.00.

6 Dorothy Gray blue enamel and silvered compact with mirror on outside lid. $40.00 – 60.00.

7 Engine-turned nickel-finish compact/cigarette case/lighter combination with raised giraffe and palm trees on lid. $125.00 – 175.00.

8 Sterling silver mini compact with yellow enameled lid decorated with flowers and finger ring chain. $60.00 – 75.00.

9 Harriet Hubbard Ayer engine-turned goldtone vanity case with center-opening compartments for powder, rouge, and lipstick (shown open). $60.00 – 80.00.

10 Double-sided painted filigree metal vanity case set with colored stones; powder and rouge compartment and hanging bead chain. $175.00 – 225.00.

11 Brown plastic compact with lid inset with embroidery under plastic; interior and exterior mirrors. $60.00 – 80.00.

1 Triangular goldtone compact with raised elephants. $40.00 – 60.00.

2 Wadsworth bolster-shaped black enamel goldtone vanity case with compartments for powder, lipstick, and cigarettes (shown open). $100.00 – 150.00.

3 Volupté satin and polished goldtone strapwork-design compact with raised flowers and small orange stones on lid. $40.00 – 60.00.

4 Richard Hudnut marbleized blue plastic vanity case with silver-plated engraved lid; powder and rouge compartments; original fitted presentation box. $80.00 – 100.00.

5 Painted plastic compact with ballet scene on lid. $60.00 – 80.00.

6, 7 Stratton blue enamel scalloped compact and matching lipstick holder. $60.00 – 80.00 set.

8 Beaded compact with multicolored beaded flowers on white beaded background, France. $75.00 – 100.00.

9 Polished goldtone oblong vanity case with leaves on lid; powder and rouge compartments. $40.00 – 60.00.

10 Vitoge polished goldtone compact and lipstick case with four-leaf clovers; protective carrying case. $80.00 – 125.00.

11 Elgin American silvered compact with engraved lid. $40.00 – 60.00.

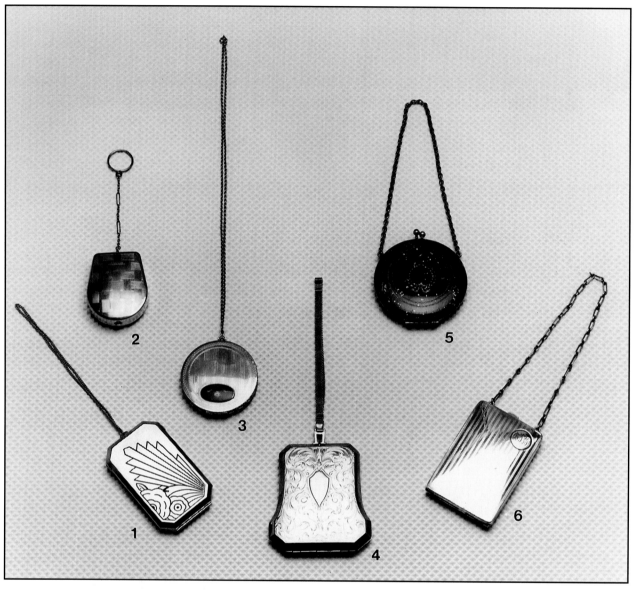

1 Melba goldtone vanity case with blue enameled flower design on lid; carrying chain and compartments for powder, rouge, and lipstick. $80.00 – 125.00.

2 Silvered-metal horseshoe-shaped vanity case with basket weave design on lid; powder and rouge compartments, swivel mirror, and finger ring chain; c. 1920s. $60.00 – 80.00.

3 D.F. Briggs Co. gold-filled engine-turned vanity case with enamel disk on lid; carrying chain and compartments for powder, rouge, lipstick, and eye make-up. $80.00 – 100.00.

4 Goldtone engraved vanity case with mesh carrying chain and compartments for powder, rouge, lipstick, and coins. $125.00 – 150.00.

5 Goldtone and green enamel vanity case with goldtone interior and green cabochon thumbpieces; carrying chain and compartments for powder and coins. $100.00 – 125.00.

6 Sterling silver hallmarked engine-turned vanity case with monogrammed lid; carrying chain and compartments for powder, coins, and bills; Continental. $150.00 – 225.00.

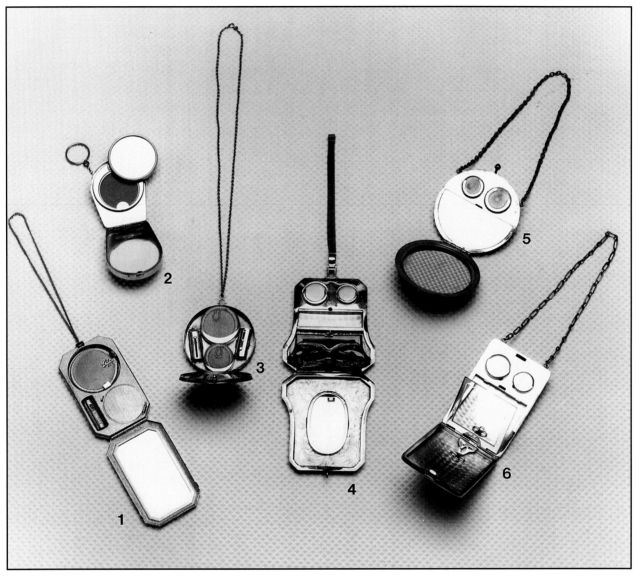

Vanity cases on page 356 shown open.

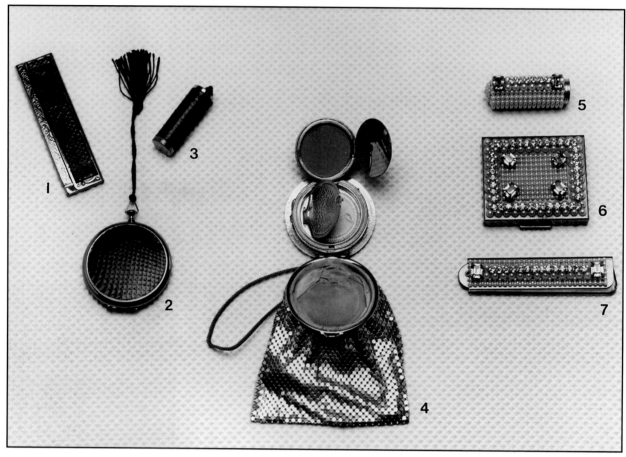

1, 2, 3 Zell Fifth Avenue brown lizard compact, lipstick, and comb set; compact designed to resemble pocket watch. $200.00 – 250.00 set.

4 Silvered-mesh vanity bag with powder and rouge compartments and carrying chain (shown open). $250.00 – 300.00.

5, 6, 7 Compact, lipstick, and comb set decorated with pearls, rhinestones, and blue stones. $125.00 – 150.00 set.

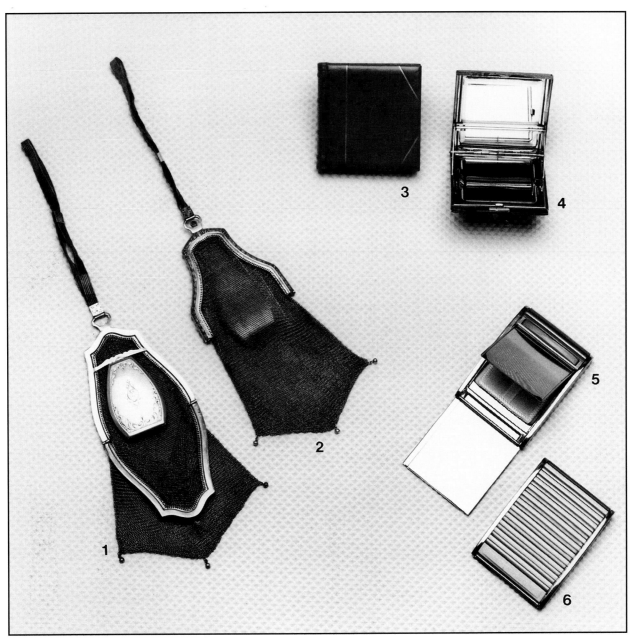

1, 2 W B silvered-metal mesh vanity bag with compact sus-
pended on bar inside bag, c. 1920s (1 shown open, 2 shown
closed). $450.00 – 550.00.
3, 4 Dunhill "Clearview" brown leather windshield-wiper com-
pact designed to resemble book, c. 1930s (3 shown closed, 4
shown open). $80.00 – 100.00.

5, 6 Blue enamel and goldtone roll-top compact; Germany, c.
1940s (5 shown open, 6 shown closed). $150.00 – 250.00.

Invention Patents

Invention patents cover the unique mechanical workings of inventions which produce utilitarian results. An invention patent is in effect, with exclusive rights for the inventor, for 17 years from date of issuance.

A GUIDE FOR DATING INVENTION PATENT NUMBERS

Patent Numbers		Dates	Patent Numbers		Dates
1	through 109	1836	488,976	511,743	1893
110	545	1837	511,744	531,618	1894
546	1,060	1838	531,619	552,501	1895
1,061	1,464	1839	552,502	574,368	1896
1,465	1,922	1840	574,369	596,466	1897
1,923	2,412	1841	596,467	616,870	1898
2,413	2,900	1842	616,871	640,166	1899
2,901	3,394	1843	640,167	664,826	1900
3,395	3,872	1844	664,827	690,384	1901
3,873	4,347	1845	690,385	717,520	1902
4,348	4,913	1846	717,521	748,566	1903
4,914	5,408	1847	748,567	778,833	1904
5,409	5,992	1848	778,834	808,617	1905
5,993	6,980	1849	808,618	839,798	1906
6,981	7,864	1850	839,799	875,678	1907
7,865	8,621	1851	875,679	908,435	1908
8,622	9,511	1852	908,436	945,009	1909
9,512	10,357	1853	945,010	980,177	1910
10,358	12,116	1854	980,178	1,013,094	1911
12,117	14,008	1855	1,013,095	1,049,325	1912
14,009	16,323	1856	1,049,326	1,083,266	1913
16,324	19,009	1857	1,083,267	1,123,211	1914
19,010	22,476	1858	1,123,212	1,166,418	1915
22,477	26,641	1859	1,166,419	1,210,388	1916
26,642	31,004	1860	1,210,389	1,251,457	1917
31,005	34,044	1861	1,251,458	1,290,026	1918
34,045	37,265	1862	1,290,027	1,326,898	1919
37,266	41,046	1863	1,326,899	1,364,062	1920
41,047	45,684	1864	1,364,063	1,401,947	1921
45,685	51,783	1865	1,401,948	1,440,361	1922
51,784	60,657	1866	1,440,362	1,478,995	1923
60,658	72,958	1867	1,478,996	1,521,589	1924
72,959	85,502	1868	1,521,590	1,568,039	1925
85,503	98,459	1869	1,568,040	1,612,789	1926
98,460	110,616	1870	1,612,790	1,654,520	1927
110,617	122,303	1871	1,654,521	1,696,896	1928
122,304	134,503	1872	1,696,897	1,742,180	1929
134,504	146,119	1873	1,742,181	1,787,423	1930
146,120	158,349	1874	1,787,424	1,839,189	1931
158,350	171,640	1875	1,839,190	1,892,662	1932
171,641	185,812	1876	1,892,663	1,941,448	1933
185,813	198,732	1877	1,941,449	1,985,877	1934
198,733	211,077	1878	1,985,878	2,026,515	1935
211,078	223,210	1879	2,026,516	2,066,308	1936
223,211	236,136	1880	2,066,309	2,104,003	1937
236,137	251,684	1881	2,104,004	2,142,079	1938
251,685	269,819	1882	2,142,080	2,185,169	1939
269,820	291,015	1883	2,185,170	2,227,417	1940
291,016	310,162	1884	2,227,418	2,268,539	1941
310,163	333,493	1885	2,268,540	2,307,006	1942
333,494	355,290	1886	2,307,007	2,338,080	1943
355,291	375,719	1887	2,338,081	2,366,153	1944
375,720	395,304	1888	2,366,154	2,391,855	1945
395,305	418,664	1889	2,391,856	2,413,674	1946
418,665	443,986	1890	2,413,675	2,433,823	1947
443,987	466,314	1891	2,433,824	2,457,796	1948
466,315	488,975	1892	2,457,797	2,492,943	1949

Patent Numbers		Date
2,492,944	2,536,015	1950
2,536,016	2,580,378	1951
2,580,379	2,624,045	1952
2,624,046	2,664,561	1953
2,664,562	2,698,433	1954
2,698,434	2,728,912	1955
2,728,913	2,775,761	1956
2,775,762	2,818,566	1957
2,818,567	2,866,972	1958
2,866,973	2,919,442	1959
2,919,443	2,966,680	1960

Patent Numbers		Dates
2,966,681	3,015,102	1961
3,015,103	3,070,800	1962
3,070,801	3,116,486	1963
3,116,487	3,163,864	1964
3,163,865	3,226,728	1965
3,216,729	3,295,142	1966
3,295,143	3,360,799	1967
3,360,800	3,419,096	1968
3,419,907	3,487,469	1969
3,487,470	3,551,908	1970

Design Patents

Design patents cover unique, ornamental exterior shapes or structures of an invention. A design patent is in effect, with exclusive rights for the inventor, for 14 years from date of issuance.

A GUIDE FOR DATING DESIGN PATENT NUMBERS

Design patent numbers are preceded with the letters D or DES.

Patent Numbers		Dates
1 through	14	1843
15	26	1844
27	43	1845
44	102	1846
103	162	1847
163	208	1848
209	257	1849
258	340	1850
341	430	1851
431	539	1852
540	625	1853
626	682	1854
683	752	1855
753	859	1856
860	972	1857
973	1,074	1858
1,075	1,182	1859
1,183	1,365	1860
1,366	1,507	1861
1,508	1,702	1862
1,703	1,878	1863
1,879	2,017	1864
2,018	2,238	1865
2,239	2,532	1866
2,533	2,857	1867
2,858	3,303	1868
3,304	3,809	1869
3,810	4,546	1870
4,547	5,451	1871
5,452	6,335	1872
6,336	7,082	1873
7,083	7,968	1874
7,969	8,883	1875
8,884	9,685	1876
9,686	10,384	1877
10,385	10,974	1878
10,975	11,566	1879
11,567	12,081	1880
12,082	12,646	1881
12,647	13,507	1882
13,508	14,527	1883
14,528	15,677	1884
15,678	16,450	1885
16,451	17,045	1886

Patent Numbers		Dates
17,046	17,994	1887
17,995	18,829	1888
18,830	19,552	1889
19,553	20,438	1890
20,439	21,274	1891
21,275	22,091	1892
22,092	22,993	1893
22,994	23,921	1894
23,922	25,036	1895
25,037	26,481	1896
26,482	28,112	1897
28,113	29,915	1898
29,916	32,054	1899
32,055	33,812	1900
33,813	35,546	1901
35,547	36,186	1902
36,187	36,722	1903
36,723	37,279	1904
37,280	37,765	1905
37,766	38,390	1906
38,391	38,979	1907
38,980	39,736	1908
39,737	40,423	1909
40,424	41,062	1910
41,063	42,072	1911
42,073	43,414	1912
43,415	45,097	1913
46,098	46,812	1914
46,813	48,357	1915
48,358	50,116	1916
50,117	51,628	1917
51,629	52,835	1918
52,836	54,358	1919
54,359	56,843	1920
56,844	60,120	1921
60,121	61,747	1922
61,748	63,674	1923
63,675	66,345	1924
66,346	69,169	1925
69,170	71,771	1926
71,772	74,158	1927
74,159	77,346	1928
77,347	80,253	1929
80,254	82,965	1930

Patent Numbers		Dates
82,966	85,902	1931
85,903	88,846	1932
88,847	91,257	1933
91,258	94,178	1934
94,179	98,044	1935
98,045	102,600	1936
102,601	107,737	1937
107,738	112,764	1938
112,765	118,357	1939
118,358	124,502	1940
124,503	130,988	1941
130,989	134,716	1942
134,717	136,945	1943
136,946	139,861	1944
139,862	143,385	1945
143,386	146,164	1946
146,165	148,266	1947
148,267	152,234	1948
152,235	156,685	1949
156,686	161,403	1950

Patent Numbers		Dates
161,404	165,567	1951
165,568	168,526	1952
168,527	171,240	1953
171,241	173,776	1954
173,777	176,489	1955
176,490	179,466	1956
179,467	181,828	1957
181,829	184,203	1958
184,204	186,972	1959
186,973	189,515	1960
189,516	192,003	1961
192,004	194,303	1962
194,304	197,268	1963
197,269	199,994	1964
199,995	203,378	1965
203,379	206,566	1966
206,567	209,731	1967
209,732	213,083	1968
213,084	216,418	1969
216,419	219,636	1970

Glossary

alloy – Base metal fused with a precious ore to change its color or to harden it.

Art Deco – (1920 – 1930). An angular style of geometric patterns and abstract designs that originated in France.

Art Nouveau – (1890 – 1910). A free-flowing style introduced in England, with emphasis on curved lines, natural motifs, and women with long flowing hair.

Bakelite – Trademark for an opaque synthetic plastic developed in 1909.

bar brooche – A narrow, horizontal decorated pin.

baroque pearl – Pearls with an irregular shape.

base metal – Any metal other than the three primary precious metals: silver, gold, and platinum.

basse-taille – A decorative enameling technique in which the metal is etched, engraved, or cut and then filled with transparent enamels. Also known as translucent enameling.

brass – An alloy composed of two-thirds copper and one-third zinc.

brocade – Silk fabric with a woven raised design.

bronze – A reddish-brown alloy of copper and tin.

cabochon – A highly polished dome-shaped stone with no facets.

cabriole – An elongated S-shaped support.

cameo – A gem, shell, or stone with a design or figure carved in relief against a background of a darker or lighter color.

carryall – Mass-produced version of a minaudiére.

celluloid – Trademark for a type of plastic developed in 1868.

champlevé – An enameling technique in which cut-out or depressed areas in the metal are filled with enamel.

chatelaine – An ornamental clasp from which five to nine chains are suspended to accommodate various small objects.

chatelette – A chatelaine with shorter and fewer chains.

chinoiserie – European decoration with a Chinese motif.

chrome – A hard, brittle gray metal used to plate other metal with a bright mirror-like finish.

circa – Approximate date an item was manufactured.

clip – A hinged support on the back of a pin or brooch that clips onto an article of clothing.

cloisonné – An enameling technique in which narrow strips of gold or silver wire are soldered to a metal base to form compartments (cloisons), which are then filled with enamel.

compact – A small portable make-up container consisting of a mirror, powder, and puff.

damascene – Decorative inlaid pattern of gold or silver on metal.

déposé – French word for patent or copyright.

enamel – A form of powdered colored glass that is fused onto metal surfaces for decoration.

engraving – A pattern or design cut into the surface of a hard material with a sharp instrument.

fede – A decorative form consisting of a pair of clasped right hands, symbolizing faith and trust.

flapjack – A slim, thin compact resembling a "flapjack" pancake.

French ivory – Trademark for plastic imitation ivory.

German silver – A white alloy of nickel, zinc, and copper. Also called nickle silver, although contains no silver.

gilt or gild – To cover a base metal with a thin layer of gold or gold color.

gold – A soft precious metal usually combined with copper or nickel, depending on the color and hardness desired.

gold-filled – A base metal (usually copper) plated with gold, usually by electroplating.

grosgrain – A stiffly corded silk fabric.

guilloché enamel – An engraved decoration on metal, usually geometric or floral, covered with a translucent enamel.

hallmark – A mark stamped on some objects of gold and silver to denote the quality, purity, origin, and manufacturer. First used in Great Britain.

inlay – A decorative technique in which a design in metal is etched or cut out and another hard material inserted in the recessed pattern to make a flat or even shape.

inro – A small compartmented and usually ornamented container that is hung from a Japanese obi (sash) to hold small objects such as medicines, perfumes or cosmetics.

intaglio – A form of engraving or carving that gives the object a hollow, three-dimensional effect; the reverse of a cameo.

jet – A glossy black variety of hard coal; a name commonly used for imitation or genuine black stones.

karat – A term denoting the amount of pure gold in an article. 24 karats equals pure gold; 18 karats equals 18 parts pure gold and 6 parts of another metal.

Limoges – A translucent enamel of colorful portraits or scenes on copper that originated in Limoges, France.

lusterware – A glaze used on pottery to give a metallic or iridescent appearance.

marcasite – Natural marcasite is crystallized white iron pyrites. Imitation marcasite is made of cut steel that is formed and faceted.

minaudière – A rigid metal, usually box-shaped evening bag with compartments for powder, lipstick, rouge, mirror, coins, and cigarettes.

mosaic – A picture or design composed of small varicolored stones or glass. A micro-mosaic is created with tiny pieces of glass or stones.

mother-of-pearl – The hard, smooth iridescent lining of pearl oyster shells.

motif – In the style of or resembling.

necessaire – Bolster-shaped version of the minaudiére with fewer compartments.

obelisk – A four-sided tapering shaft with a pyramidal top.

ojime – A sliding bead or button on a cord used to tighten or loosen an inro.

parure – A set of matching pieces of jewelry.

petit point – One-half the cross of a cross-stitch done in fine thread on a fine canvas.

pewter – A silver-white alloy of tin and lead.

plastic – Synthetic material, such as Bakelite, celluloid, or Lucite, that is molded by heat into a variety of shapes and colors. Natural, organic plastics (amber, ivory, tortoiseshell, and horn) can be softened and molded or pressed into shape.

pli – A make-up tube containing powder and a puff brush.

plique-à-jour – An enameling technique in which transparent enamel is placed across soldered bands of metal to produce a stained-glass effect.

reticule – A small handbag that is held in the hand or carried over the arm.

rhinestone – A form of rock crystal faceted to resemble diamonds.

seed pearl – A small pearl.

shagreen – Green-dyed leather made from the skin of a shark.

silver – A precious metal usually combined with copper for hardness.

Sterling silver – The purest alloy of silver, containing 0.925 parts of silver and 0.075 parts of copper.

strapwork – A pattern of crossed and interwoven bands that resembles straps.

synthetic stone – Man-made imitations of precious or semiprecious stones.

taffeta – A bright, shiny thin silk fabric.

tango chain – A short chain that attaches a compact and lipstick case.

thumbpiece – A small knob that releases a catch when pressed.

tooling – A design in leather produced by a heated tool.

tortoise shell – The translucent shell of a tortoise, which can be molded by heat.

transfer – A commercial pattern or design applied to another surface.

vanity bag – A dainty mesh evening bag incorporating a compact as an integral part of the bag.

vanity box – Fitted traveling cosmetic box.

vanity case – A compact that contains rouge and/or lipstick.

vanity clutch – A fitted cosmetic bag with sleeves attached to the inside lining to accommodate compact, lipstick, and rouge.

vanity pochette – Drawstring powder pouch with a mirror at the base.

vanity purse – Leather, fabric, metal, or beaded purse incorporating a vanity case as an integral part of the purse.

velvet – A fabric made of silk with a smooth pile surface.

vermeil – A layer of gold over silver, copper, or bronze.

vinaigrette – A small ornamental receptacle that contains scented vinegar or ammonia.

Bibliography

BOOKS

Andacht, Sandra. *Oriental Antiques and Art.*
Greensboro, NC: Wallace-Homestead Book Company, 1987.

Baker, Lillian. *100 Years of Collectible Jewelry.*
Paducah, KY: Collector Books, 1978.

Baker, Lillian. *Fifty Years of Collectible Fashion Jewelry 1925 – 1975.*
Paducah, KY: Collector Books, 1978.

Battersby, Martin. *The Decorative Twenties.*
NY: Walker and Company, 1971.

Battersby, Martin. *The Decorative Thirties.*
NY: Collier Books, 1971.

Carter, Rosalynn. *The First Lady from Plains.*
Boston, MA: Houghton Mifflin, 1984.

Chandro, Moti. *Journal of the Indian Society of Oriental Art.*
Tagore, Abanindranath, Kramrisch, Stella, Editors. Vol. VIII, – 1940.

Dike, Catherine. *Cane Curiosa.*
Switzerland: 1983. Imprimerie Rod S.A., Rolle.

Encyclopedia Britannica.
William Benton, Publisher, 1970.

de Fontenoy, The Marquise. *Eve's Glossary.*
Chicago & New York: Herbert Stone & Co., MDCCCXCVII.

Gerson, Roselyn. *Vintage Vanity Bags & Purses.*
Paducah, KY: Collector Books, 1994.

Edwards, Juliette. *Compacts.*
Surrey, England: 1994.

Haertig, Evelyn. *Antique Combs & Purses.*
Carmel, CA: Gallery of Graphics Press, 1983.

Hainworth, Henry. *A Collectors Dictionary.*
London, Boston, and Henley: Rutlege & Kegan Paul, 1981.

Heide, Robert and John Gilman. *Dime-store Dream Parade.*
New York: E. P. Dutton, 1983.

Hillier, Bevis. *The Style of the Century 1900 – 1980.*
New York: E. P. Dutton, Inc. 1983.

Hillier, Bevis. *The World of Art Deco.*
New York: Studio-Vista Dutton, 1971.

Hillier, Bevis. *Art Deco of the 20's & 30's.*
New York: Studio-Vista Dutton, 1968.

The History of Coty.
235 East 42nd Street, New York, NY. 10017.

Holiner, Richard. *Antique Purses.*
Paducah, KY: Collector Books, 1982.

Kaplan, Arthur Guy. *Official Price Guide to Antique Jewelry,* First Edition.
Orlando, FL: The House of Collectibles, Inc., 1982.

Bibliography

Kaplan, Arthur Guy. *Official Price Guide to Antique Jewelry,* Fifth Edition.
Westminster, MD: The House of Collectibles, 1985.

Kelley, Lyngerda & Nancy Schiffer. *Plastic Jewelry.*
PA: Schiffer Publishing Ltd., 1987.

Klein, Dan, Nancy A. McClelland, Malcolm Haslam.
In the Deco Style.
New York: Rizzoli, 1986.

Lester, Katharine Morris and Bess Viola Oerke.
Accessories of Dress.
Peoria, IL: Charles A. Bennett Co. Inc., 1940.

Loring, John. *Tiffany's 150 Years.*
New York: Doubleday & Co. Inc., 1987.

McClinton, Katharine Morrison. *Art Deco. A Guide For Collectors.*
NY: Clarkson N. Potter, Inc., 1972.

Mebane, John. *Collecting Nostalgia: The First Guide to the Antiques of the 30's and 40's.*
New York: Castleton Books, Inc., 1972.

Patterson, Jerry E. *Matchsafes.*
Washington, DC: Smithsonian Institution, 1981.

Sloane, Jean. *Perfume and Scent Bottle Collecting.*
Lombard, IL: Wallace-Homestead Book Company, 1986.

Whiting & Davis Co. *Tercentenary Booklet 1876 – 1930.*
Plainville, MA.

ARTICLES

Andre, Mila. "Ancient Egypt's Afterlife at the Met." *Daily News* (August 14, 1994).

Baker, Stanley L. "Collecting Compacts." *The Antique Trader Weekly* (July 27, 1977).

Bayer, Patricia. "Collecting Compacts." *Antiques World* (April, 1979).

Berg, Rona. "The Art of Beauty." *New York Times Magazine* (October 18, 1992).

Cohen, Marion. "Male Compact Collector." *Powder Puff,* Vol. 5, #1 (Fall, 1991).

Drake, Laurie. "The Powder and the Glory." *Self* (March, 1994).

Gerson, Roselyn. "Open and Shut Cases: The Wonderful World of Ladies' Compacts." *American Country Collectibles* (Winter, 1994/5).

Gerson, Roselyn. "Ladies' Vintage Compacts." *Vintage Fashions* (August, 1990).

Gerson, Roselyn. "Vintage Compacts: Coming of Age." *Lady's Gallery,* Vol. 1 Issue 1.

Kirsch, Francine. "Something from the Boys." *The Antique Trader Weekly* (November 24, 1993).

Klyde, Hilda. "Locating Ladies' Compacts in London." *Powder Puff,* Vol. 7, #2 (Winter, 1994).

Litts, Elyce. "That Mondaine Lady." *Powder Puff,* Vol. 8, #1 (Fall, 1994).

Litts, Elyce. "Compact Findings." *The Antique Trader Weekly* (Dec. 2, 1987).

"'Make-up' a Collection." *Kovels on Antiques and Collectibles,* Vol. 11 #6 (Feb. 15, 1985).

Moen, Vicki. "Texas Fair Compact Category." *Powder Puff,* Vol. 8, #1 (Fall, 1994).

Montag, Joan & Reine. "Rare Red Enamel." *Powder Puff,* Vol. 3, #2 (Winter, 1990).

Palivos, Tomi. "Antique Addict." *Powder Puff,* Vol. 7, #3 (Spring, 1994).

CATALOGS

"American Jewelry." Christie's New York, October 21, 1992.

"The American Perfumer." New York, NY, Dec. 1920.

Baird-North Co., Providence, RI, 1917.

"Year Book 1926." Baird-North Co., Providence, RI

"Exquisite Accessories." Elgin American Catalog 1952 – 1953. Elgin American Watch Case Co. Elgin, IL, September 1, 1952.

"Your Bargain Book." F. H. Sadler Co., Fall and Winter 1927 – 1928. New York Styles.

Holsman Company Chicago, IL.

"Important Jewelry." Christie's New York, December 6, 1994.

Joseph Hagn Company Catalog. Spring-Summer 1938, Chicago, IL.

Catalogue #109 Fall & Winter 1928 – 1929, Montgomery Ward & Co., Baltimore, MD.

Catalogue #97 Golden Jubilee 1872 – 1922, Chicago, IL.

"The Pohlson Colonial Gifts." Pohlson Galleries, Pawtucket, RI, 1920s.

Sears Roebuck Catalogues. 1897, 1908, 1923, 1927, 1928, 1930, 1935, 1949 Editions. Chicago, IL.

"Gifts from the Shepard Stores." Shepard Stores, Boston, MA, 1923.

MAGAZINES and NEWSPAPERS

Eastman Kodak Trade Circular, 1928.

Fortune, August, 1930.

Glamour, November 1948.

Good Housekeeping, Dec. 1928 and Dec. 1941.

Harper's Bazaar, Dec. 1943.

McCall's Magazine, June 1929.

Metropolitan Home, New York, 1987.

Mirabella, May 1993.

New York Times, July 4, 1993.

Pictorial Review – Oct. 1924, Sept. 1925, April 1927, June 1928, Jan. 1931, and Sept 1931.

Redbook, Dec. 1951 and Nov. 1954.

The Delineator, April 1919.

The Ladies' Home Journal, Dec. 1921, March 1922, March 1924, Dec. 1924, June 1925, and April 1942.

Theatre Magazine, 1919, 1920, 1926, 1927, and 1928.

Toilet Requisites, December 1921.

True Confessions, June 1946.

Vogue, August 1993.

Woman & Beauty Magazine, IPC England, November 1931.

Woman's Home Companion, Dec. 1933.

Woman's World, 1925.

Index

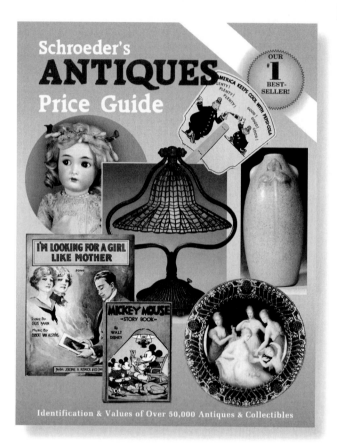